Letters from Bruce County

Written By

Pioneer Joseph Bacon

1795-1882

Dean Wheaton

authorHOUSE™

1663 LIBERTY DRIVE, SUITE 200
BLOOMINGTON, INDIANA 47403
(800) 839-8640
WWW.AUTHORHOUSE.COM

No part of this book may be reproduced, stored in a retrieval system, or transmitted by any means without the written permission of the author.

First published by AuthorHouse 7/24/2006

ISBN: 1-4208-6355-X (sc)

Printed in the United States of America
Bloomington, Indiana

This book is printed on acid-free paper.

Acknowledgment

This story of the life of Joseph Bacon would have been impossible without the contributions of many researchers who are also descendants of Joseph. They freely shared their information and answered endless questions. Through the facilities of MyFamily.com, Inc. and their offering of easy-to-maintain family websites at <u>MyFamily.com</u>, the Joseph Bacon Website researchers were able to share family history information quickly and easily. It was very fortuitous that, for the most part, at least one descendant researcher for each of Joseph's ten offspring (Joseph, Jr. never married and left no descendants) have been located and enlisted in the effort to create a family genealogy of which this story is a part. The following list gives the names and connection of researchers who made major contributions. There are others who also made contributions of one kind or other but who's names are buried in the mass of messages or with whom contact has been lost due to email address changes.

Child	Descendant Researcher
William	Douglas Bacon, Spokane, Washington
Susan	Gordon (Frankie) Harth, Red Cliff, Alberta
	Bud (Betty) Allen, Langley, British Columbia
	Dorothy Steckenreiter, Waterloo, Ontario
	Gerry (Bonnie) Adams, Edmonton, Alberta
James	Connie Goughnour, Parachute, Colorado
	Larry Phillips, Winnipeg, Manitoba
Charlotte	Winifred Price, Seattle Washington
	Janice Ohlsen, Duvall, Washington
Joseph	No descendants
John	Elaine (Routledge) Taylor, Olympia, Washington
	James Routledge, Hamiota, Manitoba
Isaac	
Elijah	Lois Lilley, Erickson, Manitoba
	Barbara Cooper, Vashon, Washington
Emma Jane	
Henry	Dean Wheaton, Clinton, Ohio
Mary Jane	Roger Clarke, Thornhill, Ontario

Dean Wheaton

Table of Contents

Acknowledgment v

Introduction.. xiii

Part I - The Letters 1

    Letter #1 - 7 Mar 1881 3

    Letter #2 - 26 Apr 1882.. 7

Part II - Narrative.. 13

    The English Years 13

    England 1835 15

    Immigration to America & Canada 16

    The Queen's Bush 18

    Settlement Roads 19

    Pioneering in The Bush.. 20

    The Settlement Process 21

    Finding Suitable Land.. 22

    Shelter 24

    Transportation 25

    Crops and Food 26

    Religion 26

    Arthur Township, Waterloo County.. 28

    Farming in Arthur Township, 1861 30

    Brant Township, Bruce County... 31

    Churches and Cemeteries 33

    The Bacon Family 35

    Crown Patents 36

    Bacon Land Records 37

    The Daughters 39

    Road Contractors 39

    Sale of the Bacon Lands 40

    The Family Scatters.. 41

    Mary Jane, Daughter or Granddaughter? 54

    Joseph & Susanna 55

    The Old Bethel Methodist/ Prior Cemetery 56

    A Small Puzzle 57

Appendix A - Family Stories 59

    Story #1 59

    Story #2 60

    Story #3 60

Story #4 60
Story #5 60
Appendix B – Crossing the Atlantic 63
   Crossing to Montreal 64
   Crossing to New York 66
   An Example Crossing and Settlement 66
Appendix C - Canada 1835-1882 69
Appendix D - Imaginary Day in the Bacon's Pioneer Life 73
Appendix E - Selected Place Names Then and Now 77
Appendix F - Geographic Places 79
   Arthur 79
   Bruce County 79
   Brant Township 79
   Vesta 80
   Walkerton 80
   Tragedy Strikes Walkerton 82
   Chronology of the Tragedy 83
Appendix G - The Cost of Things in Upper Canada 1831 85
Appendix H - Suggested Reading 87
Part III - Genealogy... 89
   Introduction 89
Modified Register for Joseph Bacon, Sr. 93
   First Generation... 93
   Source References - Joseph, Sr. 97
   Second Generation - William 101
   Source References - Williams 103
   Second Generation - Susan 105
   Source References - Susan 124
   Second Generation - James 129
   Source References - James 133
   Second Generation - Charlotte 135
   Source References - Charlotte 139
   Second Generation - John.. 141
   Source References - John.. 151
   Second Generation - Isaac.. 155
   Source References - Isaac.. 165
   Second Generation - Elijah 167
   Source References - Elijah 172
   Second Generation - Emma Jane 175
   Source References - Emma Jane 181
   Second Generation - Henry.. 187

Source References - Henry 198
Second Generation - Mary Jane 213
Source References - Mary Jane 217
Genealogy Index of Names 221

List of Figures

Figure 1, Letter #1, Page 1 of 2   3

Figure 2, Letter #1, Page 2 of 2   4

Figure 3, Letter #2, Page 1 of 3   7

Figure 4, Letter #2, Page 2 of 3   8

Figure 5, Letter #2, Page 3 of 3   9

Figure 6, Villages of Debden, Henham & Widdington
in Essexshire NNE of London   14

Figure 7, Debden Parish Church Front Facade
(1995, By the Author)   15

Figure 8, Arthur and Brant Townships, Home of the Bacons   17

Figure 9, Corduroy Road Remnant   20

Figure 10, Topographical Map of the Walkerton Area, Contours
at 10 m Intervals. The Bacon Land Along the Durham
Road North and West of the Village is Relatively
Flat. Note the Deep Valley of the Saugeen River.   23

Figure 11, An Early Settler's Clearing and Shanty   24

Figure 12, The Townships of Wellington County   28

Figure 13, Con 18 WOSR Arthur Township and the Village
of Kennilworth. The Owen Sound Road Crosses Arthur
Township diagonally from the Village of Arthur (SE) to
Mt. Forest (NW).   29

Figure 14, Townships of Southern Bruce County   32

Figure 15, The Bacon Concessions & Lots in Brant Township   33

Figure 16, Bacon Lots Near Walkerton   34

Figure 17, Vesta General Store & Post Office, 1900   42

Figure 18, Joseph Bacon, Jr. Gravestone   46

Figure 19, John & Elizabeth Bacon Gravestone   47

Figure 20, Samuel and Emma Jane Hoar's Gravestone   49

Figure 21, Henry and Elizabeth Bacon's Gravestone   51

Figure 22, Susanna & Joseph Bacon, Abt 1875   56

Figure 23, The Old Bethel Methodist/Prior Cemetery (restored)   57

Figure 24, Signatures of Joseph & Susanna Bacon, 1 Nov
1871 on Instrument #2255 Bruce County for the Sale of
Their Farm on Con 1 NDR, Lot 14.   58

Figure 25, 1983 Letter from the Royal Parks Office Baliff   59

Figure 26, Letter in Reference to Revolutionary
War Soldier Henry Bacon   61
Figure 27, Map: The British Isles   63
Figure 28, The North Atlantic from
The British Isles to North America   64
Figure 29, Gulf of St. Lawrence and the St. Lawrence River   65
Figure 30, New York City, the Hudson River
and the Erie Canal   66
Figure 31, 1852 Map: Guelph to Arthur and Brant via
the Garafraxa (A) and Elora (B) Roads; Mt. Forest (1),
Kennilworth (2), Arthur (3), Fergus (4) and Guelph (5).
The Durham Road is Chopped-out but Has Not Yet Been
Mapped.   75
Figure 32, Saugeen Foundry at Walkerton   81

List of Tables

Table 1, Crop Yields   30
Table 2, Children of Joseph and Susanna Bacon, Sr and Their
Spouses   35
Table 3, Crown Patents Received by Bacon Family Members
in Brant Township   36
Table 4, Mortgages Given by Male Members of the
Bacon Family on Brant Township Land.   38
Table 5, Final Sale of Brant Township Land Owned
by Members of the Bacon Family   41

Introduction

Two letters written in Bruce County, Ontario, one in 1881 and a second in 1882 by pioneer Joseph Bacon have survived and form the centerpiece of this memorial to his life 123 years after his death. Joseph was born in 1795 in England, married in England in 1819, immigrated to Canada in 1835 and died in Bruce County in 1882. His life story is told here in two parts:

> **Part I** - The letters. Both letters are written in Joseph's own hand to his daughter and son-in-law in northern lower Michigan where they had moved two years before. Joseph, a widower of some five years is living in the home of a widowed daughter near the former village of Vesta in northern Bruce County, wrote the first of the letters on 7 Mar 1881 and the second on 26 Apr 1882 just eight months before he passed away,

> **Part II** - A narrative of his life illustrated by original documents, photographs and maps, both contemporary and modern. Documentation of information sources in this part has been minimized for readability.

> **Part III** - A detailed genealogical record of Joseph's descendant children and grandchildren in modified register form. This provides an ample view of the geographical dispersion of Joseph's progeny without overwhelming Joseph's accomplishments. Events in addition to the normal birth, marriage, death and burial such as census, mortgages, mortgage discharges and purchases and sales of land which are recorded in public records are also included. Detailed references to all information sources are given in this part.

The author is a great great grandson of Joseph who's line of descent is as follows:
1. Joseph Bacon (1795-1882) m. 1819 Susannah Franklin (1798-1876)
  2. Henry Bacon (1839-1916) m. 1863 Elizabeth Couch (1843-1916)
    3. Lucy Violet Bacon (1886-1939) m. 1906 Warner Abner Wheaton (1885-1967)
      4. Alton A. Wheaton (1915-1987) m. 1939 Ruth Celestia Annis (1920-   )
        5. Dean Wheaton (1940-   ) m. (2) 1977 Marna Dale Miller (1947-   )

Although considerable effort has been made to gather information about Joseph's life, there is undoubtedly more awaiting other descendant researchers/ writers to find and add to this record.

Dean Wheaton
5976 Kungle Road
Clinton, Ohio 44216-9317
dean@deanwheaton.com
March 2006

Part I - The Letters

Two letters written by Joseph Bacon in Bruce County, Ontario in the very early 1880s have been preserved and passed down through the family to the writer. These letters are the focal point of Joseph's story. The letters are presented as a part of the heritage of Bruce County, the Bacon Family and other descendant families.

The letters were written by Joseph in ink on lined paper, the 1881 letter is on a single sheet 8" high by 5" wide written on both sides, the 1882 letter is on two sheets 7" high by 4.5" wide with only the first sheet written on both sides. No envelopes were preserved so the postage needed for mailing is unknown.

The letters have been scanned and digitally reproduced as written. Typed transcripts are shown in two forms:

(1) As written with the attributes of spelling, capitalization, punctuation (or lack of), formatting and pagination as close to the original as possible, and

(2) With these attributes edited to correct errors.

The original and the edited versions are presented side-by-side for ease of reading and comparison. In the edited form on the right, numerous footnotes have been inserted to explain the situations and identify the people that Joseph is writing about. The handwriting is quite good and therefore, for the most part, readability is not a problem.

The writer of the letters was Joseph Bacon, Sr., a Bruce County pioneer. Robertson[1] has this to say about Joseph:

"The land-seeker of 1850 [traveling westward on the Durham Road which was cut through in the summer of 1850], after passing the Stewarts [Con 1 NDR, Lot 21], in his westward march, in a short time came to the shanty and clearing of Joseph Bacon, who had been accompanied into the bush by his brave wife, the first woman to become a permanent settler in the township [of Brant]. Their little shanty was one whose door was ever open to offer the open-handed hospitality of the backwoods to the tired traveler."

And in a footnote on the same page Robertson says:

"Joseph Bacon was a native of Essex, England, where he was born, February 3rd,

---

[1] Robertson, Norman, *History of the County of Bruce*, William Briggs, Toronto, 1906, copyright 1960 by The Bruce County Historical Society, 4th Ed., 1988, page 281.

1795. In March, 1835, he emigrated to Canada and resided in the vicinity of Hamilton. On the opening of the Garafraxa Road he settled in the township of Arthur. When the free grants of the Durham Road were opened for settlement, he was one of the earliest to settle in Brant, taking up lot 14, on concession 1, N.D.R[2]. He had the contract for cutting out the Elora Road through the township of Carrick. Mr. Bacon was a man of marked religious principles. His death occurred December 22nd, 1882."

Joseph was age 86 years when he wrote the first letter, his wife, Susannah Franklin, had died nearly five years before and Joseph was living with his daughter Susan, wife of James Prior (deceased), and family. Susan was one of only two of his eleven children to remain in Canada. Susan lived on Con 14, Lot 9 in northern Brant Township near the small village of Vesta.

The second letter was written a year later, just eight months before his death. Joseph is still at Susan's and, as he explains, his health is not good.

---

[2] The Index of Land Instruments of Brant Township for Con 1 NDR, Lot 14, Microfilm Roll A-3-9, Walkerton Public Library, Walkerton, Ontario, page 14 shows that Joseph Bacon, Jr. received a Crown Patent for this 50 acre lot on 18 May 1854 (this is probably much after Joseph settled on the lot) and sold it to his father, Joseph, Sr., on 24 Dec 1855, recorded in Instrument #168.

Letter #1 - 7 Mar 1881

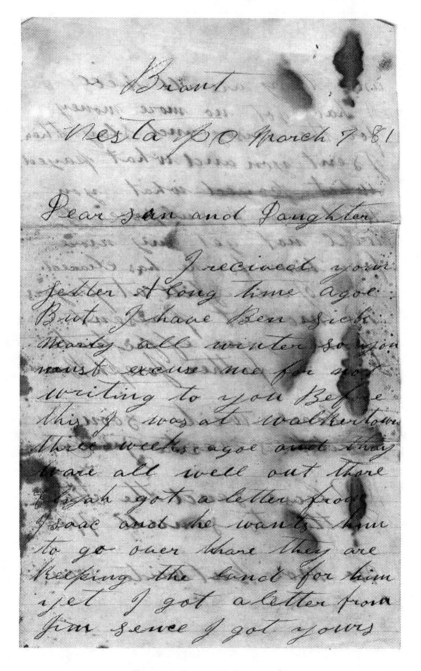

Figure 1, Letter #1, Page 1 of 2

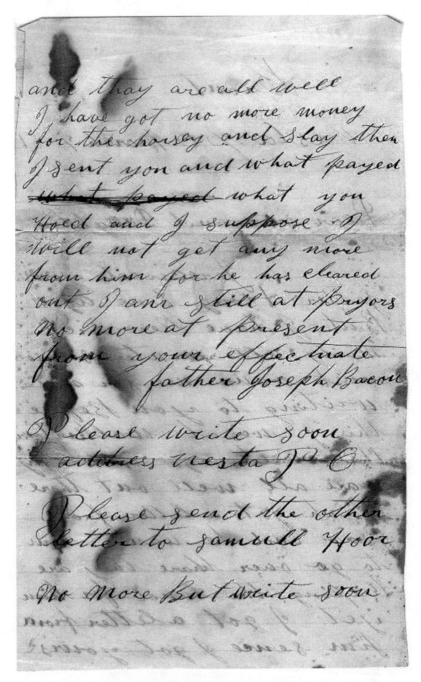

and thay are all well
I have got no more money
for the horsey and slay then
I sent you and what payed
~~what payed~~ what you
Hoed and I suppose I
will not get any more
from him for he has cleared
out I am still at Pryors
No more at present
from your effectuate
            father Joseph Bacon

Please write soon
adeures uesta P O

Please send the other
letter to samuell Hoor

No More But write soon

Figure 2, Letter#1, Page 2 of 2

Letters from Bruce County

As written by Joseph Bacon, Sr.	Punctuation and spelling corrected
Brant	Brant[3]
Vesta P0 March 7 '81	Vesta[4] PO March 7,1881
Dear Son and Daughter	Dear Son and Daughter[5],
I received your letter A long time agoe But I have Ben Sick nearly all winter So you must excuse me for not writing to you Before this I was at Walkerton three weeks agoe and thay ware all well out thare Elijah got a letter from Isaac and he wants him to go over thare They are keeping the land for him yet I got a letter from Jim Sence I got yours	I received your letter a long time ago but I have been sick nearly all winter so you must excuse me for not writing to you before this. I was at Walkerton three weeks ago and they were all well out there. Elijah got a letter from Isaac[7] and he wants him to go over there. They are keeping the land for him yet. I got a letter from Jim Sence[8]. I got yours

[3] Brant Township, Bruce County, Ontario. Brant was the original name given to Walkerton when the post office was opened there in 1852.

[4] Vesta was a small mid-1800s hamlet at the intersection of the Townline and 15th Sideroad on the border between the townships of Brant and Elderslie in Bruce County. It was at first known as Springvale. Vesta was a busy place for many years with a general store, post office, blacksmith shop, carriage or cooper shop, a Methodist Church and two homes. The coming of motor cars, rural mail delivery and the burning of the general store consigned Vesta to the history books.

[5] Son and Daughter refer to Henry and Elizabeth Bacon. Henry is Joseph's youngest son and the husband of Elizabeth Couch Bacon (daughter of Christopher Couch and Mary Ann Tyghe). They moved to Bear Lake (later Resort) Township, Emmet County, Michigan in 1879 on Gov't Lots 4 and 5, R6W, T33N, Sec 2 (135 acres). Resort Township is the southern-most township of Emmet County.

[6] Walkerton, the county seat of Bruce County, Ontario, is located in southern Brant Township on the Durham Road where it crosses the Saugeen River. Joseph Bacon had seven sons: William, James, Joseph, Jr, John, Elijah, Isaac, Henry and four daughters: Susan, Charlotte, Emma Jane, and Mary Jane. In the 1850s and 1860s Joseph and all of his sons except William owned land in close proximity a mile or two west of Walkerton. William owned land about three miles north of his father and brothers. Susan (Prior) lived several miles north of Walkerton. Mary Jane (Guinn) and Charlotte (Smith) lived near their brothers. Emma Jane (Hoar) lived few miles southeast of Walkerton in Carrick Township.

[7] Isaac had moved to Strathclair, Manitoba in 1865 and wants his brother Elijah come to Manitoba too. Elijah did move to Manitoba in 1882 about a year after this letter was written.

[8] Jim Sence is unknown, probably a neighbor.

and thay are all well
I have got no more money
for the horsey and slay then
I sent you and what payed
what you hoed and I
suppose I will not get any more
from him for he has cleared
out I am still at Priors
No more at present
from your affectionate
    father Joseph Bacon
 	
Please write soon
address Vesta PO
 	
Please send the other
letters to Samull Hoor
 	
No more But write soon
	and they are all well.
	I have got no more money
	for the horse and sleigh than
	I sent you and
	what you owed
	and I suppose I will not get any
	more from him for he has
	cleared out. I am still at Prior's[9].
	No more at present.
	From your affectionate
	    father, Joseph Bacon
	
	Please write soon
	address Vesta P0.
	
	Please send the other
	letters to Samuel Hoar[10].
	
	No more but write soon.

---

[9] James Prior married Joseph Bacon's oldest daughter Susan. Susan (James was deceased was living, at the time of the letter, on Concession 14, Lot 9, Brant Township, Bruce County, Ontario approximately two miles southwest of the Village of Vesta.

[10] Samuel Hoar was the husband of Joseph Bacon's youngest daughter Emma Jane. They were living, at the time of the letter, on the W 1/2 of SE 1/4 Sec 25, T38N, R5W, Bliss Twp., Emmet Co., Michigan. Sam and Emma Jane had immigrated there about 1879 from Carrick Township, Bruce County. Carrick Township adjoins Brant Township on the south. Bliss Township is in northern Emmet County.

Letter #2 - 26 Apr 1882

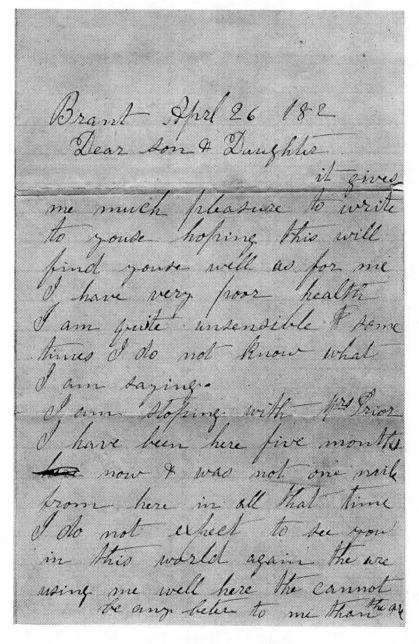

Figure 3, Letter #2, Page 1 of 3

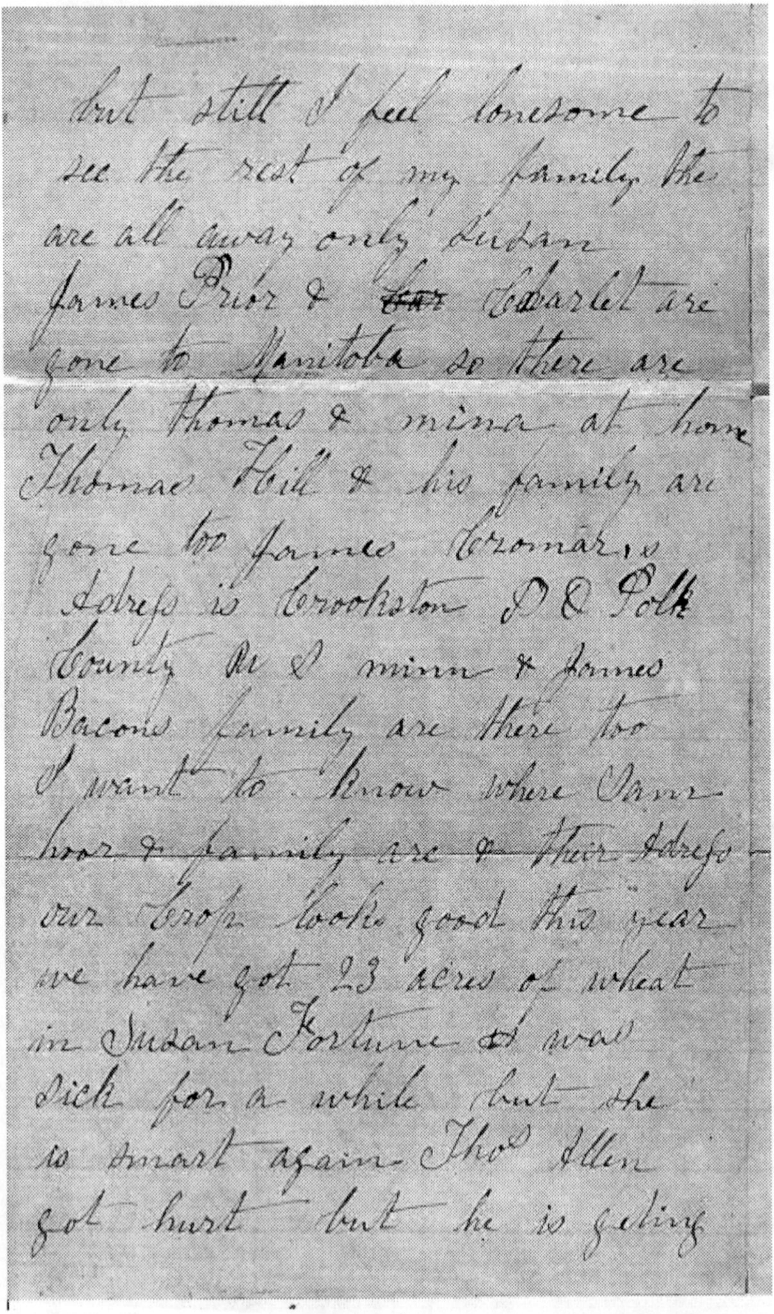

but still I feel lonesome to
see the rest of my family the
are all away only Susan
James Prior & that Scarlet are
gone to Manitoba so there are
only thomas & mina at home
Thomas Hill & his family are
gone too James Cromar,s
Adress is Crookston P O Polk
County & I minn & James
Bacons family are there too
I want to know where Dame-
broo & family are & their Adress
our crop looks good this year
we have got 23 acres of wheat
in Susan Fortune I was
sick for a while but she
is smart again Thos Allen
got hurt but he is geting

Figure 4, Letter #2, Page 2 of 3

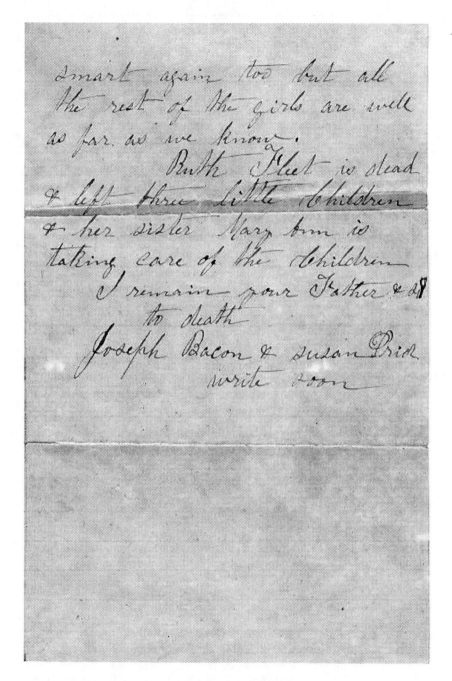

smart again too but all
the rest of the girls are well
as far as we know.
Ruth Fleet is dead
& left three little Children
& her sister Mary Ann is
taking care of the Children
I remain your Father & &
to death
Joseph Bacon & susan Prid
write soon

Figure 5, Letter #2, Page 3 of 3

As written by Joseph Bacon, Sr.	Punctuation and spelling corrected

Brant   April 26 182
   Dear Son & Daughter
	Brant[11] April 26, 1882
	   Dear Son & Daughter[12],

It gives me much pleasure to write to youre hoping this will find youre will as for me I have very poor health I am quite unsensible & some times I do not know what I am saying. I am stoping with Mrs Prior I have been here five months now & was not one mile from here in all that time I do not expect to see you in this world again The are using me well here the cannot be any better to me than the are	It gives me much pleasure to write to you hoping this will find you well. As for me, I have very poor health. I am quite insensible & some times I do not know what I am saying[13]. I am stopping with Mrs. Prior[14]. I have been here five months now & was not one mile from here in all that time. I do not expect to see you in this world again. They are using me well here. They cannot be any better to me than they are

[11] Brant Township, Bruce County, Ontario. Brant was the original name given to Walkerton when the post office was opened there in 1852.

[12] Son and daughter refer to Henry and Elizabeth Bacon. Henry is Joseph's youngest son and the husband of Elizabeth Couch Bacon (daughter of Christopher Couch and Mary Ann Tyghe). They moved to Bear Lake (later Resort) Township, Emmet County, Michigan in 1879 on Gov't Lots 4 and 5, R6W, T33N, Sec 2, 135 acres. Resort Township is the southern-most township of Emmet County.

[13] Joseph died on 27 Dec 1882, only eight months after this letter was written.

[14] Mrs. Prior is Susan Bacon Prior, the oldest daughter of Joseph Bacon and wife of James Prior. Susan (James deceased) was living, at the time of the letter, on Concession 14, Lot 9, Brant Township, Bruce County, Ontario approximately two miles southwest of the Village of Vesta.

but still I feel lonesome to see the rest of my family the are all away only Susan James Prior & Charlet are gone to Manitoba so there are only thomas & mina at home Thomas Hill & his family are gone too James Cromars adress is Crookston PO Polk County ?? ? minn & James Bacons family are there too I want to know where Sam hoor & family are & their address our crop looks good this year we have got 23 acres of wheat in Susan Fortune ?? was sick for a while but she is smart again Thos Allen got hurt but he is geting	but still I feel lonesome to see the rest of my family. They are all away. Only Susan, James Prior & Charlotte[15] are gone to Manitoba[16] so there are only Thomas & Jamina[17] at home. Thomas Hill[18] & his family are gone too. James Cromar's address is Crookston PO, Polk County[19]. ?? ? Minn[20] & James Bacon's[21] family are there too. I want to know where Sam Hoar[22] & family are & their address. Our crop looks good this year. We have got 23 acres of wheat in. Susan Fortune[23] ?? was sick for a while but she is smart again. Thos. Allen[24] got hurt but he is getting

[15] Susan is Susan Bacon Prior, Joseph's oldest daughter and wife of James Prior. James is James Arthur #2, their son. Charlotte is their daughter.

[16] Susan's brothers, James, John, Elijah, and Isaac, had moved to the Brandon area of Manitoba and the Prior's are in Manitoba to visit them and their families.

[17] Thomas and Jemina are children of James and Susan Prior.

[18] Thomas Hill is the husband of Joseph's granddaughter, Mary Margaret Prior.

[19] James Cromar was the 2nd husband of Joseph's daughter Charlotte. James held the offices of Clerk and Treasurer of Greenock Township (see Robertson, pages 403-404). Crookston, Polk County is in Minnesota about 20 miles southeast of Grand Forks, North Dakota. James & Charlotte moved to Baconsville, Dahlen Township, Nelson County, North Dakota in 1880-1881. Baconsville was named for Jerry D. Bacon, a Grand Forks business man not related to Joseph's line. The post office opened 21 Nov 1883 with James Cromar as post master. It closed 31 Oct 1905. Baconsville was west of Grand Forks. It no longer exists.

[20] It is not clear what Joseph is trying to say here. The name "minn" could refer to one of two Joseph Bacon granddaughters named Minnie, one who's parents are John and Elizabeth and one who's parents are Isaac and Margaret.

[21] James Bacon is the second oldest child of Joseph. These words seems to indicate that James is also in Minnesota, a fact not known from other sources but highly possible because James died and was buried in Bottineau, Bottineau County, North Dakota (north central part of the state).

[22] Samuel Hoar was the husband of Joseph Bacon's youngest daughter Emma Jane. They were living, at the time of the letter, on the W 1/2 of SE 1/4 Sec 25, T38N, R5W, Bliss Twp, Emmet Co, Michigan. Sam and Emma Jane had immigrated there about 1879 from Carrick Township, Bruce County. A post office was opened at Bliss in 1878.

[23] Susan Fortune is Susan Prior Fortune, Joseph's granddaughter.

[24] Thos. Allen is the husband of Elizabeth Anne Prior, Joseph's granddaughter.

smart again too but all	smart again too but all
the rest of the girls are well	the rest of the girls are well
as far as we know.	as far as we know.
Ruth Fleet is dead	Ruth Fleet[25] is dead
& left three little Children	& left three little children
& her sister Mary Ann is	& her sister Mary Ann[26] is
taking care of the children	taking care of the children.
I remain your Father & ??	I remain your father & ??
to death	to death,
Joseph Bacon & susan Prior	Joseph Bacon & Susan Prior
write soon	Write soon.

[25] Ruth Fleet is Ruth Rebecca Bacon, daughter of Isaac Bacon and the wife of William Fleet. The 1881 Ontario Census of Listowel, Perth County enumerated William Fleat (sic) with wife Rebecca age 23, with three small daughters: Charlotte, age 4, Mary, age 2, and Iva, age 1. A Mary Bacon age 19 was also enumerated in the household.

[26] Joseph's statement, "her (Ruth's) sister Mary Ann is taking care of the children" is puzzling. Ruth has no known sister named Mary. It is likely that the Mary Bacon, age 19, enumerated in the 1881 census is the same person as the Mary Ann named by Joseph but who this person is isn't known.

Part II - Narrative

The milestones of the lives of Joseph and Susannah, although given in detail in the genealogy, are important to his story and are repeated here:

Joseph
Birth: 3 Feb 1795 in Essexshire, England the son of James and Mary Stubbing Bacon.
Baptized: 29 Mar 1795 Henham Parish, Essexshire, England.
Death: 27 Dec 1882[27] in Brant Township, Bruce County, Ontario.
Burial: Old Bethel Methodist/Prior Cemetery[28], Brant Township, Bruce County, Ontario.
Marriage: Susannah Franklin, on 24 Jul 1819 in Widdington, Essexshire , England.

Susannah
Birth: 1798 in Widdington, Essexshire , England, the daughter of Henry Franklin and Sarah _____.
Death: 5 May 1876 in Brant Township, Bruce County, Ontario.
Burial: Old Bethel Methodist/Prior Cemetery, Brant Township, Bruce County, Ontario.

The English Years

The English vital records of the Bacon family are recorded in the Debden and Widdington Parish (Essexshire, England) registers with references to the Henham Parish. All three parishes are located close together in an area approximately forty miles north northeast of the center of London. On a modern map the three parishes are represented by three villages of the same names, see **Figure 6**.

The records of these parishes have now provided a path of the Bacons back to the late 16th century with the baptism of William Bacon on 9 May

---

[27] Conflicts with Robertson's date of 22 Dec 1882

[28] Neither Joseph or Susannah are included in the Bruce County Cemetery Gravestone Readings, Bruce County Archives & Museum, Southampton, Ontario. Probably because the their gravestones were destroyed before the readings were recorded.

1574 at Henham, seven generations preceding Joseph (generations 4-7 researched by English Researcher Peter C. Nutt commissioned by Douglas Bacon, Spokane, Washington).

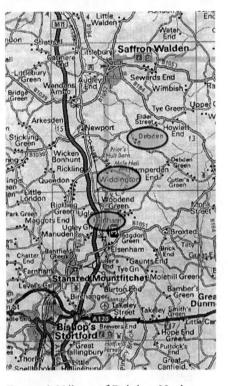

After their marriage Joseph and Susanna lived in the Debden Parish as evidenced by the recording of the baptisms/births of the first eight of their eleven children in the Debden Parish registers.

Joseph's occupation in England can be inferred from notations on some of his children's baptismal records which record simply "Labourer" in the English spelling. Some fanciful stories of his activities (champion boxer and queen's gamekeeper, etc., see Appendix A) have been authored by other descendant writers but most have not been able to be verified.

Figure 6, Villages of Debden, Henham & Widdington in Essexshire NNE of London

The family's religious affiliation in England was primarily with the Debden Parish with some association with the Hemham and Widdington parish churches. These churches were associated with the Church of England..

The Debden Parish Church, St Mary the Virgin and All Saints, dates from the thirteenth century. The church has had several repairs and additions over the intervening centuries. In current times a regular congregation of 30 to 40 meets every Sunday for worship at 9:30 AM. The church has rectors going back to before the year 1325. The Rector during the last years before Joseph and his family emigrated was William Jurin Totton who served from 1798 to 1850, a very long tenure.

As seen in 1995 by the author, the church is located down a small lane away from the village in an area of verdant farmland. The approach to the church from the car park is through a row of large pine trees to the rear of the church. Once through the trees the church lies before you. In this area is the oldest part of the churchyard from which all the gravestones have been removed (they were very old, broken and mostly unreadable). The view is of the altar end of the building looking along the right side of the building. The normally used entrance to the church is through a small vestibule on the right hand side of the building at the rear. If the visitor were to continue on, he/she would first see and then enter the newer part of the churchyard (cemetery) which is still being used for burials, the further on, the more recent the burials. Part of the churchyard was not well cared for and was grown

Figure 7, Debden Parish Church Front Farcade (1995, By the Author)

up in brambles and weeds. From the newer part of the churchyard the visitor, upon turning around, will see the front of the church building for the first time. The facade is quite imposing for a small rural church with its now unused main entrance, see **Figure 7**.

Upon entering the church the visitor sees ten rows of pews divided by a rather narrow central aisle. Overhead the ceiling is supported by arches set on large pillars. These pillars are the oldest part of the church, the northern ones constructed in 1220 and the southern ones about twenty-five years later. Overall the impression of the sanctuary and altar area is one of simplicity. Along the outer walls are a series of arched stained glass windows. The pews are standard hard-sitting wood but with an modern (1968-1972) innovation - cushions which are hung on the back of the pew in front of the parishioner when not in use. At the rear of the church is a small organ built in 1949 to replace one installed in 1880 which itself replaced the original organ destroyed by fire in 1878. On the walls are various memorial plaques.

England 1835[29]

What was going on in England in 1835 that would cause a family to give up everything and leave? The Great Reform Bill had been passed which was meant to be the answer to all men's ills when they were able to vote. It raised up men's hopes for a better life. Only it didn't work out like that as there were still restrictions and only a very small additional electorate were able

---

[29] Wheaton, Jean, Horley, England, Private correspondence, 27 Mar 2003.

to elect their MPs. This resulted in a lot of anger and discontent amongst those who were poor and who did not have the vote. Because there was a lot of unrest amongst working men the Chartist movement was started where demands included one man one vote and secret ballots. There was also a lot of upheaval in what was to become the Trade Union Movement. There were Combination Laws where individuals and groups endeavoring to form Unions were outlawed until about 1834, so this meant that even if people tried to improve their lot they were unable to do so.

The vast majority of the population lived in the country and there had also been quite a lot of problems for the poorer people who had previously managed to feed themselves from their own rented land. More and more land was enclosed, which was great for the larger landlords, but had the effect of driving the poorer countryman from the countryside (where his ancestors had lived for generations) into towns where living and working conditions were pretty dreadful. Before this time people seemed to "know their place" but with the unrest generated when the idea of "class" was introduced, and much was made about "class conflict" as a middle class came to be established - thus adding to the unease and unrest amongst the "working class" which would of course have included the Bacon Family since Joseph was a labourer. The problems really arose when a working class man, or a poor man (as he was usually) became unable to work for whatever reason. Way in the past the monasteries had taken care of the poor, then the parishes took over the role, but as the population grew the parishes could not raise enough money. What the parishes used to do was give money to those who needed it whilst they still lived in their own homes. The "poor" included the larger proportion of the population and in 1834 there was the Poor Law Act which said that there was to be no more "outdoor" relief, where men could stay with their families. Instead the families had to go into workhouses where they would be split into sections for males, females and children. There were also problems with raising bread prices due to efforts to maintain the price of home grown corn. And of course, wages were unbelievably low.

Most labourers would have had neither money or property. Very few people owned their own homes and labourers or agricultural labourers would certainly not have been among them. The gentleman farmer or yeoman might have owned his farm, but even he might have rented it from the Lord of the Manor. So, lots of people thought they would be able to have a better life anywhere other than in England.

Immigration to America & Canada

In March of 1835, Joseph, Susanna and their eight children left England. Terms of their passage assistance would have them bound for the British

Colonies of America - Canada. The children were from age fourteen (William) down to age eighteen months (the twins Isaac and Elijah). They came through the port of New York City and stopped for a short time (length unknown) in Buffalo, New York[30] where their ninth child Emma Jane was born in 1836. By the fall of 1839 the family had moved on to Hamilton, Upper Canada[31] at the western end of Lake Ontario where son Henry was born. Joseph was labeled a labourer in England in his children's birth/ baptismal records. It is highly unlikely that he

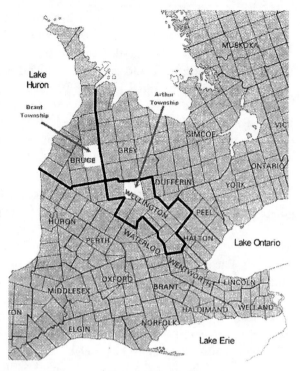

Figure 8, Arthur and Brant Townships, Home of the Bacons

was skilled at any craft and therefore likely that he was similarly occupied in Canada. Joseph is listed as an inn keeper in 1840s land documents and he is

---

[30] This route is the subject of family tradition and has not been verified. The newly discovered fact of their receiving passage assistance to the British Colonies of America casts aspersion on a route through New York but raises a conflict with Emma Jane's birth at Buffalo. Clearly, the immigration occurred sometime after the birth of the twins Elijah and Isaac, born 24 Sep 1833 in Debden. Robertson in his *History of the County of Bruce,* page 281 says, "In March, 1835, he [Joseph Bacon] emigrated to Canada and resided in the vicinity of Hamilton."

[31] The modern province of Ontario had two prior names after it was carved out of what originally was a very large area known as Quebec. In the 1791 Constitutional Act the parts of old Quebec that were to become Ontario and new Quebec were partitioned into Upper Canada (as in up the St. Lawrence River) and Lower Canada. In 1840 Upper Canada was renamed Canada West while Lower Canada became Canada East. In 1867 the Confederation of Canada was created and Canada West was renamed a third time to Ontario (Canada East became Quebec). It is customary in genealogical writings to record events using the names of places as they existed at the time that the event occurred. Upper Canada, Canada West and Ontario all refer to the same land at different times.

known to have been a road contractor in the 1850s. He likely was a farmer (like most men in Canada at this time) for most of his life.

These facts open the question of how the move of a family of ten from England to Canada was financed? The cost of food, lodging and transportation would have been substantial for such a large family. Were they assisted in some way? By the government? By their church? A possible hint can be gleaned from the following statement which appeared in the Widdington Parish Vestry Minutes: "Expenses paid for James Franklin [Susanna's brother] and family to Canada 1835."

For a view of what emigrants faced on arrival at Quebec, see the University of Waterloo's user site: http://ist.uwaterloo.ca/~marj/ and specifically the document at: http://ist.uwaterloo.ca/~marj/genealogy/emigrants1832.html, *1832 Emigrants Handbook For Arrivals at Quebec.*

As this book goes to press. Research by Peter Nutt commissioned by Douglas Bacon, Spokane, Washington has turned up the following: As authorized by a Poor Law Act of Parliment, parish Poor Law Commissioners are empowered to accept applications for the emigration of poor persons to the British Colonies of America and borrow against the Poor Rates [taxes] with repayment and interest of 5% per annum to be made over five years. Costs for families sent in 1833 for eight weeks passage: board £2 per head, passage from London to Quebec: £2, 10s per head over age 14 and £1, 5s per head under age 14; from Quebec to the head of Lake Ontario £1 per head for men, women and children. Land carriage and expenses from Debden to London were about £10 for a group of fifteen persons. The minutes of a meeting of the Debden Parish Poor Law Commissioners on 6 Mar 1835 record that Joseph Bacon, his wife and eight children were among those wishing to emigrate and requesting assistance for their passage. This has implications on their route and destination and creates a possible conflict with Emma Jane's birth at Buffalo, New York.

The Queen's Bush

The land which was eventually to bear the name Ontario was settled from the east to the west and gradually northward from the shores of Lakes Ontario and Erie. A few, mostly fishermen, lived along the shores of Lake Huron and Georgian Bay. By the1830s settlement had taken place as far as Guelph (30 miles northwest of Hamilton). Very few settlers were in the area to the northwest of Guelph which was known as The Queen's Bush. Several rivers provided access to the heavily timbered interior, the largest being the Saugeen which flowed generally northward and emptied into Lake Huron near modern day Southampton.

Settlement Roads

Settlement was aided by the government's policy of building "Settlement Roads" into the bush and making free land grants of 50 acres along the roads. First came the surveyors marking out the course of the road, the townships and lots. The surveyor's stock-in-trade for marking the course of a road or a lot boundary was the "blaze[32]" on a tree.

In the late 1830s the Government of Upper Canada decided that another road was necessary for settlement of the Queen's Bush and in 1837 Charles Rankin was hired to survey a right of way from the vicinity of Guelph to Sydenham (later changed to Owen Sound) at the south end of Owen Sound Bay. In 1840 the right of way was considerably altered by John McDonald and construction began. The road became known as the Garafraxa Road since its southern terminus was in the Township of Garafraxa in Wellington County. From Guelph the Garafraxa Road ran northwest 12 miles (a days travel by horse and wagon) to Fergus, a further 12 miles to the village of Arthur, then 12 additional miles to the village of Mount Forest, then directly northward for 50 miles to Sydenham. The construction took eight years being completed in 1848. Today's Ontario Highway 6 follows the route of the Garafraxa Road.

> Road Building in the Queen's Bush - Roads were built by contractors to the government in sections of ½, 1, 1 ½, and 2 miles depending on the terrain. The contracts specified a road width of one chain (66 ft.) to be chopped (cleared) of all timber. All trees 8 inches in diameter and under were to be cut close to the ground but all stumps, unless interfering with making the road passable, were allowed to remain. All of the timber on the road allowance was cut into logging lengths, 12-14 ft., and these, together with all brushwood and rubbish, were piled on each side of the road. These piles were left to dry and later burned. This left a span 45 feet in width in the middle of the allowance for a roadway. Timber might be felled into the woods on either side, but not into the clearings!
>
> In swamps and where causewaying (also called corduroy) was required to allow passage of wheeled vehicles, all of the timber had to be cut close to the ground for a width of 20 feet in the center of the road. Causewaying was made of straight sound logs, laid evenly and close together and at right angles to the roadway, and each log had to be 16 feet long. All bridges of 15 feet span and under were included under the head of causewaying. Contracts for chopping

---

[32] A triangular section of bark, some 40 to 60 cm on a side, was cut from a large tree, facing the route or boundary line. The next blaze would be cut on a tree further along but in sight of the previous one so that gradually a line or route could be seen connecting the blaze markings.

and logging the road varied from 23 pounds sterling to 25 pounds sterling per mile, and causewaying 7s. 6d. to 10s. per rod[33].

Note that the specifications make no mention of any improvement of the road bed. The "road" was only a cleared space in the forest covered by stumps and lined by piles of brush and logs on both sides. Its surface consisted of whatever soil was present and left in the contour in which it was found. No provisions were made for drainage of rain water or snow melt. A moments reflection on the situation will make one wonder how it could be called a road. Any vehicle would be unable to travel faster than a slow walk and would be frequently mired in sand and mud holes of staggering proportions.

Pioneering in The Bush

For centuries the Indian had lived on the land taking only what he needed and leaving the land nearly unchanged by his passage. Natural clearings were sometimes planted with corn or squash. The trees grew thick and large in dense forests. A few trails developed where it was easiest to walk. Streams were unbridged. Animals living in the forest were hunted for food only as needed. In short, the Indian accepted what he found and used it if he could by

Figure 9, Corduroy Road Remnant

adapting his needs to the land. Not so the European settler who forced the land to meet his needs. The settler found the trees an impediment to be cut and burned to make way for fields and roads. The Indian had trails which followed the contours of the land, the European forced his roads straight across the land, bridged the rivers and streams and developed vehicles to carry heavy loads. His fields were defined by straight fences and the wild animals were destroyed when they competed with his domestic ones.

---

[33] In the English monetary system of pence, shillings and pounds: 12 d. = 1s., 20 s. = £1. In linear measure: 320 rods = 1 mile.

The Indian and the European settler shared a need and usage of one aspect of the untamed land - the rivers and lakes. The Indian had learned to make small boats (canoes) and used the water for travel extensively. The European found the water was his only access on first arrival.

Because the European settler had a very different concept of the land he was entering, he found living conditions in The Bush most primitive. This was especially true for the first settlers of an area. As time passed and the density of settlers increased conditions by European standards, did improve . The truly amazing fact of settlement is that the settlers did not shy away from the hardships of The Bush. In fact, they often settled in an area only to move deeper into The Bush a few years later to start all over again. Some families even did this several times. The settler's desire for space and land to call his own was tantamount to the hardships involved.

The Settlement Process

Settlers were enticed into the Queen's Bush by free grants of 50 acre lots on each side of the Settlement Roads. Other lots away from the road were 100 acres in size and were offered for sale after the free grants were taken. The regulations of these grants required these settlers to be subjects of Queen Victoria, males, and over the age of 18 years. Twelve acres of land had to be cleared in four years, counting from the 1st of January following the taking up of the land. When chopping and logging, 5 acres of bush was looked upon as a fair winter's work; 3 acres could not be deemed excessive in the same time. Persons so taking up land had to be capable of maintaining themselves until such time as the land was self-supporting. If a lot was abandoned by a settler, the same was to be open for sale or grant to another. Settlers, on receiving a free grant had the privilege of purchasing, in addition, sufficient to make up 200 acres of land. The settler, on going to the Land Office, received a Location Ticket from the Crown Land Agent after first giving his name, age, condition, trade or profession; whether married or single, and if married the name of his wife, the number of children, and their names and ages; where he was from and the township in which he wished to settle; and a certificate of good character from a clergyman.

On receiving his Location Ticket the settler was required to take possession of his lot within 30 days after the ticket was issued and put into a state of cultivation at least 12 acres of land in the course of the following 4 years; to build a house at least 18 x 24 ft.; and to reside on the lot until the conditions of settlement were fulfilled, and then a title (Patent) was issued for the property by the Crown. Permission was granted the settler to purchase three other additional 50-acre lots at 8 shillings ($2.00) per acre.

The timber on the land was reserved by the Government, except that for the required clearings, until the land had been paid for and a Patent issued. It was to be subject to any general timber duty thereafter. The Location Ticket was not assignable without permission of the Crown Lands Agent. The License of Occupation to be null and void unless all the conditions of settlement were fulfilled, and not more than 200 acres were to be sold to any one person upon those terms.

On applying for a Location Ticket, the Crown Lands Agent gave the applicant a list of lots not already taken up. This list did not contain many lots, and was drawn out, as far as possible, with a view to prevent any two men inspecting and selecting the same lot. The Agent also planned to have people of a congenial type settle in the same locality.

When the conditions of the grant were fulfilled, the settler was eligible to receive a Crown Patent for his land. The was one catch, however. The settler had to physically appear in person at Toronto to get the patent. The usual means of transportation early days was to walk, resulting in a many days-long journey from the Queen's Bush. Hence settlers usually did not get their patent until they wanted to mortgage or sell the land. Patents were always dated as granted on the date it was received in Toronto. Therefore, dates on patents are not indicative of the date of settlement. Once the settler had his patent in hand, he still had to return to his home township and county to have the patent recorded in the Land Registry Office. All land transactions such as patents, sales or mortgages have to be registered[34].

Finding Suitable Land

A settler looking for land would set out on a prospecting tour following the surveyor's blazes. The settler had few but important preparations to make for his trip: finding a place to leave his family while he made his tour and creating his pack. The pack would sustain him in the bush and commonly contained a frying pan, cup, knife, fork, spoon, flour, salt, tea, bacon, matches, axe, gun and a blanket. His days were spent tramping on foot through the bush, at night he slept where he could find or make a little shelter at the base of a tree or beneath a crude self made lean-to with only his blanket for warmth. If he was very lucky he might find a squatter with a shanty for the night. He ate bacon and scones made from the supply of flour, salt, and water from his pack which he cooked in his frying pan over a campfire. Whatever game he could bring down with his gun was a welcome supplement.

---

[34] The documents recording such land transactions are called Instruments and are given a unique number from a sequential set maintained by each Registry Office. Instruments are then recorded in Land Instrument Indexes. A separate Index is maintained for each Concession and Lot. This is different from the system used in the U.S.

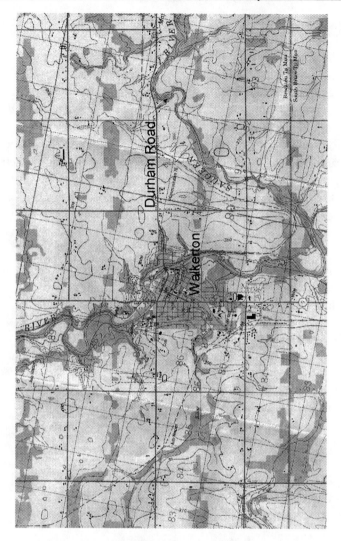

Figure 10. Topographical Map of the Walkerton Area,
Contours at 10 m Intervals. The Bacon Land Along the
Durham Road North and West of the Village is Relatively
Flat. Note the Deep Valley of the Saugeen River

Generally, the settler was looking for a lot where good hardwood timber grew indicating good soil and a nearby clear spring or stream for a water supply. When he found a suitable place, he began felling trees to make a clearing for his shanty and a sign that this lot was taken. How much he accomplished depended on his food resources but eventually he was forced

23

back to civilization to replenish and register his claim with the Crown Land Agent. His next actions depended on personal circumstances. He would go back to his lot to clear more timber and build a shanty but would he take his family with him or wait until later when his shanty was completed. If the settler was very lucky he owned a pair of oxen and cart to carry his provisions and goods provided the road to his lot was cleared. Otherwise the settler might make use of a jumper or take only what could be carried on his back.

Once the settlement road had been cleared and the free grants taken, the government opened additional land "behind" the free grants for settlement. This process served to rapidly increase the population which, in turn, brought inns, mills (both for grinding wheat into flour and for sawing logs into boards), general stores and eventually all of the other accouterments of civilization.

Shelter

The first priority of a pioneer settler was shelter from the elements. A typical situation was that of the Smith family. Brothers William and Johnston Smith came from Scotland in 1847 to The Bush of Brant Township (Con 1 SDR, Lots 21 and 22) next door to Isaac Bacon. Their sister Jane Smith left Scotland in August, 1850 to join her brothers and finds them in their shanty[35]. The shanty was built of logs 20 feet x 24 feet and eleven logs high (to allow for an eventual sleeping loft) by the brothers with the help of their neighbors. Crevices between the logs were awaiting chinking with wood chips, moss and clay. The roof was constructed of basswood logs split in half and hollowed out to form a shallow u-shape in cross section. By placing one log u-down over the joint between two logs u-up below, a lasting rain tight roof was created. There

Figure 11, An Early Settler's Clearing and Shanty

[35] McGillivray, Marion, *From City Streets to Trackless Forest: The story of Jane Smith*, The Bruce County Historical Society, 1995, pages 34-38.

were two small window openings flanking the door opening. There was no door, only a heavy woolen blanket to be hung over the opening at night. At one end of the shanty was a fireplace made from sticks and plastered over with clay. The hearth was made of flat stones carried from the river. The floor of the shanty was dirt hard packed and smoothed. Jane's bed was a frame of small poles in one corner covered with young saplings and spread with hemlock and cedar boughs. The brothers spread their blankets on hemlock boughs scattered on the floor in front of the fireplace.

Transportation

The first transportation systems were the lakes and rivers using canoes, boats and sometimes rafts. Many families built rafts at Bentinck (Durham) and floated down the Saugeen to their land. In the spring time, this mode of transportation could be very dangerous due to the high water levels, the swiftness of the current and the icy temperature of the water.

The primary form of transportation in pioneer days was right foot, left foot. In short, walking. A settler thought nothing of setting out to get supplies on a trip of tens of miles. Few if any settlers had a riding horse. Roads were non-existent to very poor especially in the spring and fall when the rains fell. The best time for travel was in winter. The snow filled in the holes and covered up the stumps and when frozen made a relatively hard smooth surface.

The settler who had more goods or materials to transport than could be carried in hand could easily construct a jumper or stoneboat from materials at hand. This device was a flat-bottomed sled with runners and a rope or chain for pulling. It could be used winter and summer although it slid easier on snow than on dirt. It could be scaled to a size to fit the task depending on the source of the towing force and the weight of the load. A settler who had a trek of fifteen or twenty miles to go for supplies in winter might construct a jumper 1½ feet wide and a few feet long which might also be called a toboggan. The settler who was clearing his land of rocks might construct a jumper of two trees six to eight inches in diameter as runners three to four feet apart. The lower front end of each runner was tapered so as to slide over the ground or snow rather than digging in. A deck of split saplings (or rough boards, if available) were fastened across the runners spaced three or four feet apart. A short chain or heavy rope hooked to the front of each runner served as a hitch point for a team of oxen.

In winter sleighs were used over the frozen snow. They could make moving very heavy loads easy.

Pioneer draft animals were exclusively oxen. Slow and plodding, oxen were far better suited to working around and between the stumps than horses.

30 Nov 1871 was a signal day in transportation for Brant Township for on that day the first locomotive steamed into Walkerton forging a link to the outside world of markets for the produce and products of the Township.

Crops and Food

The first crops planted by a settler among the stumps were potatoes, wheat and oats. The potatoes could be easily prepared by simple boiling or frying but the wheat had to be taken, sometimes many miles on a jumper pulled by hand, to a mill to be ground into flour. Early mills were not able to remove the bran from the flour. "Scones" were made from a dough of flour with a pinch of salt and some water. Baking the dough in a frying pan made an edible if not very appetizing hard bread or scone. Oats could be rolled or pounded into oat meal which when cooked in water made a nutritious porridge. Left-over oatmeal was left to harden then sliced and fried for a later meal. Sugar or molasses, salt, tea and bacon were purchased if the settler had been able to work for cash. Otherwise a little maple sugar might be available and tea improvised from burned bread crumbs or the roasted roots of certain plants.

A root house or cellar for the storage of vegetables was constructed by digging a trench 2-3 feet deep by 10 feet wide and 20 feet long which was roofed by a sloping framework of slender poles and covered with several feet of dirt. One end had a wooden door. This served as a natural refrigerator, preserving the crops but also keeping them from freezing. Field crops such as potatoes and turnips along with garden crops such as cabbage, onions and carrots were good candidates for storage in the cellar.

Pioneers also made good use of foods they found growing wild: raspberries, strawberries, blackberries, thimble berries, elderberries, various nuts and red plums. Game such as deer, bear, rabbit, squirrel and the immense flocks of passenger pigeons added meat to their diet. Fish could be caught in the Saugeen and salted or dried for winter eating. Wild honey made an excellent sweetener when it could be found.

If the settler had oxen or cows, it was necessary to have at least a rough stable to protect them from wild animals such as bears and wolves and from the harsh cold and winds of winter. For winter feed, hay was cut from beaver meadows along streams and stacked near the stable for fodder.

Religion

Joseph was apparently a man of strong religious beliefs. Even Robertson in his History of Bruce County remarked on it (page 281). In England the family was closely associated with the Church of England or Anglican faith as all their children were baptized, married and buried by that church.

When they came to Canada they soon switched to the Methodist brand of religion. Why this change was made is unknown but there must have been a compelling reason. Since Canada in the 19th century was an English colony and the dominant religion was Church of England, there certainly would have been no shortage of circuit riders of the faith even in The Bush. There were several varieties of Methodism, Joseph being sometimes recorded as an Episcopal Methodist. In his later years (after arriving in Brant Township), Joseph begins to be recorded as being of the Primitive Methodist religion. In fact, the South Line Primitive Methodist Church was built on a small hill in the northwest corner of Con 3 SDR, Lot 16 in Brant Township. This lot was granted via Crown Patent to Henry Bacon, the youngest son of Joseph. No records exist as to the date it was constructed but it is recorded that it was known as an "old church" in 1875. Popular belief in the township is that the church burned down but no record has been found to verify this.

Since his faith was so important to Joseph and Primitive Methodism is not well known, it is appropriate to include a brief description of it here. In the early 1800s the religious zeal which had earlier spread the open-air meetings of Methodism across England under the leadership of John and Charles Wesley had began to subside into more conventional channels. Two preachers in the Wesleyan Church, Hugh Bourne and William Clowes, who had strong feelings toward a return to the original Wesleyan principles, met in 1806 with Lorenzo Dow, a eccentric and powerful evangelist, who told of the amazing conversions at camp meetings in America. Fully enthused, they arranged for an all-day (6 AM to 8 PM) outdoor meeting on 31 May 1807 at Mow Cop, a rugged mountain on the border of Staffordshire and Cheshire some twenty-five miles south of Manchester. Thousands thronged to hear their message proclaimed from four preaching stands. Large numbers of those listening were converted but they were later refused admittance to the Wesleyan Church. Bourne and Clowes were reprimanded and, after continuing to hold similar outdoor meetings, were dismissed from the Wesleyan Church. In 1810 after it became clear that they and their converts would never be re-instated, they founded the Primitive Methodist Church[36, 37]. It wasn't long before the church followed its member immigrants to Canada and the U.S.

---

[36] "The Primitive Methodist Church," *LoveToKnow 1911 Online Encyclopedia*, http://35.1911encyclopedia.org/p/pr/primitive_methodist_church_the.htm

[37] "Primitive Methodist Church in the U.S.A.," www.primitivemethodistchurch.org/preface.html

Arthur Township, Waterloo County[38]

After a short time in Hamilton, Joseph moved the family northwestward into The Bush where he received a Crown Patent on 50 acres in the fourth division, east part of Lot No. 18, Concession WOSR (West of Owen Sound Road[39]) in Arthur Township, Waterloo County, Canada West on 10 Dec 1846. By the regulations governing the free grants, he would have had to

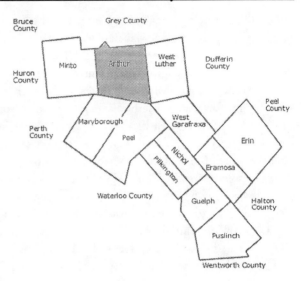

Figure 12, The townships of Wellington County

live on the land for four years before receiving his patent. Therefore, it can be assumed that Joseph arrived on this land, at the latest, in 1842[40], only a year or two after construction of the Garafraxa Road began. Joseph may have been one of the Garafraxa Road contractors. He was at various times a farmer, a road contractor and a tavern keeper. His family would have consisted of Susanna and ten children ranging in age from William, age 19, to Henry, age 2. If they came to Arthur Township in 1940 as is probable, Henry would have been a babe in arms! Their arrival in Arthur Township is bolstered by

---

[38] Wellington County was created from part of Waterloo County in 1856. Arthur Township became part Wellington County.

[39] The Owen Sound Road is also known as the Garafraxa Road.

[40] Joseph probably arrived in 1840 along with sons William and James. James would have been only age 15 years. In MacKenzie, W.F., *The County of Wellington, Township of Arthur*, pg. 17, Wellington County Museum & Archive: "The pioneers in 1840, on lot 18, and pt. 19, were Jos., William and Jas. Bacon." And on page 5 "On the O.S.R. were 35 lots of 4 parts each. On the west side the following settlers were given: ..., Lot 18, part 1, Wm. Bacon; 3 and 4, Joseph Bacon. ... ." However, William's name does **not** appear on the *Land Instrument Index*, Arthur Township, pgs. 211 & 212 for Lot 18, Con WOSR.

Figure 13, Con 18 WOSR Arthur Township and the Village of Kennilworth. The Owen Sound Road Crosses Arthur Township diagonally from the Village of Arthur (SE) to Mt.Forest(NW).

the 1841 Government Report released 24 May 1841 listing the names of the first settlers and giving their religion. Among the 42 Episcopalians are Wm. Bacon, Jos. Bacon and James Bacon. In addition, there were 19 Presbyterians, 15 Roman Catholics and 4 Wesleyan Methodists[41]. Their eldest daughter, Susan, married James Prior about 1839 in Arthur Township. James and Susan owned two 50 acre parcels in Lot 18 EOSR across the road from her parents and adjacent to the village-to-be of Kennilworth[42]. It is probable that the two oldest sons, William, age 21 and James, age 16, built a second shanty for their domicile on their father's property. Joseph's eldest daughter, Susan, was married and living across the Garafraxa Road from her parents. This left the parents and only seven children living in the family shanty, still a rather crowded situation especially in the winter months.

No doubt Joseph had a pair of patient and enduring oxen, a much more efficient draft animal among the stumps, trees and roots than a high strung horse for pulling a cart, timbering and tilling the land. Imagine traveling into

---

[41] First Settlers in Arthur Township, Wellington County Virtual History Book (www.wcm.on.ca/tweedsmuir/idex.php), Wellington County Museum & Archives, 1841 Government Report, Elora Observer, 24 May 1861, Former Editor Richard Mills' Papers [WWD320].

[42] This was a very busy period in the lives of the Bacons: Henry was born 11 Oct 1839 in Hamilton, Susan married James Prior about 1839 and had her first child on 12 Jul 1840 in Arthur Township. This in addition to moving the entire family approximately 60 miles into the bush, clearing land and building a cabin, possibly more than one.

an unsettled wilderness with such a family. Life would have been difficult at best living in a log cabin with no nearby store or a mill to grind wheat (if they had any) for flour within many days travel. Having sixteen and twenty-one year old sons would have been a great help. The soil, when cleared of trees and brush, was rich and black yielding 50-70 bushels of wheat per acre, a very substantial yield.

On 6 Jun 1848 Joseph mortgaged his lot to a group of three men for £24. The reason for the borrowing this money is unknown. The loan was repaid and the mortgage discharged on 6 Aug 1849. Two days later on 8 Aug 1849, in the eleventh year on the land, Joseph & Susanna sold their 50 acre farm to James MacKay for £132, £131, 5s. to Joseph and 5s. to Susanna for her dower rights.

Farming in Arthur Township, 1861 [43]

The census of 1861 included an agricultural part. Although the Bacons had already left the area, a brief review of that census will provide some insight into late-day pioneering farming. After twenty years from first settlement on the land, the settlers had an average of thirty-five percent of their lots under cultivation. This cultivated land was split 65%-35% between crops and pasture. The remaining 65% of the lot was still in forest or wild. The average cash value of a farm was $15.11 per acre. The average cash value of farm equipment was $105 per farm.

Spring wheat was universally grown on from 15% to 60% of the land under cultivation. On average 30% of land under cultivation was used to raise spring wheat. Nearly all farmers grew peas, most grew oats, 62% grew potatoes and 54% grew turnips. Average yields for these crops are shown in adjacent table. Hay was nearly universally harvested, averaging a little over three tons per farm.

Crop	Yield, Bu./Acre
Wheat	10
Peas	12
Oats	37
Potatoes	50
Turnips	216

Table 1, Crop Yields in 1861

Although the census asks about the following additional crops, none were reported grown: buck wheat, mangel wurtzel (sugar beets), orchards, carrots, beans, hops and cider. Neither did

---

[43] 1861 Agricultural Census of Canada West, Wellington County, Arthur Township, page 86, lines 1-25 except 11. The group of twenty-four farms enumerated in this sample were neighbors in the area near where the Bacons lived and includes 150 acres (lines 24-25) once owned by Joseph (and possibly William & James) Bacon on Lot 18 Con OSR.

anyone report owning a pleasure carriage. Only five of the farms reported producing maple sugar and of those only 64 lbs. on average.

Eighty percent of the farms reported having one or two horses and/or a team of oxen. Slightly more than one half had oxen and one half had horses. Of those with horses 25% also had oxen. Nearly all farms with horses also had one or more colts (horses under three years of age). Nearly 25% of farms had neither horses or oxen with little or no correlation to the amount of land under cultivation. The average value of a horse was $62.

Other livestock enumerated in the census were milch cows, sheep and pigs. Nearly every farm had pigs, typically three, and most farms had milch cows and sheep. The average number of milch cows per farm was 2.26 with a farm with cows having between one and four. These farms also tended to have a number of young (under three years) cattle. The average number per farm was 3.81. The number of sheep on a farm was between two to sixteen with the average number being seven.

Other farm produce immediately usable as food was butter, cheese, beef and pork. While most farms reported producing butter (average 144 lbs) only two farms reported making even a small amount of cheese. Twenty of twenty-four farms reported producing pork (average 468 lbs.) but only nine reported producing beef (average 467 lbs.). No mention is made of raising or consuming chicken either in the census or in contemporary literature. Likewise with consumption of mutton. Apparently the sheep were raised primarily for their wool. Ten of the twenty-four farms reported making an average of 25 yds. of flannel .

Based on the data from this census, the diet of a farm family in 1861 can be assumed: bread made from their own wheat, potatoes, turnips, peas, oat meal, pork, some beef, milk, butter but little or no cheese.

Brant Township, Bruce County

As in the case of the free grants along the Garafraxa Road, Joseph's sons seem to have been attracted by free grants along the Durham Road in Brant Township, Bruce County, Canada West. As road contractors the planned opening of more roads may also have been an attraction to Joseph and his sons. It must have taken some special fortitude to have worked hard for several years carving a farm and home out of dense forest of Arthur Township only to give it up and move into a more distant part of the Queen's Bush to do it all over again.

The Durham Road, another Government Colonization Road, was first surveyed in 1848-49. Its route began at the village of Bentinck (later Durham), 17 miles north of Mount Forest, on the Garafraxa or Owen Sound Road and ran westward to Buck's Crossing (later Hanover) on the Saugeen River and then to Walkerton. Later it was continued westward to the village of Penetangore (later Kincardine) on the Lake Huron shore. The Durham Road was constructed in sections east to west. The Durham to Hanover section was completed in 1849. Construction of the section through Brant County began on 10 Jul 1850, was completed 1 Oct 1850 and the eleven contractors were paid a total of £665 4s. 9d. during November. The Brant Township section included two bridges over the Saugeen which cost £277 10s, nearly one half of the cost of the road through the township. Modern highways 4 (Durham to Walkerton) and 9 (Walkerton to Kincardine) basically follow the route of the original Durham Road, the biggest exception being at Walkerton where the Durham Road continued straight west not jogging south as Highway 9 now does.

Figure 14, Townships of Southern Bruce County

Six concessions of free grant lots of 50 acres each (one half the normal size) were surveyed along the Durham Road in Brant Township, three north of the road (NDR) and three south (SDR) of it. These lots were opened to settlement in August 1848 but were stopped for a time until the township survey was completed in 1849. Early in May 1849 Joseph L. Lamont and his wife became the first settlers in the township[44]. Soon after (Robertson doesn't say when) James Bacon [2], son of Joseph [1], and his wife settled in the Township[45]. Mrs Lamont, nee Elizabeth Jasper, had the honor of being the first white woman to enter the township but the honor of being the first permanent white woman settler goes to Mrs. Bacon, nee Mary Norris.

Churches and Cemeteries

It is not known what church the Bacons attended but some possibilities include the following possibilities. The Old Bethel Methodist Church[46] was located on Con 1 SDR, Lot 11 a short way west of the Bacon lots. Records are sketchy but it is recorded that a field meeting was held there on 19 Jul 1863 by Rev. Jonathan Pike. The chapel was completed in 1865. In 1867 is was described as a hewed log church 18 ft. x 24 ft., nicely fitted up with seats and pulpit and valued at $200.

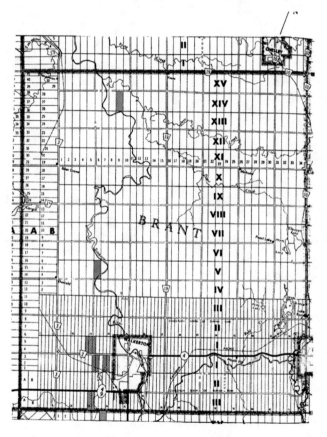

Figure 15, The Bacon Concessions & Lots in Brant Township

---

[44] Ibid, Robertson, page 34.

[45] Ibid, Robertson, page 35.

[46] Gateman, L. M., Ed., *The History of the Township of Brant 1854-1979*, The Brant Township Historical Society, Elmwood, Ontario, 1979, page 254.

Lot	Con 3 SDR	Con 2 SDR	Con 1 SDR	Con 1 NDR	Con 2 NDR	Con 3 NDR
12	Herman Ridel	John MacNeil	James Black	Jno. Wilson	Richard McConnell	Wm. Denny
13	Wm J Moore	James Moore	James MacGilvary	Wm. Morton	Edmond Godfrey	Jas. Dennis
14	Louis Fountain	Wm. Chesney	James MacGilvary	Jos Bacon	Partick Godfrey	Kno. H. Runions
15	Geo. Smith	Henry Chesney	Angus Kerr	Henry Bacon	Jno. Bartes	Joseph Allen
16	Henry Bacon	Jno. Chesney	Jno. Bacon	Wm. Gywnne, Jr.	Jno. MacDonald	Jas. Wilson
17	Jas. Richardson	Thomas Whitney	James Bacon	Jas. Gwynne	James MacDonald	Jas. Wilson
18	Richard Whitney	Wm. Whitney	James Scott	Wm. Gywnne, Sr.	Wm. MacDonald	Jas. Wilson
19	David Smith	David Smith Jr.	Elijah Bacon	Richard Gwynne	Thos. Cockburn Kerr	Jas. Wilson
20	David Smith Jr.	Johnston Smith	Isaac Bacon	Geo. Briggs	Mary Ann Phelan	Partick Monnahan
21	Robert Wallace	Robert Wallace	Wm. Smith	Arch Steward	Jas. Kingshall	Partick Monnahan
22	Robert Wallace				Wm. Reid	John Monnahan
23	Philip Geeson				Joseph Furgeson	Jno. Monnahan
24	Jas. B				Angus MacDonald	Rev. Robert C. Moffatt
25	Jas. B				Partick Mannahan	Rev. Robert C. Moffatt
26	Geo. Jackson				Arch MacDonald	James Graham
27	Geo. Jackson				James Bell	James Graham
28	Joshua Jamieson				Hugh Bell	Samuel Bell
29	Sam B. Foste				Jno. Harkey	Abraham Rowand
30	Sam B. Foste				Wm. I. Hislop	Abraham Rowand
31	Henry Etsell	Henry Estell			Hugh H. Todd	Thomas Craig
32	Marla Jasper	Jacob L. Keifer	Wm. Jasper	Thos. Todd	Wm. Greirson	Thomas Todd, Sr.

Figure 16, Bacon Lots Near Walkerton

Surnames of member families were Wellwood, Ferrier, Taylor, Scott, Hodgkinson, Wakely and Agnew but not Bacon. When the Walkerton Methodist church opened (ca 1870) the two congregations joined in services there. A companion cemetery, the Old Bethel Methodist/Prior Cemetery was located on across the Durham Road from the church on Con 1 NDR, Lots 13 and 14. The cemetery has been restored (pre-1979) to a portion of its original. Burials recorded begin in 1858 and include surnames Prior, Ibson, Jarvis, Bacon, Wilson, Grainger, Mordem and Smith. How the name Prior became associated with the cemetery is unknown.

Child	Birth Date	Spouse	Marriage Date
William	22 Aug 1821	Ellemena Pavers	4 Jan 1846
Susan	5 May 1823	James Prior	Abt 1839
James	4 Mar 1825	Mary Norris	1 Feb 1847
Charlotte	31 Jul 1827	John Smith (2)	1845
		James Cromar (1)	24 Oct 1878
Joseph, Jr	13 Dec 1829	Never married	
John	31 Dec 1831	Elizabeth Hunter	Abt. 1856
Elijah	24 Sep 1833	Maria McNeil	27 Jan 1863
Isaac	23 Sep 1833	Margaret _____	Abt. 1854
Emma Jane	17 Jul 1836	Samuel Hoar	Abt. 1854
Henry	11 Oct 1839	Elizabeth Couch	27 Jan 1863
Mary Jane	22 Jan 1847	William Guinn	13 Feb 1866

Table 2, Children of Joseph and Susanna Bacon, Sr and Their Spouses

The South Line Primitive Methodist Church[47] was built near the northwest corner of Con 3 SDR, Lot 16 by a group of settlers who wanted a place of worship near their homesteads. The church's construction date can not be found but it was called "old" in an 1875 document. In the 1883 annual report member surnames included Mary Shelton, George Merritt and James Ramage but again, no Bacon. However, they should not be expected since the Bacons had emigrated before this time. By inference it is near certain that this was the Bacon Family's church, they are known to have espoused Primitive Methodism and Henry Bacon was the owner of Lot 16 until 15 Apr 1875 having been the grantee of the Crown Patent for the lot on 21 Nov 1872.

The Bacon Family

Joseph and Susanna were the parents of eleven children, nine of them born in England and the last two in North America. Seven of the children were boys and four were girls. All married except one (Joseph, Jr.) and one (Charlotte) married twice. Most of the children had large families with a total of eighty-eight grandchildren born. Discounting William who had only one child and Joseph, Jr. who had none, that is an average of 9.2 grandchildren per child.

---

[47] Ibid, Gateman, Page 263.

Crown Patents

Name	Con	Lot	Date Rcv'd
Elijah	1 SDR	19	17 May 1854
Isaac	1 SDR	20	17 May 1854
John	1 SDR	16	17 May 1854
Joseph, Jr	1 NDR	14	18 May 1854
Mary Jane (Wm Guinn, Jr)	1 NDR	16	18 May 1854
Henry	1 NDR	15	01 Oct 1857
James	1 SDR	17	01 Oct 1857
William	5	6	16 Feb 1864
Henry	3 SDR	16	21 Nov 1872
Susan (James Prior)	14	9	22 Feb 1887

Table 3, Crown Patents Received by Bacon Family Members in Brant Township

Crown Patents (deeds) are given to the first holder of the land originally belonging to the Crown, in the Bacon's case, Queen Victoria of England. The land was sometime given as a free grant and sometimes had to be purchased at a small fee. There were six concessions set aside for free grants along the Durham Road: 1, 2 & 3 north of the road (NDR) and 1, 2 & 3 south (SDR) of the road. These concessions were surveyed into lots of 50 acres, one half the normal size. Each of the six concessions contained 74 lots. All other concessions in the Township had typically 34 lots of 100 acres each which were sold to settlers for 8 s. per acre.

There were ten Crown Patents received by members of the Bacon family in Brant Township. Nine were free grants of 50 aces and one was a 100 acre lot purchased by William. For reasons set out earlier, the date of receiving a Patent has nothing to do with when the settler arrived on the land. A study of **Table 3** will show the surprising result that Joseph, Sr. was not an early landowner in Brant Township nor did he ever have a Crown Patent there. He did, however, purchase land (Con 1 NDR, Lot 14) from his son Joseph, Jr. on 24 Dec 1855, see **Table 5**. This was about five years after the family arrived in Brant Township from Arthur Township. There is no single record that identifies exactly when Joseph and his sons came to Brant Township. But a good guess based on the available evidence would be early 1850 when they moved onto the land of their choice and took out applications for free grants. Certainly very soon after they arrived settlers began to pour in to the area taking up unclaimed land rapidly.

Bacon Land Records

The land transaction records required to be registered in Land Registry Offices are a rich source of information. Three unusual transactions were found in the records for land owned by Bacons:

1) On 3 Jun 1857 a mortgage was given for a loan of $1,200 which was secured by the lands of Joseph, Sr., Isaac, John, Henry, Elijah and Joseph, Jr., a total of 300 acres. The mortgage was discharged in 1864.

2) A Deed Poll[48] was granted by John Macdonald, Sheriff of the United Counties of Huron & Bruce to Samuel Regent McIlroy on 6 Jul 1864 for the sum of $80. This was land originally granted to Joseph, Jr. in 1854 and later sold to Joseph, Sr. On 20 Sep 1864 Samuel McIlroy sold the land back to Joseph, Sr.

---

[48] A Deed Poll is normally used to change a person's name similar to a woman when she marries. In this situation that is not the case. For some unknown reason the county sheriff was selling Joseph's land to a third party.

Name	Con	Lot	Date Mort.	Instr. No	Amt	Date Dischg'd	Instr. No.	Notes
John	1 SDR	16	3 Jun 1859	205	$1,200	27 Sep 1864	255	(1)
			15 Jun 1864	526	$400	21 Jul 1870	1846	
			5 Jun 1868	1042	$600	29 Jul 1870	1847	
			1 Jul 1870	1848	$1,375	11 Mar 1876	3646	(2)
			20 Feb 1876	3647	$1,850	1 Aug 1878	4524	
			1 Aug 1878	4525	$1,550	5 Dec 1885	7291	
			1 Aug 1878	4526	$521	10 Nov 1881	6021	
Joseph, Jr.	1 SDR	17	3 Jun 1859	205	$1,200	27 Sep 1864	255	(1)
			15 Jun 1864	523	$350	21 Oct 1870	1918	
			13 Apr 1867	828	$140	26 Feb 1869	1294	
			26 Feb 1869	1295	$888	6 Apr 1870	1751	
Elijah	1 SDR	19	3 Jun 1859	205	$1,200	27 Sep 1864	255	(1)
			15 Jun 1864	527	$400	9 Apr 1867	8221	
Isaac	1 SDR	20	3 Jun 1859	205	$1,200	27 Sep 1864	255	(1)
Henry	3 SDR	16	25 Oct 1872	2542	$500	2 Jul 1875	3409	(3)
Joseph, Sr.	1 NDR	14	14 Jul 1858	169	£36 3s 6p	26 Jul 1859	3	
			3 Jun 1859	205	$1,200	27 Sep 1864	255	(1)
			3 Jun 1859	525	$350	8 Oct 1869	1538	
			11 Oct 1869	1532	$600	20 Dec 1871	3142	
Henry	1 NDR	15	3 Jun 1859	205	$1,200	27 Sep 1864	255	(1)
			11 Jun 1864	524	$350	28 Apr 1868	1015	
			16 Jun 1867	861	$303	22 Apr 1868	1012	
			22 Apr 1868	1013	$678	4 May 1871	2172	
			10 Mar 1871	2085	$1,000	14 Mar 1876	3658	(4)
William	5	6	1 Dec 1863	461	$600	- - - - -	461	(5)

Notes:

(1) This mortgage was given on 3 Jun 1859 by Joseph, Sr. & wife Susanna, Isaac & wife Margaret, John & wife Elizabeth, Henry, Joseph, Jr. and Elijah to the Trust and Loan Company of Upper Canada for the loan of $1,200 at an interest rate of 8% per year secured by Lot 14, Con 1 NDR (Joseph, Sr.); Lot 15, Con 1 NDR (Henry); Lot 16, Con 1 SDR (John); Lot 17, Con 1 SDR (Joseph, Jr.); Lot 19, Con 1 SDR (Elijah); and Lot 20, Con 1 SDR (Isaac). This mortgage was discharged on 27 Sep 1864, a term of 5 years, 3 months, 24 days. Why this loan was taken out and what this considerable sum of borrowed money requiring 300 acres of prime farm land as collateral was used for is unknown.

(2) Indicative of the increase in value of the land. A $1,200 mortgage eleven years earlier required 300 acres as collateral.

(3) This mortgage was given nearly a month before Henry received the Land Patent and was sold with the land to be paid by the new owner although no assignment was recorded.

4) Became unsecured when Henry sold the land 5 Aug 1871.

5) No discharge is recorded for this mortgage. It defaulted to the Grantor's spouse after the grantor's death.

Table 4, Mortgages Given by Male Members of the Bacon Family on Brant Township Land

3) Some unusual and unknown situation occurred in early June 1864 causing John, Joseph, Jr., Elijah, Joseph, Sr., and Henry to give nearly simultaneous mortgages to the Huron & Erie Savings & Loan Society for $400, $350, $400, $350, and $350, respectively, for a total of $1,850. While no information is recorded about the use of money received for a mortgage, it is possible that some of the money went to subscriptions for the construction of facilities such as mills (saw and/or grist) or even the railroad as such subscriptions were known to occur.

Several other mortgages, see **Table 4**, were made and discharged on the lots owned by members of the family. In no case is the reason for the mortgage known. John, Joseph, Sr., Joseph, Jr., and Henry were very active in borrowing money while Elijah and Isaac took out only one or two mortgages and James none. The Bacons were good borrowers, always repaying their mortgages faithfully with but one exception. William failed to pay any of the principle or interest on his $600 1863 mortgage and the mortgage went into default.

The Daughters

Nothing has been said of the family's daughters in Bruce County except their spouses and dates of marriage in Table 2. All four remained for a time in Bruce County. Susan and James Prior lived in the north of Brant Township on Con 14, Lot 9[49]. Where Charlotte and first husband George Smith lived in the township is uncertain but it is quite likely that Charlotte's husband is the George Smith listed as the Crown Patent grantee of Con 3 SDR, Lot 15 adjacent to Henry Bacon's lot. George died in 1873 after twenty-eight years of marriage and Charlotte married a second time in 1878 to James Cromar. Charlotte and James lived in Greenock Township. Later they moved to Minnesota, North Dakota and British Columbia. Emma Jane and Samuel Hoar lived in Carrick Township and later moved to northern lower Michigan Mary Jane and William Guinn, Jr. lived near her brothers in Brant Township on Con 1 NDR, Lot 18. Later they moved to the Toronto area.

Road Contractors

Another of the Government Settlement or Colonization Roads was the Elora Road which runs from Elora, twelve miles northwest of Guelph, northwest to Southampton along the routes of modern highways 7, 9 and 3 The section through Brant Township was chopped out during the summer

---

[49] The Prior's lot has sometimes been reported as Con 14 Lot 8. This is incorrect.

of 1851. In the list of contractors[50] are Joseph Bacon [Sr.] and James Bacon. It is reported[51] that Joseph, Sr. also had a contract for a section of this road in Carrick Township and possibly sections of it in other townships/counties. Joseph received £330 in 1854 for road work in Carrick Township[52]. It is possible that Joseph, Sr. and James also had additional contracts for chopping out other roads in Bruce County. It is known, for example, that Joseph Sr., James and William had contracts on the Owen Sound Road in Arthur Township, Wellington District before they came to Brant.

Be aware that a mid-19th century road contractor in Canada was vastly different from a road contractor in the late 20th and 21st centuries. Then a road contractor cut and removed the trees from the right-of-way (the stumps were left as cut), surfaced extremely wet or swampy sections with corduroy and built wooden bridges. Vehicle speeds were from a slow walk by oxen (normal) to a few miles per hour (rare). Modern road contractors use huge machines to shape the right-of-way to a predetermined grade, surface the graded right-of-way with concrete or asphalt and build bridges of all types and sizes. Vehicles range in weight up to twenty tons traveling at speeds of seventy or more miles per hour.

Sale of the Bacon Lands

Joseph Bacon's sons took up 50 acre free grants in southern Brant Township about 1850 and remained on their lands for approximately twenty years. The dates of the sale of their land, see Table 5, is indicative of the time in which they decided to leave Ontario and move west or, in the case of Joseph, Sr., it probably marks his retirement from farming and road building as he would have been nearly 76 years old.

---

[50] Ibid, Robertson, page 53.

[51] Ibid, Kalbfleisch, page 1.

[52] Ibid, Robertson, page 66.

Name	Con	Lot	Date Sold	Buyer	Amount
John	1 SDR	16	20 Jul 1870	WG&B Railroad *	$100
John	1 SDR	16	3 Nov 1881	Duncan Kerr, Sr.	
James	1 SDR	17	28 Dec 1858	Joseph Bacon, Jr.	
Joseph, Jr.	1 SDR	17	25 Feb 1869	Thomas Campbell	$1,800
Elijah	1 SDR	19	1 Mar 1867	Alex McCarter	$1,325
Isaac	1 SDR	20	25 Feb 1865	Andrew Thompson	$1,000
Henry	3 SDR	16	15 Apr 1875	RH Middaugh	$1,485
Joseph, Jr.	1 NDR	14	24 Dec 1855	Joseph Bacon, Sr.	£200
Joseph Sr.	1 NDR	14	1 Nov 1871	Uriah Roswell	$2,100
Henry	1 NDR	15	5 Aug 1871	Uriah Roswell	$1,050
William	5	6	25 Jan 1867	Eliza McKeller **	$600
Thomas Pryor ***	14	9	1 May 1936	Richard McCurdy	$3,000
Wm James Guinn ****	1 NDR	16	Aft 1897		

* Wellington Bruce & Grey Railroad purchased 1.8 acres of John's Lot 16 for a right-of-way for their track. Although the railroad appears to also cross Lot 17 and possibly Lot 19, no sale of such a right-of-way(s) is recorded.

** William defaulted on a $600 mortgage on this property to Eliza McKellar who then sold it for $750 to Frances Smith on 25 Jan 1867.

*** Thomas inherited the property from Susan Prior (mother). Thomas died in 1928, the land is being sold by his Administratrix, Susan Prior Fortune.

**** Wm James inherited the property from Wm Guinn, Jr. (father).

Table 5, Final Sale of Brant Township Land Owned by Members of Bacon Family

The Family Scatters

Like their father, the Bacon sons seemed to have had a yen for pioneering. Well before the end of the 19th century, all of Joseph's sons and two of his four daughters had left Bruce County to pioneer again in the Michigan, Minnesota, North Dakota or Manitoba. Two of the four daughters remained in Ontario. Although this story is about Joseph, Sr., it is in order to discuss his children briefly since their lives reflect on Joseph's later years.

1. William

William was born 22 Aug 1821 in England and came with his family in 1835 to Buffalo, New York; then to Hamilton, Upper Canada in 1839. At age 19, he accompanied his parents when they moved to Arthur Township in 1840. He is credited by MacKenzie with being an 1840 pioneer settler on Lots 18 and 19 with his father and brother James[53]. William and brother-in-law

James Prior chopped out miles 45 and 46 of the Garafraxa Road in northern Arthur Township on both sides of the Saugeen River in the spring of 1840[54]. Following the time in Arthur Township, William exhibited considerable independence from his family. In 1846 he was in Brant

Figure 17, Vesta General Store & Post Office, 1900

Township, Bruce County where he married Ellemenia Pavers. William and Ellemenia were enumerated by the 1851 census in Onondaga Township, Brant County with eleven year old George Pavers (Ellemenia's brother or nephew) living in a round-log house. Their first and only child was born 19 Jul 1855 in Brant Township, Bruce County and Ellemenia died there on 12 Jan 1856. The 1861 Canadian Census enumerated William as widower in Brant Township, Bruce County living with his parents. His son, six year old Hiram, is not mentioned in this census. William received a Crown Patent for Con 5 Lot 6 (100 acres) in Brant Township, Bruce County on 16 Feb 1864[55].

---

[53] MacKenzie, W.F., The Guelph Evening Mercury, 7 Dec 1907 and The Guelph Weekly Mercury and Advertiser, 19 Dec 1907, Wellington County Museum and Archives, Fergus, ON. MacKenzie was a local historian who traveled through Arthur Township collecting oral histories which he then wrote in a narrative which was published in the Guelph Mercury in 1906-1909.

[54] Sworn Testimony in *Mount Forest vs Murphy* by John Horsborough on 27 Sep 1892, Mount Forest Transportation, Wellington County Museum & Archives, Fergus, Ontario. Horsborough testified that he lived along that section of the road for seven years from Christmas time of 1839 onward..

In his 1912 Declaration of Intent for U.S. citizenship, Hiram, son of William, declares that he immigrated to the United States at Port Huron, Michigan on 27 Mar 1867. It is probable that his father immigrated with him on that date also as Hiram would have then been only 12 years old. Both William and Hiram were enumerated three years later by the 1870 U.S. Census as the only members of a household in Ionia Township, Ionia County, Michigan (about 130 miles due west of Port Huron). The 1880 U.S. Census enumerated William and Hiram in Two Rivers Township, Morrison County, Minnesota (about 25 miles northwest of St. Cloud). Hiram married in Morrison County on 25 Feb 1882 and we lose track of William. William's death and burial places are unknown.

2. Susan

Susan was born 5 May 1823 in England and came with her family in 1835 at age 12 to Buffalo, New York; then to Hamilton, Upper Canada by 1839 and finally to Arthur Township, Wellington District, Canada West a short time later. About 1839 she married James Prior born 1815 in England (it is believed that James came from England with the Bacons). Fifteen children were born to this marriage between 1840 and 1871, ten girls and five boys. The marriage likely took place in Arthur Township where James was granted a patent on 50 acres in the 4th Quarter of Lot 18 EOSR[56] on 1 Nov 1847. This land was on the opposite side of the Owen Sound Road from Susan's parents and adjacent to the Village of Kennilworth. James and family were enumerated by the 1851 census in Arthur Township living in a one story log house. By the summer of 1855 James had twelve acres cleared, fenced and under crop. James purchased

---

[55] The ownership of this lot is a rather curious situation. William did not take advantage of the free grants along the Durham Road as did his siblings. Lots were opened for purchase in Brant Township on 5 Aug 1851 at twelve shillings and sixpence ($2.50) per acre. William purchased a lot (Con 6 Lot 5) of 100 acres for which he would have paid $250. His Crown Patent is dated 16 Feb 1864 but this gives no information as to when he settled on the lot (settlers had to personally appear in Toronto to get their patent and they didn't usually make the trip until they wanted to sell). William gave a mortgage secured by the lot to Duncan McKellar for $600 on 1 Dec 1863 and then sold his lot to Mary Bacon (his sister) on 21 Apr 1864. There is no discharge of this mortgage recorded nor is a sale of the lot by Mary Bacon recorded. The only sale recorded (in the early years of the lot's land index) is by Eliza McKellar on 25 Jan 1867 [Brant Township Land Instrument #486]. This instrument records Eliza's sale of the land to Frances Smith for $750 and the following information: William never paid any of the principle or interest on the $600 mortgage and it was in default. The original grantee, Duncan McKellar, died on 16 May 1864 and his wife Eliza inherited the land and the mortgage. Was Mary out her $600? And William $1,200 to the good?

[56] EOSR: East of Owen Sound Road. Sometimes called the Garafraxa Road.

an additional 50 acres for £25 in the 3rd Division, Lot 18 EOSR and received a patent for it on 15 Feb 1856. By 1861 they had moved to Brant Township, probably to their farm of 100 acres on Con 14 Lot 9[57] for which $142 was paid. This lot was bordered on the south by the Saugeen River and is several miles north of her brother's farms in the Bacon enclave near Walkerton. They were enumerated in the 1861 Census of Brant Township living in a one story log house with ten children, all the children born up to that time except Mary Margaret. James was listed as a farmer.

Their farm was approximately two miles west and one mile south of the Village of Vesta. Recall that Joseph's first (Mar 1881) letter gives "Vesta PO" as his address. See Appendix F for a description of the village. Figure 17 is a photo of the Vesta General Store and Post Office in 1900. The proprietor, John Connelly, is standing in front of the horse. Connelly was the last Vesta postmaster serving from 1905 to 1814 when rural mail delivery forced the office to close.

James Prior died 14 Mar 1879 in Brant Township of injuries received while digging the well on Con 14 Lot 9. The 1881 Census enumerated Susan as a widow age 57 and a farmer in Brant Township. Susan obtained a Crown Patent for the farm on 22 Feb 1887[58] just before selling it to her son Thomas Henry Prior on 16 Mar 1887. In the deed Susan reserved access to the river for boats. Susan Bacon Prior followed her husband in death on 10 May 1904 in Brant Township. Both were buried in the Old Bethel Methodist/Prior Cemetery in the township. The Priors were affiliated with the Church of England in Canada.

The farm stayed in the family with son Thomas until he died in 1928. It was then sold by his niece and administratrix, Susan Jane Fortune (granddaughter of Susan Bacon Prior and daughter of Susan Jane Bacon Fortune), to Richard McCurdy on 1 May 1936 for $3,000.

3. James

James was born 4 Mar 1825 in England and came with his family at age 10 in 1835 to Buffalo, New York; then to Hamilton, Upper Canada by 1839 and to Arthur Township, Wellington District, Canada West in 1840.

---

[57] Many family documents report the Prior's as owning Con 14, Lot 8. This is incorrect. Lot 9 is correct.

[58] Without a copy of the original paperwork, this appears to be a classic case of taking up Crown Patent land but not making the trip to Toronto until years later to obtain the actual Patent in order to sell the land. It is highly likely that the patent was applied for by James in the early 1850s when the township was settled. Since James was deceased, Susan's dower rights made her holder of the patent.

He married Mary Norris, born about 1827 in England, on 1 Feb 1847 in the Wellington District, Canada West. They had a family of ten children, four girls and six boys born between 1848 and about 1871. MacKenzie credits James an 1840 pioneer in Arthur Township owning land in Lot 18 but the Land Instrument Index does not list him as a lot owner. In the census of 1851 he was enumerated as a farmer living with his wife and two children in Brant Township. James was also a pioneer road contractor in Ontario. He worked on the Garafraxa Road, the Elora Road and probably others. He received a Crown Patent on Lot 17, Con 1 SDR on 1 Oct 1857 and sold it a short time later on 28 Dec 1858 to his brother Joseph, Jr. Robertson credits James as one of the earliest settlers of Brant Township with his wife, Mary, as the first white woman settler. Possibly James lived in Saginaw, Michigan before moving to North Dakota. James and his family were enumerated by the 1885 Dakota Territory Census in Lakota Township, Nelson County next door to his sister Charlotte and her husband James Cromar. James Bacon died 7 Oct 1906 in Bottineau, North Dakota and was buried in Bottineau. Mary died 3 Apr 1894 and was buried in Bottineau.

4. Charlotte

Charlotte, born 31 Jul 1827 in England, came with her family in 1835 at age 8 to Buffalo, New York; then to Hamilton, Upper Canada by 1839 and to Arthur Township, Wellington District, Canada West in 1840. She married (1) George Smith, born 13 Mar 1814 in Ireland, in 1845 in Hamilton, Canada West. On 18 Jul 1845 Mr. & Mrs. George Smith were transported by train from Hamilton to Preston with 300 pounds of baggage[59]. In the period 1854-56 George was listed in the original handwritten bylaws of the Township of Greenock and Culross written by James Cromar, Township Clerk and George Cromar, Town Reeve[60]. George & Charlotte had a family of twelve, eight girls and four boys between 1846 and 1869. The 1871 Canadian Census enumerated the Smith family in Brant Township, Bruce County. There is a George Smith on Lot 15, Con 3 SDR[61] (Crown Patent) next to Henry Bacon's lot. It is not known for certain if this is Charlotte's husband but the odds are good that it is. George died 2 Jul 1873 in Brant Township and was buried in the Old Bethel Methodist/Prior Cemetery

---

[59] Preston is 28 miles northwest of Hamilton and fourteen from Guelph. In 1846 it had 600 inhabitants, daily post and a wide variety of merchants. Researched by Wini Prince.

[60] James Cromar Journal, researched by Wini Price

[61] Gateman, Laura M., *The History of the Township of Brant: 1854-1979*, The Brant Township Historical Society, Elmwood, Ontario, 1979, page 480 in a list of township Crown Deed holders.

there. Five years later Charlotte married (2) James Cromar, born abt. 1836 in England, on 24 Oct 1878 at Teeswater, Culross Township, Bruce County. In the September 1880 James and Charlotte entered the U.S. at Duluth, Minnesota where James filed his Intent to become a U.S. citizen. Later they moved to Crookston, Polk County, Minnesota and a short time later to Baconsville, Dahlen Township, Nelson County, Dakota Territory (named for Jerry Dempster Bacon, no relation to "our Bacon Family"). On 21 Nov 1883 the Baconsville farm post office was established in Section 35-154-57 in Dahlen Township, three miles south of Dahlen village, with James as Post Master[62]. The post office was moved in 1904 to a new location three miles west of Dahlen with a new postmaster. This post office closed in 1905. In 1885 James and Charlotte were enumerated by a Dakota Territory Census in Lakota Township, Nelson County (later North Dakota[63]). Charlotte's brother James Bacon and family were neighbors as evidenced by their appearance immediately previous in the census. On 29 Sep 1888, James received a land patent for 160 acres in Nelson County, North Dakota. On 7 Dec 1897, James received a Homestead Patent on three adjacent parcels totaling nearly 160 acres in Bottineau County. James, Charlotte and a twenty year old son named George were enumerated by the 1900 U.S. Census of North Dakota, Bottineau County, Bottineau Village. In 1902 they returned to Canada; to Hill Hall (now Benson), Saskatchewan[64]. Charlotte died 31 Jan 1905 in Hill Hall and was buried in the Woodley-Cromar Cemetery at Hill Hall. James died at Hill Hall in 1907.

5. Joseph, Jr.

Joseph, Jr., born 13 Dec 1829 in England, came with his family in 1835 at age 5 to Buffalo, New York; to Hamilton, Upper Canada by 1839 and to Arthur Township, Wellington District, Canada West in 1840. About 1850 he moved to Brant Township, Bruce County just west of the Village of Walkerton with the family. He received a Crown Patent on Con 1 NDR Lot 14 on 18 May 1854 and sold it

Figure 18, Joseph Bacon, Jr. Gravestone

---

[62] Wick, Douglas A., *North Dakota Place Names*, Hedemarken Collectibles, Bismark, Page 10 [WWD317].

[63] North and South Dakota gained statehood on 2 Nov 1889.

[64] 1906 Census of Saskatchewan, Researched by Wini Price.

to his father in 1855. He was active in buying and selling land and had several mortgages, some in conjunction with his brothers. Joseph was enumerated by the 1861 census of Brant Township as single and living with his parents at age 30 with his widowed brother William. Joseph never married. He died young on 20 Apr 1870 at age 40 leaving no descendants. He also was buried in the Old Bethel Methodist/Prior Cemetery. His gravestone survives, see Figure 18.

6. John

John, born 31 Dec 1831 in England, came with his family in 1835 at age 3 to Buffalo, New York; then to Hamilton, Upper Canada by 1839 and to Arthur Township, Wellington District, Canada West in 1840. He married Elizabeth Hunter, born 1837 in Quebec, about 1856. They had six children, five girls and one boy between 1858 and about 1869. The first five were born in Ontario. John received a Crown Patent on Lot 16, Con 1 SDR on 17 May 1854 and sold the lot on 3 Nov 1881. On 13 Jun 1882 he made entry on the SE 36-12-25 W1 in the RM[65] of Woodsworth, Manitoba

Figure 19, John & Elizabeth Bacon, Gravestone

and received a patent for the land on 31 Oct 1892. John was probably a farmer in both Ontario and Manitoba. He died 16 Feb 1917 in Manitoba. Elizabeth died 25 Mar 1919 in Manitoba. Both are buried in the Kinsmore Cemetery on the NE 1/4-29-12-24 W1 in the R. M[66]. of Woodsworth (four miles west and four miles north of Kenton). John was originally buried in the Scotia Cemetery but was reinterred in the newly opened Kinsmore Cemetery.

7. Elijah - Nickname "Lige"

Elijah, twin of Isaac, was born 24 Sep 1833 in England and came with his family in 1835 at age 18 months to Buffalo, New York; then to Hamilton,

---

[65] It is customary to give prairie province land descriptions as three numbers separated by dashes. The numbers are the values of the: 1) Range, in the part of Manitoba of interest here, west of a prime meridian; 2) Township north of base line (here the U.S.-Canadian border); and 3) the Section. Ranges and townships are in multiples of six miles. In Canada section numbers are 1-36 but run differently than in the U.S. In Canada they begin in the southeast corner of the section going to six in the southwest corner. The second tier of sections run from seven in the west eastward to twelve. Section 36 is then in the northeast corner.

[66] Rural Municipality, a Canadian political subdivision roughly equivalent to a county.

Upper Canada in 1839 and to Arthur Township, Wellington District, Canada West in 1840. He married Maria Elizabeth McNeil, born 1843 in Carrick Township, Bruce County, on 27 Jan 1863 in Brant Township. They had nine children, five girls and four boys between 1863 and 1882. Elijah received a Crown Patent on Lot 19, Con 1 SDR in Brant Township on 17 May 1854 and sold it on 1 Mar 1867 to Alex McCarter[67] for $1,375. No information is known about where he was between 1867 and 1882 except that his children, for the most part, were recorded as being born in Walkerton[68], son Joseph in 1880. Possibly he lived on his brother John's land as John didn't sell until November 1881. In the spring of 1882 he began a move to Strathclair, Manitoba with his family - eight children and a pregnant wife. They left Brant Township on April 1, 1882. By July they were in Portage La Prairie, Manitoba, where Maria died at the birth of their daughter who was named Maria in honor of her mother. Maria McNeil Bacon was buried in an unmarked grave in the northwest corner of the Hillside Cemetery at Portage La Prairie. The records for that part of the cemetery were lost or destroyed many years ago. After burying their mother, the family continued on to Strathclair where daughter Lucy who was fifteen on 11 Jul 1882 raised the family. Elijah and his twin brother Isaac homesteaded at Strathclair, Manitoba on 31-16-21 for some time and then Elijah moved his family about 1886 to another homestead approximately five miles west of his brother John. He built his log buildings on a hill side above the Assiniboine River about 12 miles southwest of Crandall, Manitoba. He filed for this homestead on 8 Nov 1897 on one quarter of land, 12-25-30 NE. For many years he raised sheep. He died about 1907 but there is no record of his death because the records were burned in a fire in the 1920s. He is buried in the Scotia Cemetery six miles north and three west of Kenton, Manitoba in an unmarked grave.

8. Isaac

Isaac, twin of Elijah, was born 24 Sep 1883 in England, came with his family in 1835 at age 18 months to Buffalo, New York; then to Hamilton, Upper Canada by 1839 and to Arthur Township, Wellington District, Canada West in 1840. He married Mary Margaret Wilson about 1854. Mary was born in England about 1836. They had nine children, six girls and three boys between 1855 and 1876. Isaac received a crown patent for Lot 20, Con 1 SDR, Brant Township,

---

[67] Alex McCarter is the son-in-law of Elijah's sister Mary Jane.

[68] Although there is no evidence that any of the Bacons ever resided in the village of Walkerton, many of the records list it as the place of events in their lives. This was customary during the pioneer times to give the nearest town as their address.

Bruce County, on 22 Mar 1854. He sold this farm on 1 Mar 1865 to Andrew Thompson for $1,000 and moved to Strathclair, Manitoba. There, he lived on and farmed 31-16-21 (Donald Lucy's farm) for a short time. In 1883 the family moved to Springbend area just north of Enderby, British Columbia where he purchased 19-9-14SW on 7 Mar 1899. On 28 May 1904 Isaac sold this property to Wm. Tomkinson. In later times, the property was owned by the SpringbendCommunity Club. Isaac became ill and went to Vancouver, British Columbia where he died at the Essondale Asylum in New Westminster. He was likely buried at Essondale. His wife Margaret is buried in Lansdowne Cemetery. Isaac was a Methodist Minister.

Figure 20, Samuel and Emma Jane Hoar's Gravestone

9. Emma Jane - "Jane"

Emma Jane was born 17 Jul 1836 in Buffalo, New York and came with her family to Hamilton, Upper Canada by 1839 and to Arthur Township, Wellington District, Canada West in 1840. She married Samuel John Hoar(e), Sr., born 2 Nov 1832 in England, about 1854 in Bruce County. They had ten children, six girls and four boys between 1855 and about 1875. The first four children are enumerated in the 1861 census of Carrick Township[69], Bruce County, Canada West where Samuel and Emma lived on a farm near Walkerton. All of their ten children were born on this farm, three boys and

---

[69] Carrick Township lies immediately adjacent to and south of Brant Township.

[70] Kalbfleisch, R. W., *The Hoar Family Record*, Privately published, 1868, 26 pages. Records found in the Walkerton Public Library (*Index of Land Instruments of Brant Township, Bruce County, Ontario*, microfilm A3-9) and at the Bruce County Land Registry in Walkerton: (Instr #1829) John & Caroline Hoare sell Con 2 SDR, Lot 35 to George Lambertus on 8 Jul 1870 for $1,400; (Instr #2029) Samuel & Elizabeth Hoare sell Con 2 SDR, Lot 36 to John Hoare on 20 Jun 1870 for $1,000; (Instr #2030) John & Caroline Hoare sell Con 2 SDR Lot 36 to Martin Hessnauer for $500. Samuel & Elizabeth are the parents of Emma Jane's husband Samuel and John and Caroline are Emma Jane's Husband Samuel's brother.

seven girls. Samuel's parents and brother lived in Brant Township[70]. About 1879, the family immigrated to Michigan and settled in Bliss Township, Emmet County, Michigan. Bliss Township was not organized until 9 Oct 1876 and by 1880 its population only amounted to 192. Records indicate that in 1878 Bliss Township had two school districts, sixteen students, and no school buildings. The 1880 US census lists Samuel and "Jane E" as living on a farm in Bliss Township with children Elizabeth, Samuel, Joseph and granddaughter Carrie Carlton. Samuel was a farmer and a well known lay preacher.

The 1894 Michigan state census lists him as owning 40 acres in Bliss Twp valued at $1000 and producing $200 in farm products. The 1902 plat book of Emmet County shows his farm as the W 1/2 of SE 1/4 Sec 25, Bliss Township, 80 acres with an additional 80 acres directly east of Samuel's as belonging to Jane Hoar (his wife). His farm is listed in the 1903 Polk's Directory of Emmet County as 80 acres in Sec 25 and had an assessed value of $1960. The 1984 Michigan census lists his son Joseph as renting 120 acres. Does this imply that at the time of the census Samuel was working 40 acres and Joseph the other 120 acres of the 160 acres listed to Samuel and Jane in the 1902 Plat Book? Samuel died 22 Sep 1883 in Levering, Emmet County, Michigan and was buried in the Bliss Township Cemetery at Bliss (Emmet Co.).

Emma Jane married for a second time to David B. Hoar, her first husband's brother, born 1 Apr 1848 in England, on 29 Mar 1894 in Bliss, Michigan. This was David's third marriage. They did not have any children. According to the 1894 Michigan Census, David owned 40 acres of land in Bliss Township, Emmet County, Michigan valued at $1000 (land & buildings). The 1902 Plat Book of Emmet County shows it in Bliss Township, Sec 35, SE 1/4 of SW 1/4, 40 acres. He sold this farm to Andrew Hoar a few years later. In 1903 this property had an assessed value of $550 and a mailing address of Canby. David died 21 Jan 1908 in Levering, Michigan.

Emma Jane died 29 Oct 1907 in Petoskey, Michigan at age 71 of Brights Disease. Her funeral was on 29 Oct 1907. Burial was in the Bliss Township Cemetery at Bliss. A large stone marks her and Samuel's grave, see Figure 20.

10. Henry

Henry was born 11 Oct 1839 in Hamilton, Gore District, Upper Canada and came with his family to Arthur Township, Wellington District, Canada West in 1840 as an infant. He married Elizabeth Couch[71], born 16 Aug 1843 in Peterborough, Upper Canada, on 27 Jan 1863 in Brant Township,

Figure 21, Henry and Elizabeth Bacon's Gravestones

Bruce County, Canada West. They had ten children, six girls and four boys born between 1863 and 1886. Henry received Crown Patents on two 50

---

[71] There is an interesting story about Elizabeth becoming Henry Bacon's wife and their takeover of her brother Henry Couch's homestead. Elizabeth's father, Christopher Couch, immigrated to Douro Township, Peterborough County, Canada West with his parents from Ireland in 1825 as part of the Peter Robinson Settlers assisted immigration scheme. Christopher's father died about a year after arriving in Canada leaving 18 year old Christopher as head of the family. After living in Douro Township for nearly forty-five years, Christopher moved to Carrick Township, Bruce County about 1870. On 12 Jul 1875 he received a Crown Patent on Con 15, Lot 7, 120 acres (this was not a free grant like the Bacon's received). This lot adjoins the Carrick-Brant township boundary as does Henry Bacon's land in Brant, Con 3 SDR, Lot 14 about one half mile east of Henry's - very close neighbors for those days! In 1875 when homestead land became available in Emmet County, Michigan, Christopher and his four sons moved to Emmet County where each of the four sons took out a homestead in Resort Township. Son Henry applied for his homestead on 21 Jan 1876, and, in the process of clearing the heavily timbered land, Henry was struck and killed by a falling tree limb on 18 Oct 1876. Christopher, Henry's sole heir and by now very elderly, tried to continue the process of homesteading the land. He was barely succeeding and was finally forced to summon his daughter and son-in-law, Elizabeth and Henry Bacon, from Bruce County in 1879 to take over the homestead. Although the homestead was a Couch one, it became popularly known as the "Bacon Homestead" throughout the surrounding area.

acre free grants in Brant Township: Con 1 NDR, Lot 15 on 1 Oct 1857 and Con 3 SDR lot 16 on 21 Nov 1872. Lot 15 was sold on 5 Aug 1871 to Uriah Roswell for $1,050. Lot 16 was sold on 15 Apr 1875 to Randolph H. Middaugh for $1,485.

Henry and son Isaac came to the Resort Township, Emmet County, Michigan (near Petoskey) in June 1879 and took over the homestead of Elizabeth's brother Henry on the north shore of Walloon Lake, Gov't Lots 4 & 5, Sec 2, R33N, R6W, 135 acres[72]. Later, in the summer of 1879, they and other settlers cut the first trail through on what is now Resort Pike. This was done so Henry could bring his family (wife Elizabeth and four children ages one to nine) out to the homestead in a wagon drawn by a yoke of oxen. The homestead was bordered on the east by Resort Pike and to the south and west by the lake. Some of the land was cleared for farming and the lake front subdivided into cottage lots[73]. Henry later had a small grocery on what is now the west side of Resort Pike. He had a large dock built to accommodate the passengers who came from the many cottages around the lake by steamer.

In 1903 Henry owned 66 acres in Section 2 of Resort Township (the Bacon Homestead at the end of Resort Pike and on the shore of Walloon Lake) which was assessed a value of $1900. In September 1903 a barn raising was held on the Bacon Homestead which was reported in The Star Monthly with photos and description by Dr Clarence Hemingway[74]. The homestead log cabin burned to the ground on 20 Feb 1907. The 1910 Census for Resort Township, Emmet County, Michigan enumerated the following in the household: Henry, head, Elizabeth, wife, Houston, son, age 34 (never married), Dolly, daughter, age 29 (had a mental illness), Alfred Couch, nephew, age 8 (son of Edward T. Couch, Elizabeth's brother). In an act typical of them, Henry and Elizabeth set money aside for Alfred's education. By the end of the 20th century the majority of the Bacon Homestead was owned by the Little Traverse Conservancy and was reforested in pine trees which were 4 in. to 6 in. in diameter and 40 ft tall in the summer of 1993. Henry

---

[72] It was measured as 79.10 acres by the original survey in 1840 which laid out an artificial lake shore by means of a meander line. In actuality there was approximately 135 acres when the land between the meander line and the lake shore was included. The land patent certificate Christopher received on 5 Jul 1883 used the original survey size. A later survey corrected the problem.

[73] Three of these lots (19, 20, & 21) were sold to Dr. Clarence E. Hemingway, father of author Ernest Hemingway, in 1898. Dr. Hemingway built Windemere, the family's summer home on the three lots. Windemere is now in the National Register of Historic Places.

[74] A copy of the article and photos is reproduced in *Resort Township Remembers*, Rehpkof, Mildred, Ed., Printed by Mitchell Graphics, Petoskey, Michigan, 1992, pages 97 and 146.

was deeply religious and he passed this sentiment on to his children. He led the family in prayers twice a day and often read them passages of the Bible. Henry was a long time member of the Resort Township School Board and the Emmet County Fair Board. There was talk of closing the Fair in his honor for his funeral but the Bacon family refused to allow it since it was to be children's day at the fair. Elizabeth took ill and died rather suddenly in a Petoskey Hospital on 20 Jun 1916. Her death is listed as the result of "age". She was 72 years old. Services were held at Stone Funeral Home in Petoskey on 22 Jun 1916 at 10:30 AM with Rev Shepard of Clarion, Michigan conducting the services. Henry died three months later at his home in Resort Township of heart failure and gangrene of one foot. His funeral was on Wednesday, 13 Sep 1916 at the Resort Township Methodist Episcopal Church at 10:30 AM with Rev Shepard of Clarion conducting services. Both Henry and Elizabeth were buried in the Greenwood Cemetery at Petoskey in the Bacon plot, see Figure 21.

11. Mary Jane

Mary Jane was born 22 Jan 1849 in Middletown Township, Middlesex County, Canada West[75]. She married William Guinn, Jr.[76], born in 1834 in Montreal, Canada East, on 13 Feb 1866 in Brant Township, Bruce County. They had six children between about 1866 and about 1876, three girls and three boys. Before her marriage Mary Jane bought[77] Con 6 Lot 5 in Brant Township from her brother William on 21 Apr 1864 for $600. This purchase was subject to a $600 mortgage made by William on which he eventually defaulted. No mention is made of Mary's interest when the lot was sold 25 Jan 1867 following foreclosure by the mortgage holder. Was Mary out her $600? Four Guinns received Crown Patents for 50 acre free grants in Brant Township in Con 1 NDR, Lots 16, 17, 18, and 19 adjacent to the Bacon lots in Con 1 SDR and Con 1 NDR: William, Jr. on Lot 16, James on Lot 17, William, Sr. on Lot 18, Richard on Lot 18, all four received their patents on 18 May 1854. Like the Bacons, the Quinns[78] were a father and sons.

---

[75] No such township exists today and no record has been found for a former one. Mary Jane's birth is recorded only by family records, no independent record of it has been found.

[76] In early documents this name was spelled Gwynn later it was changed to Guinn.

[77] Instrument #498 was registered 28 Apr 1864. Mary's and William's brothers Isaac and Elijah were witnesses to this bargain and sale instrument. It references the subject mortgage with the grantor as being the Church Society of the Diocese of Huron. The actual grantor was one Duncan McKellar, Esq. of the Township of London, County of Middlesex (Brant Township Instrument #461).

Although William, Jr. received the Crown Patent on Lot 16, it was part of William, Sr.'s estate[79] at his death in 1895 and was inherited by Mary Jane and her son William James. James received the Crown Patent on Lot 17 but he sold the lot to Mary Jane and William, Jr. in 1859. They owned it for nearly seventeen years before selling it back to James for $2,000 in 1876 a few months before William's death. William died 26 Sep 1876 in Brant Township and Mary Jane abt. 1905. William's and Mary Jane's burial places are unknown.

Mary Jane, Daughter or Granddaughter?

The eleventh child, Mary Jane, born in 1847 is attributed as a daughter of Joseph and Susanna. However, there is some feeling in the family that Mary Jane is a granddaughter of Joseph and Susannah rather than a daughter[80]:

1. There is a large gap of more than nine years between the birth of Mary Jane, born 22 Jan 1849, and her next youngest sibling, Henry, born 11 Oct 1839. All of the other children were born at approximately two year intervals.
2. Susannah would have been approximately age 49 years when Mary Jane was born, not an impossible age but an unlikely one.
3. Mary Jane's birth is given as being Middlesex County, two counties south of any known places that Joseph and Susanna lived.
4. There is no Middletown Township in Middlesex County, past or present.
5. Based on the sale of their Arthur Township land, Joseph and Susanna were Arthur Township until August, 1849.
6. William was placed in Arthur Township in 1840 by MacKenzie.
7. William does not appear in any of the writings about Brant Township but he did own land in Brant Township, Lot 6, Con 5, 100 acres for which he received a Crown Patent on 16 Feb 1864. See the footnote on page 43 in the discussion of William referring to this lot.

---

[78] There are at least four generations with a William in the direct line in addition to some brother's sons who were also named William. Hence it may be difficult to positively identify a particular William in a given situation.

[79] It is far from clear exactly how this happened from the Index to the Land Instruments for Brant Township.

[80] In an interview with Ruth Bacon Bates[4] (Joseph Elias Bacon[3], Henry Bacon [2], Joseph Bacon [3]) that was conducted on 20 Jul 1994 in Kentwood, Michigan (a Grand Rapids suburb) by Dean Wheaton. Ruth stated that "Mary Jane is the daughter of William Bacon (b. 1821) and his wife who died at Mary Jane's birth. Mary Jane was then adopted by her grandparents Joseph & Susannah". Ruth died at age 94 in November following the July interview. She was fully alert and possessed of her faculties when she was interviewed.

Possibly Mary Jane is the daughter of William, Joseph's and Susannah's oldest son. Since William would have been age 25 when Mary Jane was born, it is certainly not impossible. William was not a family person as indicated by being the only one of the children to completely strike out on his own separately from his siblings in later years after all the rest of his brothers and two sisters had left Ontario for Manitoba, North Dakota or northern lower Michigan[81]. This would be consistent with Mary Jane being born in Middlesex County, a location where no one else in the family lived.

Joseph & Susanna

It must be said that Joseph and Susanna led full lives forsaking their English homeland after nineteen years of marriage and eight children, crossing the Atlantic on an immigrant ship with eight children including twin boys just 18 months of age, living in Buffalo, New York and Hamilton, Upper Canada for short times with the birth of a child in each, pioneering in the Queen's Bush[82] for several years in Arthur Township and then pulling up stakes again to move further into The Bush in Brant Township[83] where they lived in a log shanty 12 ft x 16 ft. When they came to Arthur Township in 1840 they were one of only eighty families in the entire township. During their lives they followed the Church of England (Anglican) faith in England, the (Episcopal) Methodist faith in Arthur Township, and the Primitive Methodist faith in their later years.

Their last owned property was sold in November, 1871, four and one half years preceding Susanna's death on 5 May 1867. Where they lived during the intervening time between sale of the farm and Susanna's death is unknown. At death Susanna was age 78 and Joseph was age 81. It likely that they went to live with one of their children, most probably Susan as she was the

---

[81] Kalbfleisch, Raymond W., *The Bacon Family*, self published about 1980, 8 pages. Raymond, an Emmet County, Michigan historian and genealogist, reports on page 4 that "William lived in Saginaw, Michigan and had a family of seven children". William was enumerated in Ionia County, Michigan by the 1870 U.S. Census and in Two Rivers Township, Morrison County, Minnesota by the U.S. 1880 Census. In both of the census William and son Hiram are together with no other family. In 1870 they are living with an unrelated farm family employed as laborers. In 1880 they are in a separate household with William listed as a farmer and Hiram has no occupation given.

[82] See Brown, W.M., M.D., *The Queen's Bush*, John Bale, Sons & Danielsson, LTD., London, 1932, 295 pages, 4.75" x 7.5", paperback for stories of pioneering in the Bush. Includes mentions of the Bacon Family.

[83] See Robertson, Norman, *History of the County of Bruce*, William Briggs, Toronto, 1906, copyright 1960 by The Bruce County Historical Society, 4th Ed., 1988, 560 pages, hardback for stories of pioneering in Bruce County including several mentions of Joseph, Sr. and James Bacon.

only child remaining in Brant Township. Recall that James and Susan Prior lived in the northern part of the township near the village of Vesta and that James had died in early in 1879. After Susanna's death and probably until his own on 27 Dec 1882, Joseph lived with Susan as the two letters that are the center pieces of this story indicate. Although the gravestone records for the cemetery do not record their burial place it is nearly certain that both were buried in the Old Bethel Methodist/Prior Cemetery very near the land owned by their sons.

Figure 22, Susanna & Joseph Bacon, Abt 1875

The Old Bethel Methodist/ Prior Cemetery

This cemetery, see Figure 23, is located on Con 1 NDR, Lot 12, Brant Township, Bruce County, Ontario. Today a mile or so west of the town of Walkerton. This location was also known as Johnson's Corners[84]. Many of the Bacon family are buried there. Some years ago the cemetery was in great disrepair with broken stones, weeds, etc. It is suspected that a farmer-owner of the land attempted to return the land to cultivation, removing all of the gravestones in the process. Fortunately, someone or some organization took up the task of restoring it to the condition seen in Figure 23. This photo was taken in October, 2002 looking northeast across the Durham Road. The surviving stones have been reset in asphalt paving and a modern gravestone of red marble installed for the Prior family. Although torn down many years ago,

---

[84] Named for William Johnson (sometimes Johnston), one of the first six settlers of Brant Township who arrived in 1849.

Figure 23, The Old Bethel Methodist/Prior Cemetry(restored)

a church (The Old Bethel Methodist) once stood next door to the cemetery on Lot 13 (to the right in the picture).

Figure 24, Signatures of Joseph & Susanna Bacon, 1 Nov 1871 on Instrument #2255 Bruce County for the Sale of Their Farm on Con 1 NDR, Lot 14.

A Small Puzzle

As a final challenge, the reader is left with a small puzzle. The two center piece letters of this document were certainly written by Joseph. However, on two legal documents requiring Joseph's signature, a mortgage to the Trust and Loan Company of Upper Canada on 3 Jun 1859 and the deed for the sale of his farm on 1 Nov 1871, his signature is written in with the words "His Mark" and an "X".

Usually this is an indication that the signer is unable to write his/her name. It is difficult to believe that Joseph who wrote so well in the letters learned to write between 1871 and 1881 when the first letter was written.

Appendix A - Family Stories

In the Bacon Family as in most families, stories of one kind or other have grown up over the passing years. Like the game "Telephone[85]" which most children participated in elementary school, the message or story changes with each telling. The changes are not made maliciously, they occur because the communication channel between the teller and the listener is imperfect. Often there is some kernel of truth to a story, the problem is to sort out the kernel from the chaff. Such is the case of these Bacon Family Stories. It is left to the readers to form their own opinion.

Story #1[86]

Joseph was reputed to have been one of the champion boxers of England. This accomplishment led to a job as Queen Victoria's (b.1818, reigned 1837-1901) game keeper in charge of the Royal Parks in London.

On Sundays and holidays one of the favorite past times of the people of London was a walk in one of their beautiful and spacious parks such as Richmond Park or Bushy Park. Herds of a hundred or more deer roamed the park and were a pleasant source of interest and a special joy to children. However, the deer population was being rapidly reduced by poachers who were

Figure 25, 1983 Letter from the Royal Parks Office Baliff.

---

[85] This game probably pre-dates the telephone but its pre-telephone name is unknown.

[86] This story was related to Raymond W. Kalbfleisch of Petoskey, Michigan in 1968 by Joseph E. Bacon (1870-1972, son of Henry, grandson of Joseph) and privately published by Raymond in *The Bacon Family* before 1994. Raymond was a historian and genealogist in Emmet County, Michigan.

taking the deer in the dark of night. It was a serious matter, previous game keepers, in their efforts to apprehend and stop the poachers, had been beaten.

Joseph was brought onto this scene in hopes that his reputation as a champion boxer might halt the poaching. Night after night Joe and his assistants watched and waited, often hiding in the bushes in various locations in the park. Finally, late one night dark shadows appeared - evidently a group of men intent on getting their deer. Joe immediately accosted them inquiring as to the purpose of their presence in the park in the middle of the night. The answer was a swift and vicious attach upon Joe. He knocked several to the ground even before his assistants, who were nearby, could reach the scene of the melee. Seven men were captured, tried, and all were hung within a few days.

In spite of efforts by Manitoba Bacon descendants, this story cannot be verified, see **Figure 25**.

Story #2

Joseph E. Bacon [3] (1870-1972) related that his grandfather Joe was acquainted with Wm Gladstone, Prime Minister of England, who visited Ontario about 1876 and he was taken by his grandfather to the railroad station in Walkerton to see Gladstone. William Ewart Gladstone served as Prime Minister of England in 1868-1874, 1880-1885, 1886 and 1892-1894.

Story #3[87]

Joseph E. Bacon [3] (1870-1972) remembers how his English grandmother, Susanna Bacon, wrathfully referred to Benjamin Franklin as a rebel cousin and a traitor. He had become a loyal and famous American. The Christian or given name of Susanna's father is unknown [since found, his name is Henry. Susanna also had a sister Anne, baptized 13 Feb 1785 in Widdington]. And an examination of the Franklin family tree fails to shed any light upon the matter. However, Joe states that his grandmother Susanna was definitely a cousin of the famous American.

Story #4[88]

Another facet of family information related by Joseph [3] (1870-1972) pertained to Susanna's sister Mary Ann. She married William Reed an iron monger (hardware merchant) of London where they lived throughout their life. They had no children. The pastor of the Church of England at Widcombe wrote Joe a letter saying "Wm & Mary Reid formerly owned the parsonage where I live. Their graves are in this church yard." The story was also published by R.W. Kalbfleisch in The Bacon Family and is quite likely true but it has not been verified.

---

[87] Ibid, Kalbfleisch, *The Bacon Family*, page 3.

[88] Ibid, Kalbfleisch, *The Bacon Family*, page 3.

Story #5[89]

Also related by Joe Bacon [3] (1870-1972): Henry Bacon, possibly an uncle of my grandfather came to America during the Revolution and is buried in Arlington National Cemetery, see **Figure 26**. He came as a British soldier, subsequently deserted and joined the American forces. He is reputed to have been a general in both forces. He had a son in the American army who fought in the Indian campaigns in Michigan.

A quick Google search of the world wide web for "Henry Bacon" yields nearly one million hits. Many, many Henry Bacons in many professions are represented.

Figure 26, Letter in Reference to Revolutionary War Soldier Henry Bacon

Story #6

This very small story concerns Mary Jane Bacon and was related by Ruth Bacon Bates [4](1900-1994), daughter of Joseph Bacon [3]. "Mary Jane married the Mayor of Toronto after her husband William Guinn, Jr. died."

Facts: Mary Jane's <u>daughter</u>, Mary Quinn (abt 1866-1934), was married to Thomas Bruce Clarke who was the brother of Toronto's mayor Edward Frederick Clarke. Edward Clarke was Mayor of Toronto and local Member of the Provincial Parliament 1888-1892. Edward was later a Member of Parliament during the Governments of John A. MacDonald and Robert Borden.

---

89 Ibid, Kalbfleisch, *The Bacon Family*, page 7.

Appendix B – Crossing the Atlantic

It has been recorded that Joseph and Susanna Bacon with their then family of eight children left England for New York in the early spring of 1835. No collaborating sources (passenger lists) have been found but the general scenario is supported by hand-me-down stories from several branches of the family. At least three of the children, William age 14, Susan age 12 and James age 10, were old enough to understand the move and therefore would have been able later to pass the story on. In stark contrast, the story of the Couch family's 1825 move from Ireland[90] to the wilderness near present-day Peterborough is known in great detail thanks to the meticulous records kept by Peter Robinson.

This appendix discusses only the routes available to the Bacon family. The other details of immigration are fascinating reading and sometimes describe situations that are hard to believe. A good source is Guillet's The Great Migration[91]. If a library nearby doesn't have a copy, search for out of print books on the web at www.amazon.com, www.barnesandnoble.com and others. Your author found a signed copy in excellent condition with a dust jacket for $41.00 on amazon.com.

Figure 27, Map: The British Isles

Ports of embarkation in the British Isles for immigrant ships to America and Canada were typically Cork on the south coast of Ireland or Liverpool on the west coast of England, see Figure 27. However, many other ports were also used. In all likelihood, the Bacons embarked at one of these other ports, possibly London. Immigrant ships were notorious for being overcrowded with abysmal conditions. Parliament

---

[90] Henry Bacon, son of Joseph, was to marry Elizabeth Couch, daughter of Christopher, on 27 Jan 1863 in Walkerton.

[91] Guillet, Edwin C., The Great Migration: The Atlantic Crossing by Sailing Ship 1770-1860, Thomas Nelson and Sons, Toronto, London, New York, 1937, Hardback, 298 pages with illustrations (photos and drawings).

passed several Passenger Vessel Acts in an attemp to curb the worst abuses. The last before the Bacons sailed was the Act of 1823 which required the ship to carry 50 gallons of pure water and 50 pounds of bread, biscuit, oatmeal or breadstuff for each passenger; a £20 fine for dumping passengers a Quebec when they had contracted and paid for passage to Montreal; and a between-decks space of 5 ½ feet. Ships were allowed to carry three passengers for every four tons of the ship's register which resulted in each passenger receiving 20 ½ inches of deck space - a condition hardly paralleled in slave ships.

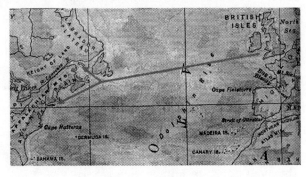

Figure 28, Map: The North Atlantic from The British Isles to North America

Once aboard ship there was approximately 3000 miles of the North Atlantic Ocean to be crossed, see Figure 28, in a sailing ship totally at the mercy of the weather. In fair weather with favorable winds, the crossing could be made in thirty days, with contrary winds it might take up to sixty days. Other hazards of the crossing were fog, ice bergs, and violent storms especially if encountered near the end of the crossing to Canada in the shallow waters of the Grand Banks. Because of the difficulties of sailing up the St. Lawrence, crossings to Canada usually took longer than crossings to New York. Since the passenger records for the Bacons have not been located, nothing is known of their crossing.

Keep in mind that the trials of immigration did not end with arrival in North America. The immigrant, as he moved westward, was at a distinct disadvantage - he was unfamiliar with the new territory that he was traveling though. As a result he was beset on every hand by cheats, scoundrels, pick pockets, dishonest inn keepers and ship's captains and miscrants of every stripe.

Crossing to Montreal

Arrival in North America was generally in either New York or Montreal. Other arrival ports were used but not as frequently. For ships bound to Montreal, the excitement at the first sight of land after the rigors of the ocean crossing was New Foundland and it was, in a way, just a tease. Nothing in his experience had prepared the immigrant for the vastness of the new land.

The whole of the British Isles were hardly 625 miles in north-south extent, the total land area of the United Kingdom (England, Scotland, Wales and northern Ireland) was only twice the size of the state of New York. The unwary immigrant not knowing that nearly a 1000 miles of dangerous and time consuming travel awaited before arrival at Kingston on Lake Ontario, three quarters of it to be endured before he could leave the ship at Montreal.

The way was fraught with danger from the very entrance to the Gulf of St. Lawrence. When passing between New Foundland and Cape North (Cape Breton Island, Nova Scotia) the ship had to avoid Isle St. Paul[92], ten miles off the cape. Next came the Bird Rocks raising 400 ft. perpendicularly from the sea. Then came Anticosti Island without bay or harbor jammed almost like a cork into the mouth of the St. Lawrence. Beyond Anticosti were

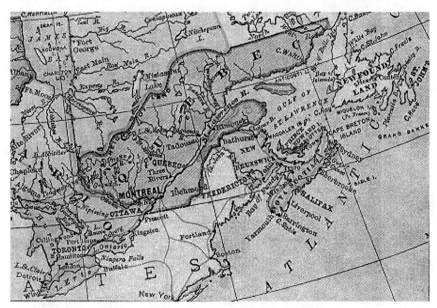

Figure 29, Gulf of St.Lawrance and the St. Lawrence River

more than 500 miles of the ever narrowing St. Lawrence to be navigated, see **Figure 29.**

At Montreal navigation was blocked by the Lachine Rapids and the ship could go no further. At last, the immigrants could disembark. Ahead was a nine mile hike around the rapids while their baggage was transported by

---

[92] A huge isolated rock divided at the top into three conical peaks rising boldly from the sea and surrounded by strong currents. A very dangerous place in fog.

ox cart. Immigrants bound for Upper Canada had next to board bateaux paddled by French-Canadian crews for the trip to Prescott, a little more than 100 miles, which took six to twelve days. Above Prescott, the river was free of rapids and sailing vessels again became practical. Although steamships first arrived on Lake Ontario in 1817, it wasn't until the 1830s that they came into wide spread and affordable use. After 1831 the immigrant ships had a man-made obstacle in the St. Lawrence near Quebec - the Grosse Isle quarantine station - an attempt by the authorities to control the ever increasing numbers arriving with contagious diseases. By the 1840s, a series of canals and the steamship had reduced the passage time from Lachine to Kingston, a distance of some 250 miles, to twenty-six hours in first class accommodations for $12, a sum far beyond most immigrants. Most would have been hard pressed to pay the $3 steerage passage and make the trip in three days. Once at Kingston all of the Great Lakes were accessible via steamship at low fares.

Crossing to New York

The second major route for immigrants to Canada was through New York City. In contrast to the St. Lawrence route, the immigrant arriving at New York was very near to disembarkation when land was first sighted after the crossing. Of course, immigrants headed for Canada still had a way to go, about 500 miles to Buffalo, but at least they were free of the ship's confines.

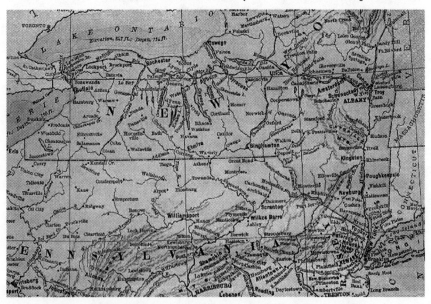

Figure 30, Map: New York City, the Hudson River and the Erie Canal

Early Canada bound immigrants went up the Hudson River by sailing sloop. Early steamships on the Hudson, like those on the St. Lawrence, were too expensive for most immigrants. The 150 miles of river between New York City and Albany was unobstructed by rapids which led to "floating towns" of canal boats four or five abreast and up to one half mile long towed by steamships. At Albany the way north and westward on lakes and rivers was as varied and primitive as any other waterway of the time. In late October, 1825 the Erie Canal opened between Albany and Buffalo, a distance of 362 miles which took about six days by canal boat. Once at Buffalo, although at the opposite end of Lake Ontario, the immigrant was at the same advantage as one who had arrived at Kingston via the St. Lawrence but was much less stressed by a far easier journey.

An Example Crossing and Settlement

This example of the Henry Couche family's journey from Ireland to Scott's Plains (Peterborough) in 1825 is presented because their immigration was meticulously documented. It is unusual because the Couches were part of a large assisted immigration scheme. Further, the Couch family was to become joined to the Bacon family in 1863 when Henry Bacon married Elizabeth Couch albeit not until both families had migrated to Bruce County.

In 1825 the British Government appropriated £30,000 to fund an assisted emigration project for poor Irish Catholics. The anticipated emigrants would be mainly farmers with a few trades people. Henry Couche being a shoemaker was one of this latter group. Peter Robinson, a Canadian, was appointed to organize and supervise the project. After broadsides were posted in southern Ireland in the Spring of 1825, Robinson received applications from more than 50,000 Irish when only 1500 had been planned for. Settlers were promised and, surprisingly, received transportation from Ireland to Canada, 100 acres of land in Canada, a shanty on their land, a cow, free provisions for one year, and tools to work their land. Robinson pared the list to 2,024, all of whom are listed by ship with name and age. Nine were Henry Couche, his wife, Susanna, and their seven children ages 3 to 19. Susanna was pregnant with an 8th child which was born 2-3 months after they reached Canada. They were among the 227 settlers aboard the converted navy ship Resolution which they boarded on 5 May 1825 at Cork. Anthony Ward, Master, was in charge of the ship and G.H. Reade, Surgeon, was responsible for the immigrants. Resolution sailed 10 May 1825 and arrived at Quebec on 15 Jun 1825, a very short, uneventful voyage.

The settlers then traveled by steamer to Montreal, by ox cart to Lachine, and bateaux to Prescott and Kingston. In Kingston they were placed in tents on the beach awaiting Robinson's arrival while the temperatures soared to over

100 degrees for days on end[93]. On 9 Aug 1825 Robinson arrived and on 11 August 1825 approximately 500 settlers were embarked for a 24 hour voyage by steamboat to Cobourg. The remaining settlers were brought up in three more weekly trips. After ten days repairing the road from Cobourg to Rice Lake and an additional eight days building two special scows to handle the extremely low water in the Otanabee River, the first group of settlers arrived in Scott's Plains (later Peterborough) about 1 Sep 1825. By approximately 30 Oct 1825 all the settlers had been brought up to Scott's Plains.

At Scott's Plains began the arduous tasks of cutting trails through the heavily wooded and untracked wilderness, locating their lots and building a shanty before the onset of the Canadian winter. Somehow by 24 Nov 1825 it was accomplished. Nearly all, if not all, of the settlers were taken sick along the way with ague (paroxysms of chills, fever and sweating) and other problems. Several died.

Once in Douro Township and located on their lot, Henry's family was given a provisions allocation of meat and flour apportioned by age and sex. For adult males it was one pound of each per day ranging downward to one quarter pound for infants. The total allocation for the ten members of the Couche family was 5 lb 8 oz meat and 6 lb 8 oz flour per day. From the records available during the period 25 Jun 1826 to 24 Nov 1826, the family received a little more than would be indicated by the daily allocation: meat, 1298 lbs by allocation vs 1575.5 lbs dispensed; flour, 1534 lbs allocated vs 1779.5 dispensed

The family was also allotted one cow, two axes, and three blankets. The account also listed pickaxes, augers, crosscut saws, whip saws, adzes, bill hooks, hoes, and wedges but none allocated to the family. Why the family did not receive more tools is unknown. In another account, it was noted that the three blankets were dispensed to the family on December 23. This seems a rather sparse number of blankets for a family of nine or ten and rather late in the season.

---

[93] The weather in the early 1800s appears to be more variable than today. Nine years earlier, 1816 was the year without summer when frost occurred every month of the year and caused wide-spread crop failures. The cause has been attributed to a of number of major volcanic eruptions preceding 1816: Soufriéére and St. Vincent in 1812, Mayon and Luzon in the Phillippines during 1814, Tambora in Indonesia during 1815. The Tambora eruption has been estimated to be the most violent in historical times. The explosion is believed to have lifted 150 to 180 cubic kilometres of material into the atmosphere. For a comparison, the infamous 1883 eruption of Krakatau ejected <u>only</u> 20 cubic kilometres of material into the air, and yet it affected sunsets for several years after.

Appendix C - Canada 1835-1882

Although Joseph lived the Canadian part of his life in The Bush far from most amenities of civilization, there were significant events in the outside world that would have effected him or he would have heard about. Some of the more significant ones are listed below.

1837 The Victorian Era began when Victoria succeeded to the British Throne on 20 Jun 1837. Much celebrating would have occurred across the Empire at her crowning on 28 Jun 1838 and again on her marriage to Prince Albert on 10 Feb 1840.
The Upper Canada Rebellion breaks out lead by the former mayor of Toronto, William Lyon Mackenzie. Mackenzie escapes to the United States and the rebellion is quickly put down.

1840 Upper and Lower Canada are united by the Act of Union. Upper Canada becomes Canada West and Lower Canada becomes Canada East.

1841 Canada West's population is about 450,000.

1844 Construction began on the first railroad in Canada.

1846 The Oregon Boundary Treaty is signed by Queen Victoria and U.S. President James Polk which defines the western boundary between the United States and British North America. This was to become important to the Bacon sons who later moved to Manitoba.

1848 An ice jam at the entrance of the Niagara River completely blocks the flow of Niagara Falls for the only time on record.

1849 The first Canadian money is printed and placed in circulation.

1851 Canada's first postage stamp, the three penny beaver, is issued.

1857 Queen Victoria names Ottawa as the capital city of Canada.

1858 The first Canadian coins go into circulation in denominations of 1, 5,10 and 20 cents.

1859 Blondin crosses Niagra Falls on a tightrope watched by 25,000 spectators.

1860 The Prince of Wales visits Canada.
Maple Leaf is first used a symbol of Canada.
The Civil War begins in the United States.

1861 The population of Canada West is 1.4 million.

1864 The first formal steps toward Confederation takes place in Charlottetown, Prince Edward Island and the City of Quebec.

1865 The Civil War in the United States ends.

1866　The Fenians (Irish loyalists intent on Irish independence from Britain) riot and raid Canada from the United States. American authorities and 10,000 Canada militia quell the riots and put down the raids. Fenianism unites Canada as it moves toward Confederation.

1867　The Confederation of Canada creates the Dominion of Canada. It leads to a Dominion wide holiday, Canada Day, every July 1st (the Canadian equivalent of America's 4th of July).

1869　The Red River Rebellion by Métis landowners lead by Louis Riel occurs in Manitoba.

1870　Manitoba becomes the fifth province of Canada.

1871　British Columbia becomes the sixth province of Canada.
　　　　The population of Ontario reaches 1.6 million.

1876　Alexander Graham Bell makes the first long distance telephone call between Brantford and Paris, Ontario, a distance of 13 Km.

During his long life, Joseph experienced a great many changes. Probably the change most effecting him during his years in Canada was the coming of the railroads. The railroad's had their Canadian beginnings in 1844 and by 1860 200 miles of track had been laid, much of it in Canada West. Railroad fever caught the attention of Bruce County in 1868 with two main propositions vying for go-ahead: the Toronto, Grey and Bruce Railroad proposed to build a narrow gauge line to Kincardine while the Wellington, Grey and Bruce Railroad proposed to build a standard gauge line to Southampton. After a long and bitter fight at many excited meetings in towns, villages, and district school-houses, the issue was placed on the ballot by the County Council on 2 Nov 1869. By a vote of 2,911 to 2,626, a plurality of only 285 votes or 5%, the Wellington, Grey and Bruce Railroad was awarded a free grant of $250,000 to build their line from the southeast line of the county near Clifford to Southampton. Construction was completed in 1872. In the fall of 1873 a line was completed to Kincardine and in 1874 another was completed to Teeswater.

Imagine the thoughts and feelings of an elderly man born in the 18th century to these happenings. A man who pioneered the untracked, unbroken forests of The Queen's Bush. A man who would have thought nothing of walking from Guelph to Owen Sound or of carrying a 100# bag of flour on his back from Hanover to Walkerton. First came the roads (which he helped build), then came ox-carts which gave way to teams of horses pulling wagons (summer) and sleighs (winter). Just twenty years later the iron horse was spreading rapidly across the land. Now for the price of a ticket one could be whisked from town to town at average speeds of 25 mph to 35 mph!

This mode of travel must have been as shocking to Joseph as an idea presented on the Discovery Channel last evening (brought to your author's flat screen, high definition, digital TV via Earth synchronous satellite 22,500 miles over-head). The concept was a New York to London submerged floating tunnel. The trip would take about 1.25 hours on trains carrying a 1000 people traveling 5000 mph in a high vacuum. The steel alone needed to construct such a tunnel was estimated to equal the entire output of the world's steel mills for a year.

Appendix D - Imaginary Day in the Bacon's Pioneer Life

Imagine what life was like on a cold February day for the Bacon Family in their self constructed log shanty on their newly claimed land in Arthur Township that first winter of 1840-41. None of the things we take for granted today were available or were even a thought in an inventor's dreams: electricity, clocks, running water, bath room, bath tub, lights, automatic heat, sink, drain, newspaper, tooth brush, tooth paste, soap, cooking stove, microwave, toaster, refrigerator, clothes washer, clothes dryer, packaged foods, insulation, paint, etc. All these things were far in the future.

With only the help of a few neighbors, the shanty was constructed on their fifty acre free grant just outside the limits of the Village of Kennilworth on the newly opened Garafraxa or Sydenham Road. The shanty was completed just ahead of the first snow which, we will imagine, came in late November that year. The family was very happy to be under a dry roof at last and was settling down for the winter. They had found in the five years since leaving England that the weather of a Canadian winter was nothing like that which they had experienced back home where snow was a rare occurrence. It is February 12, 1841, mid-winter and one week following Joseph's 46th birthday.

Outside, the first light of the breaking dawn was erasing the stars and a pink glow was spreading on the thin clouds above the trees in the southeast. The temperature was near zero with the snow lying heavy and white across the small clearing. A path of sorts leads from the door of the shanty through the waist deep snow to the wood pile nearby, beyond the wood pile the path next leads to the spring where clear icy cold water bubbles out of the ground, a branch in the path goes around to the lean-to shelter at the back of the shanty for the oxen and another branch leads off in the opposite direction to the outhouse. Inside, the only light comes from the heath of the shanty's fireplace where father had restarted the fire using last night's carefully banked hot embers. Since "lights" or glass window panes were scarce and very expensive, the shanty has none. The two older boys, Joe and Jim, ages 11 and 9, are responsible for stocking an inside store of kindling and firewood near the fireplace and refilling the family's two precious buckets at the spring the evening before. Mother with the help of Charlotte, age 13, was busily preparing a hearty breakfast of porridge simmering in a cast iron pot hung on a crane hook above the fire. Charlotte has broken the ice out of the buckets to get water for the porridge as the family as yet had no cow for milk. She

73

then placed the buckets on the hearth where the ice would melt as the fire gained hold.

As the shanty began to warm, Charlotte woke Lige, Isaac, the twins, age 7, and Jane, age 4, and changed baby Henry, age 16 months, while Joe and Jim got dressed for breakfast. All the children took their turn on the chamber pot as it was far too cold to attempt using the outhouse. Later, it would be twins responsibility to dump and rinse it.

By the time everyone was dressed, the water in the bucket nearest the fire was tepid. Charlotte poured out a small amount into a large wooden bowl so everyone could wash the sleep from their faces and hands. While the porridge was cooking over the fire, mother had set out small wooden bowls for everyone on the rough table that had been made by William after the shanty was raised. Father had chair at the table's end while everyone else sat on rough benches along each side of the table. Father said the prayer then mother served the porridge with a special surprise of wild honey that the boys had found in a bee tree just before the snow had come. The late fall cold had made the bees so lethargic that not one of the boys was stung.

As the family ate there was a discussion of the tasks to be undertaken for the day by the various family members. Mother and Charlotte listened politely because they knew that cooking the family's meals, straightening the shanty and caring for the younger children would keep them busy all day. The major discussion was about replenishing the supply of oatmeal, a major ingredient in the family's food supply. Father and William were making plans for making the thirty mile each way journey with the jumper to get more from the mill at Guelph. The first eighteen miles from Kenilworth to Fergus would be the most difficult as there would be only the survey blazes to follow and few people were traveling to create a track through the deep snow. The last twelve miles from Fergus to Guelph was expected to be easier with more traffic and the possibility that the road had been chopped out. The return trip would be the most difficult since pulling the loaded jumper was always harder than pulling it empty. Because of a late start today, they planned to stop over-night at the tavern in Arthur. The second day should be an easy trek to Fergus. An early start from Fergus on the third day should make their arrival at Guelph early enough to purchase the oatmeal and other supplies before the mill and General Store close for the day. If there was a good track through the snow on the road, it might be possible with a very early start from Fergus and a long day on the march to make the homeward trip in two days. Father charged Joe as the oldest with responsibility for the family while he would be gone. Father admonished both Joe and Jim to make sure that they brought in the firewood each evening and to feed the oxen from the stacks of meadow hay near the lean-to as he and William set out.

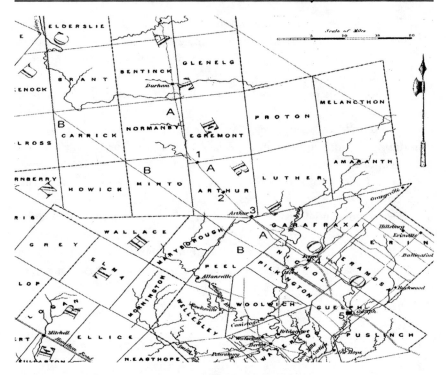

Figure 31, 1852 Map: Guelph to Arthur and Brant via the Garafraxa (A) and Elora(B) Roads; Mt. Forest (1), Kennilworth (2), Arthur (3), Fergus (4) and Guelph (5). The Durham Road is Chopped-out but Has Not Yet Been Mapped.

With father absent, the children were a little less inhibited than usual. Because of the deep snow and intense cold they were confined to the shanty. Joe, Jim and Charlotte had adult tasks to do leaving the younger children to their own devices. Mother planned dinner a little later than if father had been home. Dinner consisted of a stew of potatoes, turnips and a few carrots from the root cellar and venison from the deer hunted by William last week along with plenty of bread that mother had baked on the hearth. The afternoon was essentially a replay of the morning except the younger children were put to bed for naps with the twins being allowed to nap on their parent's bed.

Sleeping arrangements for the family consisted of mother and father's bed built in one corner of the shanty. It was constructed of two small poles driven into the walls about two feet above the floor and supported at their outer corner by a cedar post. Another pair of small poles ran along the shanty walls. Saplings were then laid on this frame work and covered by aromatic hemlock and cedar branches. The girls slept on a layer of cedar and hemlock branches laid on the packed dirt floor in the opposite corner. The boys except baby Henry slept in a loft at one end of the shanty on similar branches. The loft had the advantage of being warm in the evening but it was also bitterly cold on winter mornings. Baby Henry slept in a cradle made by father from basswood and cedar bark.

For supper this day, mother sliced and fried the oatmeal leftover from breakfast along with strips of venison that everyone thought looked like the pork they didn't have. Since everyone had entertained themselves reasonably well during the long afternoon, a special desert of dried berries picked from the neighboring forest was served. After the boys fed and watered the oxen and got in a supply of firewood and water for morning it was already dark. Since father was absent, mother read a chapter from the bible by the light of a single precious candle. Then she then banked the fire and the family retired for the night.

In due time the nearly full but waning moon shown its silver light down on the snow blanketed earth. If anyone had been awake, they would have heard the cry of hungry wolves on the hunt.

Appendix E - Selected Place Names
Then and Now

Over the years names given to places have been changed especially, it seems, in Upper Canada/Canada West/Ontario. The names were changed for a variety of reasons, some forgotten. The following were selected[94] because they pertain to places in Joseph Bacon's story.

Original Name	Modern Name
Bentinck	Durham
Buck's Crossing	Hanover
Bytown	Ottawa
Brant	Walkerton
Johnston	Chatsworth
Penetangore	Kincardine
Saugeen	Southampton
Springvale	Vesta (no longer exists)
Sydenham	Owen Sound
York	Toronto

---

94 Robertson contains a long list in Appendix N on page 538

Appendix F - Geographic Places

Arthur

The first settlers (including the Bacons) arrived at the future location of the village of Arthur in 1840. However, the village was not officially surveyed until 1846. Arthur took root as the southern terminus of the Grafraxa Road to Sydenham. A saw mill and grist mill were established which further promoted Arthur as a market center for the area's agricultural products. A post office was established in 1851 and the first church and school were organized followed by a newspaper (The Enterprise). In 1872 Arthur was incorporated as a village and received a huge economic boost by the establishment of the Toronto, Grey and Bruce Railroad station. Arthur was named for Arthur Wellesley, Duke of Wellington (1769-1852).

Bruce County

In 1836 a treaty was signed with the Indians for a very large tract of land including what would become the southern half of Bruce County. Part of the tract was sold and part retained by the government. It became known unofficially as The Queen's Bush and officially as the Huron District. On 19 Apr 1847 an Order-in-Council was passed to open the lands of the district for settlement and in May the Commissioner of Crown Lands directed Alex Wilkinson, PLS, to survey the lands. Wilkinson laid out the southern boundary of Bruce County and then the townships.

Brant Township

On 26 Aug 1848 a second Order-in-Council authorized the survey of a colonization or settlement road from the village of Durham on the Owen Sound or Grafraxa Road through the Townships of Bentinck, Brant, Greenock and Kincardine to Lake Huron at the mouth of the Penetagore River. This road became known as the Durham Road. The order also laid out the rules for obtaining free 50 acre grants on either side of the road. By 1850 the entire township had been surveyed.

The Durham Road was surveyed by blazing trees along it route. In 1850 eleven contracts were let to chop-out the road.. Richard Quinn, brother-in-law to Mary Jane Bacon, had one of the contracts. By November, the job was completed including two large bridges over the Saugeen River, one at Hanover and one at Walkerton.

The land to be Brant Township was very attractive to settlers with its hardwood timber, fertile soil and fresh water. So attractive that many squatters did not wait for the official opening and proper surveying. The result was a major headache for the Land Agent and fights over lots were not unusual.

The Township does not have a "founder" and there is no official record of why it was named Brant. It has become accepted that the Township was named for the great Indian Chief Joseph Brant or Thayendanegea (1742-1807)[95].

Vesta

Early in the settlement of Bruce a small village known as Springvale was established on the border of Brant and Elderslie Townships at the 15th Sideroad. Later the village name was changed to Vesta. A nearby spring-fed stream attracted Richard Blakeway to build a sawmill powered by the stream. The village had a general store, a blacksmith shop, a carriage or cooper shop, a Methodist Church and two homes. In 1860 a post office was established, generally located in the home of the current postmaster. The post office was closed when rural mail delivery began in 1914. A log school was build a short way east of the village. It was used until it was replace by a two-room brick building a mile and a half south of the village. Years later the general store burned down and the village past into history.

Walkerton

The town of Walkerton owes its name and, perhaps its very existence, to an Irishman named Joseph Walker. In May 1850, Walker and his son William settled on Con 1 NDR, Lots 27 and 28 and Con 1 SDR, Lot 29. Walker was a miller by trade. Later that spring he left the area with three friends looking for a site to construct a sawmill. The group set out on foot north to Owen Sound, then south via the "Gimby Trail" to the mouth of the Saugeen and on to Kincardine looking for possible sites. Finding none, Walker and his friends headed east along the blazed line of the Durham Road. His friends found satisfactory farm land in Greenock but Walker continued on until he came to the Saugeen River. Here he decided to locate his mill. Crown Lands Department records show that on 15 Jul 1851 Walker was recommended as the locatee of a mill site and lands where the Saugeen crossed the Durham Road. This recommendation was approved by the Department eleven days later.

Walker's cabin soon turned into a tavern for settlers traveling into The Bush and the location became known as Brant. A mercantile business was

---

95 See Reville, F. Douglas, History of the County of Brant, The Hurley Printing Company Ltd., Brantford, Ontario, 3rd printing, 1982 for information about Brant

soon opened by Jardine and Valentine directly opposite Walker's Tavern. Shortly thereafter a second store was opened by John Shennan on the East side of the river. These businesses and Walker's sawmill saved many a settler the thirty-four mile round trip to Durham for supplies. In 1852 a post office was opened in Shennan's store with the name "Brant." This was the third post office in Bruce County. The other two being established at Kincardine and Southampton in 1851.

Figure 32, Saugeen Foundry at Walkerton, 2002.

Walker spent much effort in establishing the town. Within six years he and his son had acquired ten of the twenty-eight Crown lots that would eventually become Walkerton. He chopped out and clear parts of the Durham Road, contracted to build the two original bridges in the township over the Saugeen and built the first saw mill in the area with a very creative design for the dam on the Saugeen to power the mill. In 1853 Walker steered the location of a grist mill from Maple Hill to Brant and convinced the local farmers to put up $1,600 for the mill. Following the grist mill into the growing town was a tannery, an oatmeal factory, a planing mill and a woolen mill. In 1864 a foundary and machine shop opened. Figure 52 is a modern view of the Saugeen Foundry built in Walkerton in 1873 and certainly a sight with which the Bacons would have been familiar.

In 1854 Brant Township had become incorporated as a municipality with Walker appointed Reeve[96]. In 1855 a survey was made to divide the Crown lots into town lots but it faded away. In 1857 Walker & son hired another surveyor to remake the survey. This survey was successful and resulted in the post office and town name being changed to Walkerton. This year also saw Walker step down to Deputy Reeve and take on the task of making Walkerton the County Town[97].

This goal was finally attained but it took nine years and much political infighting. Walker was the instigator, commander-in-chief, hard-nosed politician, leader and finally the winner in a classic battle. In 1865 Parliament

---

96 AKA a township supervisor in the U.S.

97 County Seat in the U.S

declared Walkerton the County Town of Bruce County. The county buildings (courthouse and goal[98]) were completed in 1866 and opened for business 1 Jan 1867. Since Walkerton had never been incorporated as a village, even though warranted by the population, there was a slight embarrassment over its official status. Another Act of Parliament passed 15 Feb 1871 gave Walkerton the right to become a separate municipality and a full-fledged town. Joseph Walker rightfully received the honor of being the town's first mayor.

In 1901 Walkerton reached a population of 2,971 which continued to increase to 10,163 in 1996. Since that time the population has been decreasing.

The Municipality of Brockton was amalgamated in 1999 and consists of the former Township of Brant (incorporated in 1854), Township of Greenock (incorporated in 1856), and the Town of Walkerton (incorporated in 1871).

A rather complete community profile can be seen at: http://town. walkerton.on.ca/Economic%20Development/CommunityProfile.pdf

Tragedy Strikes Walkerton

On 12 May 2000 a torrential downpour set Walkerton up for an infamous reputation that it did not desire. A combination of unusual weather, poorly understood water supply well design and sighting, budget cuts in the Environmental Ministry and potentially criminal actions of water department employees came together to create a tragedy which medical experts termed Canada's worst and the world's second-worst instance of e-coli contamination spread through a water system.

Walkerton's water supply was a system of wells, at least one of which was very shallow and susceptible to the incursion of surface runoff in an area of intensive livestock operations. On May 12 torrential rains saturated the Walkerton area. E-coli were eventually found in the town's water supply. Hundreds of Walkerton's citizens are taken ill and seven died.

Walkerton's water system had been plagued with problems for years. In 1998 the Ontario Ministry of the Environment made recommendations to the Walkerton PUC regarding the use of chlorine, the training of staff and the testing of the water supply. The Ministry failed to ensure that its recommendations were implemented. And it did not act on several reports early in 2000 that showed contaminants were getting into the Walkerton water supply. The Ministry's failure to intervene in Walkerton was bound up with a drastic downsizing of its operations.

---

98 Jail in the U.S

Chronology of the Tragedy

May 12:   Torrential downpour washes bacteria from cattle manure into shallow town well.

May 17:   Residents complain of bloody diarrhea, vomiting, cramps, fever -- symptoms of E. coli poisoning.

May 18:   Tests of water sampled May 15 reveal E. coli contamination. Water manager Stan Koebel fails to notify public or public health office.

May 19-21:   Hundreds fall ill; Koebel does not mention knowledge of E. coli in water to health authorities.

May 21:   Public health unit begins independent water testing, issues boil-water advisory.

May 22:   First death directly linked to E. coli.

May 23:   Health unit tests reveal water contaminated with deadly E. coli O157:H7. Two-year-old girl dies, more than 150 people seek hospital treatment, another 500 complain of symptoms.

May 24:   Medical officer of health, Dr. Murray McQuigge, declares E. coli outbreak Canada's worst. Two more die.

May 25:   Fifth person dies. At least four children in critical condition. McQuigge declares tragedy preventable. Outside agency takes over water system. Stan Koebel leaves town, goes on sick leave.

May 26:   Tory Premier Mike Harris denies government cuts to blame for tragedy, points finger at changes made by previous NDP government. Proposed class-action lawsuit launched. Provincial police begin probe.

May 29:   Sixth death. Province admits knowing for six years water system flawed; announces new rules to protect drinking water.

May 30:   Seventh death.

The tragedy in Walkerton has raised issues of water contamination in other parts of rural Canada and the U.S.A. from intensive livestock operations (ILOs) designed for the large scale factory farming of animals. Critics of industrialized agribusiness have raised concerns about the environmental sustainability of this food regime including air, water and soil quality, and threats to human health. ILOs produce an added challenge to sustainability with their requirements for the assimilation of vast quantities of animal waste. Factory farming and corporate concentration in agriculture pose the question of which governance strategies may best be employed to ensure that these operations are regulated in the public interest.

Appendix G - The Cost of Things in Upper Canada 1831[99]

Item	Min Cost			Max Cost			Ave Cost			Ave Cost	Cost in Days of Common Labour
	£	s	p	£	s	p	£	s	p	£	
Horse	7	10	0	10	0	0	8	5	0	8.2500	47.14
Oxen for labour, per pair	15	0	0	17	0	0	16	0	0	16.0000	91.43
Milch Cow	3	15	0	5	0	0	4	5	6	4.2750	24.43
Wagon for a pair of horses	20	0	0							20.0000	114.29
Harness for a pair of horses	10	0	0							10.0000	57.14
A plough	3	0	0							3.0000	17.14
Brake harrow	2	0	0							2.0000	11.43
Long chains to drag trees, each	1	5	0							1.2500	7.14
Double horse sleigh	7	0	0							7.0000	40.00
Common ox sleigh	2	0	0							2.0000	11.43
Wheat per bushel	0	3	6	0	5	0	0	4	3	0.2125	1.21
Barley per bushel	0	2	6	0	3	0	0	2	9	0.1375	0.79
Oats per bushel	0	1	6	0	2	0	0	1	9	0.0875	0.50
Indian corn per bushel	0	1	6	0	2	6	0	2	0	0.1000	0.57
Peas per bushel	0	2	6	0	3	0	0	2	9	0.1375	0.79
Potatoes per bushel	0	1	6	0	2	0	0	1	9	0.0875	0.50
Hay per ton	2	0	0	2	10	0	2	5	0	2.2500	12.86
Hire of a man for farm work with board per month	2	10	0							2.5000	14.29
Hire of female for ordinary housework per month	1	10	0							1.5000	8.57
Carpenter per month	6	10	0							6.5000	37.14
Blacksmith on job per month	4	5	0							4.2500	24.29
Blacksmith for a set of shoes	0	10	0							0.5000	2.86
Chopping per acre	1	10	0							1.5000	8.57
Logging (collecting & dragging) per month	1	0	0							1.0000	5.71
Ordinary fencing of split rails per rod	0	1	1							0.0542	0.31
Post and rail fence per rod	0	1	10							0.0917	0.52
Harrowing and sowing per acre	0	5	0							0.2500	1.43
Reaper's wages (find themselves) per acre	0	5	0							0.2500	1.43
Common labour at Indian corn or potato work	0	3	6							0.1750	1.00
Wheat reaped, hauled & stacked per acre	1	0	0							1.0000	5.71
Threshing & winnowing per bushel	0	0	6							0.0250	0.14
Handsome sideboard two doors & five drawers	15	0	0							15.0000	85.71
Secretary or writing table	10	0	0							10.0000	57.14
Sofa	12	0	0	15	0	0				12.0000	68.57
Dining tables, three to a set	7	0	0							7.0000	40.00
Bureaus, six drawers	5	0	0							5.0000	28.57
Breakfast tables	1	5	0							1.2500	7.14
Black walnut chairs, hair bottoms, each	1	15	0							1.7500	10.00
Common Windsor chairs, each	0	5	0							0.2500	1.43
Drawing room table, claw feet	7	10	0							7.5000	42.86
Drawing room table, plain	4	10	0							4.5000	25.71
Bedsteads, high posts	2	0	0							2.0000	11.43
Tent, high posts	1	10	0							1.5000	8.57
Dressing table & wash stand	1	10	0							1.5000	8.57
Double washstand	1	10	0							1.5000	8.57
Light washstand	0	12	0							0.6000	3.43
Ladies work table	1	10	0							1.5000	8.57

99 Reville, F. Douglas, History of the County of Brant, The Hurley Printing Company, Brantford, First printing 1920, Third printing 1982, pages 270-271

Notes:

(1) The furniture articles are handsomely and substantially made of native woods: bird's eye maple, black walnut, birch, elm, oak, cherry, etc. the supply is excellent and with beautiful materials.

(2) Conversions: £1 = 20 shillings, 1 shilling = 12 pence, 40 rods = 1/4 mile.

(3) 1 month = 26 days (6 day week, 30 days per month).

Appendix H - Suggested Reading

The books listed here tell the story of life as lived by pioneers of Bruce County in the 1840s and 1850s. Most of these books mention Bacon family members. They are highly recommended for the reader who wishes to develop an understanding the trials and tribulations faced by these hardy people.

1. Kennedy, David, Sr., *Pioneer Days at Guelph and the County of Bruce,* Toronto, 1903, Reprinted by The Bruce County Historical Society, 1973 & 1991, paperback, 135 pages.

    Personal experiences of the author in settling in Bruce County mainly in 1851.

2. Gateman, Laura M., *The History of the Township of Brant: 1854-1979,* The Brant Township Historical Society, Elmwood, Ontario, 1979, hardback, 484 pages.

    No index, Bacons are listed in a table of township Crown Deeds by Concession and Lot beginning on page 480.

3. Robertson, Norman, *History of the County of Bruce,* The Bruce County Historical Society, 1906, hardback, 560 pages.

    Bacons are mentioned on pages 34, 35, 53, 66, 281 and 337.

4. *Surname Index to The History of the County of Bruce,* The Bruce County Historical Society, 2000, paperback, 35 pages.

    The index to Robertson's *History* only contained some 295 surnames compared to the 1,600-1,700 indexed here by a group of historical society members.

5. McGillivray, Marion, *From City Streets to Trackless Forest: The Story of Jane Smith,* The Bruce County Historical Society, 1995, paperback, 53 pages.

    Eighteen year old Jane Smith travels from Scotland to join her two brothers who had settled on Con 1 SDR, Lot 20, Brant Township adjacent to Isaac Bacon. Jane Smith's brother William is a nephew by marriage to Mary Ann Bacon Guinn, daughter of Joseph. The Bacons are mentioned on several pages.

6. Brown, W.M., *The Queen's Bush: A Tale of the Early Days of Bruce County*, John Bale, Sons & Danielsson, LTD., London, 1932, reprinted by The Bruce County Historical Society, 1992, paperback, 295 pages.

   Bacons are mentioned on pages 96, 112, 125, 133, 134, and 153.

7. Smith, Wm. H., *Smith's Canadian Gazetteer of Canada West*, H. & W. Rowsell, 1846, reprinted by Coles Canadiana Collection, 1970, paperback, 285 pages with foldout map.

   Not especially readable but contains lots of interesting information.

Part III - Genealogy

Introduction

The genealogy is a structured account in modified register format of the spouse and parent-child relationships with dates and places of events (birth, marriage, death and burial) of the descendants of Joseph Bacon to the third generation. .

Generation [1]: ID 1, Joseph Bacon
Generation [2]: IDs 2-12, Children of Joseph Bacon (12)
Generation [3]: IDs 13-97, The grandchildren of Joseph Bacon (85)
Generation [4]: A statement for each set of parents of the number of male and female great grandchildren

Like Joseph and Susanna, their children [2] had yearnings for a better place and they scattered widely from their child-hood home in Ontario. It was left to the grandchildren [3] to consolidate and people these new places. The places where the genealogical events in the lives of the grandchildren took place provide a fascinating view of the resulting migration.

Although Joseph's parents and grandparents have been known for some time and very recently his ancestry to eight generations has been determined by an English researcher commissioned by Douglas Bacon of Spokane, Washington, a descendant of Joseph's son William, none has been included in this story.

Auxiliary Events

Auxiliary events such as Census, Land Patent, Purchase or Sale of land, Obituary and Biography have been included in the genealogy for two reasons:

1) They provide information about the family's migration across the United States and Canada,

2) They provide specific references and the all important geographic location where the reader may find that and other family information.

Census: Children are considered part of their parents family for census events if they are living in the family home unless they have married. Wives are considered as part of the husband's census event.

Biography: Reference citations have been included as an indication of the amount and richness of the information and, as stated above, to provide clues to where it can be found.

Source Reference Citations

Significant efforts have been made to include source reference citations. Your author had hoped to find primary sources[100] for all genealogical facts. However, it quickly became obvious that there were not enough years in a lifetime to accomplish that objective. Therefore, your author has used data compiled by other descendant authors. Generation [1] events in England are sourced through a paid researcher to primary (church) records but the specific references were not provided. In Canada a mixture of primary and secondary sources[101] are cited. For Henry [2] and his sister Emma Jane [2] the objective of citing only primary sources is approached through your author's personal research. For the remaining sibling lines, compiled sources are generally cited and are believed to be reliable and based on primary sources.

Sometimes more than one citation is given for a specific event. This is done to establish credibility of the source(s).

Referencing Individuals

Where it is necessary to refer to an individual descendant, that individual has been identified by generation indicators in his/her line counting down from Joseph Bacon, Sr., i.e., Michael the great grandson of Joseph and his line of descent would be given as Michael [4], Joseph [3], Henry [2], Joseph [1].

Walkerton

The Bacons lived near the village of Walkerton in Brant Township, Bruce County, Ontario. Walkerton was the largest town in the Township and the County Town. Many documents refer to the Bacons as though they lived in Walkerton. There is no evidence that any Bacon event took place in the

---

[100] A Primary Source is data recorded at or near the time of the event by someone with personal knowledge of the facts or someone authorized to record the facts. For example, the earliest records generally available in Canada are church records created by the parish priest or minister recording marriages, baptisms and burials. Beginning in the 1860s for the United States and Canada, county clerks were authorized to by law to record and maintain public records of births, marriages and deaths.

[101] A Secondary Source is data recorded either after the fact and therefore depends on someone's memory of the event or the data has been compiled and published in a book or other document. Although recording errors do occur in primary records, errors are more likely in secondary records

village other than possibly buying food or other supplies, attending church or filing papers at the county land registry. Walkerton is wholly within Brant Township so your author has changed compiled source references that record an event as occurring in Walkerton to occurring in Brant Township without loss of accuracy. In later years, some of Susan Bacon Prior's grandchildren are known to have been buried in the Walkerton Protestant Cemetery.

Technical Tools

The genealogy was created using Ancestry Family Tree (AFT), Ver. 9.0.3, by Incline Software, LC and MyFamily.com, Inc. AFT is available for free download from www.MyFamily.com. Photos were cropped, edited and otherwise manipulated by Corel Photo-Paint 8. They were stored as media in the AFT database. Several new events, i.e., mortgage, land purchase and sale, were added to the basic AFT event set. The data was output in modified register format as a series of WordPerfect documents, edited and assembled into final form using Corel WordPerfect 12.

Modified Register for Joseph Bacon, Sr.

First Generation

1. **Joseph Bacon Sr.** was born[1] 03 Feb 1795 in Essexshire, England, the son of James Bacon and Mary Stebbing, and was baptized[2] 29 Mar 1795 in Henham, Essexshire, England. He died[3,4] 27 Dec 1882 in Brant Township, Bruce County, Ontario from consumption and was buried[5] in Old Bethel Methodist/Prior Cemetery, Brant Township, Bruce County, Ontario.

Joseph pursued the occupation[6] of labourer before 1835 in England. He pursued the occupation[7] of farmer & road contractor in Canada. He emigrated[8] Mar 1835 from Debden, Essexshire, England. He immigrated Mar 1835 to near Hamilton, Gore District, Upper Canada. He received a Crown Patent[9,10] for Lot 18 Con WOSR, 4th Div., East Part (50 acres) on 10 Dec 1846 in Arthur Township, Bruce County, Canada West. He gave a mortgage[11,12] on Lot 18, Con WOSR, 4th Div., East Part to James Ropo, et al for 24 Pounds Sterling on 06 Jun 1848 in Arthur Township, Wellington County, Canada West. He pursued the occupation[13] of Tavern Keeper 1848 in Arthur Township, Wellington District, Canada West. He and his wife received a discharge of mortgage[14,15] on Lot 18, Con WOSR from James Ropo, et al on 06 Aug 1849 in Arthur Township, Wellington County, Canada West. He sold[16,17] Lot 18, Con WOSR, 4th Div., East Part (50 acres) to James MacKay on 08 Aug 1849 in Arthur Township, Wellington County, Canada West. He was enumerated in a census[18] 1851 in Bruce County, Brant Township, Canada West. He purchased land[19] Lot 14, Con 1 NDR (50 acres) from son Joseph Bacon, Jr. for 200 Pounds Sterling on 24 Dec 1855 in Brant Township, Bruce County, Canada West. He gave a mortgage[20] on Lot 14, Con 1 NDR (50 acres) for 36 Pounds, 3 Shillings & 6 Pence to Jno. Bruce on 14 Jul 1858 in Brant Township, Bruce County, Canada West. He gave a mortgage[21] on Lot 14, Con 1 NDR (50 acres) for $1,200 to the Trust & Loan Company of Upper Canada on 03 Jun 1859 in Brant Township, Bruce County, Canada West. He and his wife received a discharge of mortgage[22] on Lot 14, Con 1 NDR (50 acres) from Jno. Bruce on 26 Jul 1859 in Brant Township, Bruce County, Canada West. He was enumerated in a census[23] 1861 in Brant Township, Bruce County, Canada West. His religion[24,25,26] was

Primitive Methodist 1861/1881 in Brant Township, Bruce County, Ontario. He gave a mortgage[27] on Lot 14, Con 1 NDR (50 acres) for $350 to The Huron & Erie Savings & Loan Society on 11 Jun 1864 in Brant Township, Bruce County, Canada West. He lost[28] Lot 14, Con 1 NDR (50 acres) 06 Jul 1864 in Brant Township, Bruce County, Canada West. He purchased land[29] Lot 14, Con 1 NDR (50 acres) from S.R. McIllroy for $175 20 Sep 1864 in Brant Township, Bruce County, Canada West. He and his wife received a discharge of mortgage[30] on Lot 14, Con 1 NDR (50 acres) from the Trust & Loan Company of Upper Canada on 27 Sep 1864 in Brant Township, Bruce County, Canada West. He and his wife received a discharge of mortgage[31] on Lot 14, Con 1 NDR (50 acres) 08 Oct 1869 in Brant Township, Bruce County, Ontario. He gave a mortgage[32] on Lot 14, Con 1 NDR (50 acres) for $600 to Findlay McCallum et-al on 11 Oct 1869 in Brant Township, Bruce County, Ontario. He sold[33] Lot 14, Con 1 NDR (50 acres) to Uriah Roswell for $2,100 on 01 Nov 1871 in Brant Township, Bruce County, Ontario. He and his wife received a discharge of mortgage[34] Lot 14, Con 1 NDR (50 acres) 20 Dec 1871 in Brant Township, Bruce County, Ontario. He was enumerated in a census[35] 1871 in Bruce County, Brant Township, Ontario. He was enumerated in a census[36] 1881 in Brant Township, Bruce County South, Ontario. He resided[37] Dec 1881 - Apr 1882 in Con 14, Lot 9 near Vesta, Brant Township, Bruce County.

Joseph married[38] **Susannah Franklin** "Susan", daughter of Henry Franklin and Sarah, on 24 Jul 1819 in Widdington, Essexshire, England. Susan was baptized[39] 07 Sep 1798 in Widdington, Essexshire, England . She died[40] 05 May 1876 in Brant Township, Bruce County, Ontario and was buried in Old Bethel Methodist/Prior Cemetery, Brant Twp, Bruce County, Ontario.

They had the following children:

+2 M   i.   **William Bacon** was born 22 Aug 1821 in Debden, Essexshire, England and was baptized 07 Oct 1821 in Debden, Essexshire, England.

+3 F ii. **Susan Bacon** was born 05 May 1823 in Debden, Essexshire, England and was baptized 03 Aug 1823 in Debden, Essexshire, England. She died 10 May 1904 in Brant Township, Bruce County, Ontario and was buried in Old Bethel Methodist/Prior Cemetery, Brant Township, Bruce County, Ontario.

+4 M iii. **James Bacon Sr** was born 04 Mar 1825 in Debden, Essexshire, England and was baptized 12 Jun 1825 in Debden, Essexshire, England. He died 07 Oct 1906 in Bottineau, Bottineau County, North Dakota and was buried in Bottineau, Bottineau County, North Dakota.

+5 F iv. **Charlotte Bacon** was born 31 Jul 1827 in Debden, Essexshire, England and was baptized 06 Jan 1828 in Debden, Essexshire, England. She died 31 Jan 1905 in Hill Hall, Saskatchewan and was buried in Woodley-Cromar Cemetery, Hill-Hall, Saskatchewan.

6 M v. **Joseph Bacon Jr.** was born 13 Dec 1829 in Debden, Essexshire, England and was baptized 24 Jan 1830 in Debden, Essexshire, England. He died 20 Apr 1870 in Bruce County, Ontario from consumption and was buried in Old Bethel Methodist/Prior Cemetery, Brant Township, Bruce County, Canada West.

+7 M vi. **John Bacon** was born 31 Dec 1831 in Debden, Essexshire, England and was baptized 26 Aug 1832 in Debden, Essexshire, England. He died 16 Feb 1914 in SE 36-12-25 w1, near Crandall, Manitoba and was buried in Kinsmore Cemetery, RM of Woodworth, Manitoba.

+8 M vii. **Isaac Elisha Bacon** was born 24 Sep 1833 in Debden, Essexshire, England and was baptized 22 Oct 1833 in Debden, Essexshire, England.

He died 24 Jan 1895 in New Westminster, British Columbia and was buried in British Columbia.

+9 M viii. **Elijah Bacon** "Lige" was born 24 Sep 1833 in Debden, Essexshire, England and was baptized 22 Oct 1833 in Debden, Essexshire, England. He died about 1907 in Pope, RM of Hamiota, Manitoba and was buried in Scotia Cemetery, RM of Hamiota, Manitoba.

+10 F ix. **Emma Jane Bacon** "Jane" was born 17 Jul 1836 in Buffalo, New York. She died 27 Oct 1907 in Petoskey, Emmet County, Michigan from bright's disease and was buried in Bliss Township Cemetery, Bliss, Emmet County, Michigan.

+11 M x. **Henry B. Bacon** was born 11 Oct 1839 in Hamilton, Upper Canada. He died 12 Sep 1916 in Resort Township, Emmet County, Michigan from gangrene and was buried 14 Sep 1916 in Greenwood Cemetery, Petoskey, Emmet County, Michigan.

+12 F xi. **Mary Jane Bacon** was born 22 Jan 1847 in Middletown Township, Middlesex County, Canada West. She died about 1905.

Source References - Joseph, Sr.

1. Robertson, Norman, *History of the County of Bruce* (William Briggs, Toronto, 1906, Reprinted by The Bruce County Historical Society, 1960), Page 281, The Collection of Dean Wheaton, 5976 Kungle Road, Clinton, OH 44216-9317. "Joseph Bacon was a native of Essex, England, where he was born, February 3rd, 1795." Text from a footnote at the bottom of the page.

2. Wilcock, Ruth, Report of Bacon Family Research in England, Debden Parish Registers, Essex, England, Unpublished, Nov 1982, Commissioned by Betty Allen, Langley, B.C., Line 45, The Collection of Dean Wheaton, 5976 Kungle Road, Clinton, OH 44216-9317. [BFR002]

3. Robertson, Norman, *History of the County of Bruce*, Page 281. "His death occurred December 22nd, 1882." Text from a footnote at the bottom of the page.

4. Death Registrations of Bruce County, Office of the Registrar General, 70 Lombard Street, Toronto, Ontario. [KRW001, 1]

5. Betty Allen, 21107 88th Avenue, Langley, British Columbia, Compilation of Bacon Family Information , Unpublished, Page 4, The Collection of Dean Wheaton, 5976 Kungle Road, Clinton, OH 44216-9317. [REV001, 11]

6. Wilcock, Ruth, Report of Bacon Family Research in England, Debden, Lines 5-12. All of Joseph's children's baptismal records have Occupation of Father given as "Labourer".

7. Robertson, Norman, *History of the County of Bruce*, Page 53, Footnote #1, 1906.

8. Robertson, Norman, *History of the County of Bruce*, Page 281. "In March, 1835, he emigrated to Canada and resided in the vcinity of Hamilton."

9. Wellington County Land Registry, Land Abstract Index: Arthur Township, Wellington County, Registry Office, Wellington County, Canada West, Book 1, 4th Div., Page 212, Wellington County Museum & Archives, RR #1, Fergus, Ontario N1M 2W3. WOSR = West of Owen Sound Road. Two concessions were laid out along the Owen Sound (Garafraxa) Road, one on each side, east and west. The concessions were divided into 35 Lots which were subdivided into four Parts of 50 acres each. Land in both concessions was available to settlers as free grants. [LAI001]

10. Crown Deed to Joseph Bacon, Arthur Township, Waterloo County, Wellington District, Researched by Betty Allen, Lot 18 WOSR (part), 20 Jan 1847, Library & Archives of Canada, 395 Wellington Street, Ottawa, Ontario, Canada K1A 0N4. [LLE003]

11. Wellington County Land Registry, Land Abstract Index: Arthur Township, Book 1, 4th Div., Instr. #502, Page 212, 07 Jun 1848.

12. Land Instruments of Arthur Township, Wellington District, Canada West, Instr. #502, Liber N, Folio 1, 07 Jun 1848, Wellington County Land Registry Office, 1 Stone Road West, Guelph, Ontario N1G 4Y2. Joseph & Susan mortgage their land for twenty-four pounds (part of Lot 18, West of Owen's Sound Road, 50 acres). Joseph is recorded as a Tavern Keeper. [WLI001]

13. Land Instruments of Arthur Township, Wellington District, Canada West, Instr. #502, Liber N, Folio 1, 07 Jun 1848. Joseph is recorded as a tavern keeper in this mortgage.

14. Wellington County Land Registry, Land Abstract Index: Arthur Township, Book 1, 4th Div, Instr. #1230, Page 212, 15 Aug 1849. Discharges mortgage of Instr. #502.

15. Land Instruments of Arthur Township, Wellington District, Canada West, Instr. #1230, Liber N. Folio 2, 15 Aug 1849. Discharge of Joseph Bacon mortgage made 6 Jun 1848. Joseph is again referenced as a Tavern Keeper.

16. Wellington County Land Registry, Land Abstract Index: Arthur Township, Book 1, 4th Div., Instr. #1231, Page 212,, 15 Aug 1849.

17. Land Instruments of Arthur Township, Wellington District, Canada West, Instr. #1231, Liber N, Folio 10, 15 Aug 1849. Sold to James Mackay, the younger, for 132 pounds, 131 pounds and five shillings to Joseph and five shillings to Susan for her dower interest.

18. 1851 Canada West Census of Bruce County, Brant Township, Reel #C-11715, Researched by Betty Allen, Langley, BC, Lines 30-34, 1851, Library & Archives of Canada, 395 Wellington Street, Ottawa, Ontario, Canada K1A 0N4. "Farmer, Age 60, Episcopalian, Log shanty 12 x 16; Susan, Age 60; Henry, Labour, Age 15; Isaac, Age 16; Joseph, Age 23, Labour." [LLE003]

19. Bruce County Registrar, Land Records of Bruce County, Ontario, Microfilm Series A, Roll A-60, Instr #168, 12 Dec 1858, Bruce County Registry Office, 203 Cayley Street, Walkerton, Ontario N0G 2V0. NDR = North of Durham Road. Six concessions of free grants of 50 acres each were laid out along the Durham Road, three north of road and three south of road. [OBC001]

20. Bruce County Registrar, Index of Land Instruments for Bruce County, Ontario, Microfilm A-3-9, Page 248, Instr. #169, 21 Dec 1858, Walkerton Branch Library, 253 Durham Street East, Walkerton, Ontario N0G 2V0. [OBC002]

21. Bruce County Registrar, Index of Land Instruments for Bruce County, Ontario, Microfilm A-3-9, Page 248, Instr. #205, 24 Jun 1859. This is a curious mortgage in that Joseph and five of his sons (John, Joseph, Jr., Elijah, Isaac & Henry) all gave mortgages on their land (a total of 300 acres) for $1,200, a very large sum for those times, for an unknown purpose.

22. Bruce County Registrar, Index of Land Instruments for Bruce County, Ontario, Microfilm A-3-9, Page 248, Instr. #3, 12 Aug 1859. Discharges mortgage in Instr. #169.

23. 1861 Canada West Census of Bruce County, Brant Township, Researched by Betty Allen, Reel #C1010, Page 6, Lines 47-50, 1861, Library & Archives of Canada, 395 Wellington Street, Ottawa, Ontario, Canada K1A 0N4. "Joseph, Age 66, Primitive Methodist; Susana, Age 64; William, Age 40, Widower; Joseph, Age 30, Single, Labour.". [LLE003]

24. 1861 Canada West Census of Bruce County, Brant Township, Reel #C1010, Page 6, Lines 47-50, 1861. "Religion: Primitive Methodist."

25. 1871 Census of Canada - Ontario: Searchable Database of Heads & Strays, http://db.library.queensu.ca/dbtw-wpd/exec/dbtwpub.dll, Dist. 27, Subdist. H, Div. 1, Page 9, 1871, Queen's University Libraries, 99 University Avenue, Kingston, Ontario K7L 3N6. "Religion: Primitive Methodist." [QUL001]

26. 1881 Canadian Census of Ontario, Bruce County, Brant Township, FHL Film #1375911, NA Film # C-13275, Page 82, Household 347, 1881, FamilySearch Online, www.familysearch.org, Family History Library, Salt Lake City, Utah. "Religion: Primitive Methodist." [CCB001]

27. Bruce County Registrar, Index of Land Instruments for Bruce County, Ontario, Microfilm A-3-9, Page 248, Instr. #525, 28 Jul 1864. There is a line entry preceding this one (#525) for Instr. #002 for 17 Jun 1864 but no other data is entered.

28. Bruce County Registar, Land Records of Bruce County, Ontario, Microfilm A-61, Instr. #533, 30 Aug 1864. A Deed Poll is normally used by an individual to change their name. In this instance, however, a Deed Poll was used to convey title (as in a sale) by the Sheriff of Huron & Bruce Counties of Joseph's land to Samuel Regent McIlroy of Hamilton, Wentworth County for $80. Why this event occurred is not recorded in the records.

29. Bruce County Registar, Land Records of Bruce County, Ontario, Roll A-64, Instr. #1531, 30 Sep 1869. Joseph buys the land back from S.R. McIlroy for $175.

30. Bruce County Registrar, Index of Land Instruments for Bruce County, Ontario, Microfilm A-3-9, Page 248, Instr. #255, 08 Oct 1864. Discharges mortgage in Instr #205.

31. Bruce County Registrar, Index of Land Instruments for Bruce County, Ontario, Microfilm A-3-9, Page 248, Instr. #1538, 13 Oct 1869. Discharges mortgage in Instr. #252 (002).

32. Bruce County Registrar, Index of Land Instruments for Bruce County, Ontario, Microfilm A-3-9, Page 248, Instr. #1532, 05 Oct 1869.

33. Bruce County Registrar, Land Records of Bruce County, Ontario, Microfilm A-65, Instr. #2255, 19 Dec 1871.

34. Bruce County Registrar, Index of Land Instruments for Bruce County, Ontario, Mircofilm A-3-9, Page 248, Instr. #3142, 02 Oct 1874. Discharges mortgage in Instr. #1532.

35. 1871 Census of Canada - Ontario: Searchable Database of Heads & Strays, Dist. 27, Subdist. H, Div. 1, Pg 9, 1871. "Joseph, age 76, farmer, Primitive Methodist."

36. 1881 Canadian Census of Ontario, Bruce County, Brant Township, Page 82, Household # 347, 1881. "Birth Year = 1795, Birthplace = England, Age = 86, Marital Status = Widowed, Occupation = Retired Farmer, Religion = Primitive Methodist."

37. Bacon, Joseph, Letter To Henry & Elizabeth Bacon, 26 Apr 1882, The Collection of Dean Wheaton, 5976 Kungle Road, Clinton, OH 44216-9317. "I am stopping with Mrs. Prior. I have been here five months." [DB0003]

38. Wilcock, Ruth, Report of Bacon Family Research in England, Debden, Lines 2-3. "Marriage: Joseph Bacon of Debden Parish, bachelor and Susannah Franklin of Widdington, spinster by Banns 24 July 1819, R. Birch, Rector, Both marks, Witnesses: Charlotte Franklin, George Freeman."

39. Wilcock, Ruth, Report of Bacon Family Research in England, Widdington Parish Registers, Essex, England, Unpublished, Nov 1982, Commissioned by Betty Allen, Langley, B.C., Line 9, The Collection of Dean Wheaton, 5976 Kungle Road, Clinton, OH 44216-9317. Susannah's baptism records gives her parents as Henry and Sarah. [BFR002]

40. Bacon, Joseph, Family Information, The Collection of Dean Wheaton, 5976 Kungle Road, Clinton, OH 44216-9317. A typed list of information which appears to have come from a family Bible obtained from Ruth Bacon Bates, Kentwood, Michigan on 10 Apr 1994. [WWD055, 18]

Modified Register for Joseph Bacon, Sr.

Second Generation - William

2. **William Bacon** was born[1] 22 Aug 1821 in Debden, Essexshire, England and was baptized 07 Oct 1821 in Debden, Essexshire, England.

    William was enumerated in a census[2,3] in 1851 in Onondaga Township, Brant County, Canada West. He was enumerated in a census[4] in 1861 in Brant Township, Bruce County, Canada West. He gave a mortgage[5] on Lot 5 Con 6 (100 acres) for $600 to Duncan McKellar 01 Dec 1863 in Brant Township, Bruce County, Canada West. He received a Crown Patent[6] for Lot 6 Con 5 (100 acres) 16 Feb 1864 in Brant Township, Bruce County, Canada West. He sold[7] Lot 5 Con 6 (100 acres) to Mary Bacon, his sister, for $600 on 21 Apr 1864 in Brant Township, Bruce County, Canada West. He was enumerated in a census[8] in 1870 in Ionia Township, Ionia County, Michigan. He was enumerated in a census[9] 25 Jun 1880 in Two Rivers, Morrison County, Minnesota.

    William married[10] **Ellemena Pavers** on 04 Jan 1846 in Brantford, Brant County, Canada West. Ellemena was born[10] 25 Jun 1813 in Germany. She died[10] 12 Jan 1856 in Brantford, Brant County, Canada West and was buried[10] in Batson & Tranquility Methodist Cemetery, Brantford, Brant County, Canada West.

They had the following child:

13 M i. **Hiram William John Bacon** was born[11] 19 Jul 1855 in Brant Township, Bruce County, Canada West. He died[11] 09 Mar 1927 in Minnewaska, Polk County, Minnesota and was buried[11] in Glenwood City Cemetery, Glenwood, Polk County, Minnesota.

     Hiram was enumerated in a census[8] 05 Aug 1870 in Ionia Township, Ionia County, Michigan. He was enumerated[9] in a census 25 Jun 1880 in Two Rivers, Morrison County, Minnesota. He was enumerated in a census[12] 01 Jun 1900 in Copley Township, Beltrami County, Minnesota. He filed a Declaration Intent to obtain U.S. Citizenship[13] 07 Aug 1912 in Roseau, Roseau County, Minnesota. He was enumerated in a census[14] 13 Jan 1920 in Grove Park Township, Polk County, Minnesota.

Hiram married[15] (1) **Margaret Rachel Kiley** on 25 Feb 1882 in Two Rivers, Morrison County, Minnesota. Margaret was born[11] 03 Jun 1860 in Mt. St. Patrick, Renfew County, Canada West. She died[11] 07 Aug 1939 in Palouse, Whitman County, Washington and was buried[11] 11 Aug 1939 in Palouse, Whitman County, Washington.

Hiram also married[11](2) **Nancy A. Brayman** on 1892 in Minnesota. Nancy was born[16] Sep 1861 in Minnesota.

Hiram and Margaret had two children, a boy and a girl, born in 1883 and 1885.
Hiram and Nancy had one child, a boy, born in 1893.

Source References - Williams

1. Report of Bacon Family Research in England, Line 30. [BFR002]

2. GEDCOM: 212467.ged, William Bacon Descendants, 27 Feb 2000, Page 1. [BDL002]

3. 1851 Canada West Census of Brant County, Onadago Township, Reel #s C-11713 & C-11714, Page 101, Lines 4-6, 1851. [LLE003]

4. GEDCOM: 212467.ged, William Bacon Descendants, 27 Feb 2000, Page 1.

5. Land Records of Bruce County, Ontario, Instrument #461, Page 500, 26 Dec 1863. [OBC001]

6. Index of Land Instruments for Bruce County, Ontario, Microfilm A-3-9, page 500. [OBC002]

7. Land Records of Bruce County, Ontario, Microfilm Records, Instrument #498, Page 539, 28 Apr 1864.

8. 1870 U.S. Census of Michigan, Ionia County, Ionia Township, Page 469, Lines 28-29, 05 Aug 1870. [CMB004]

9. 1880 U.S. Census of Minnesota, Morrison County, Two Rivers, Page 427D, Lines 22-23, 25 Jun 1880. [CMB003]

10. William Bacon Timeline, Page 3. [BDL003]

11. GEDCOM: 212467.ged, William Bacon Descendants, 27 Feb 2000, Page 2.

12. 1900 U.S. Census of Minnesota, Beltrami County, Copley Township, Page 218B, Lines 88-90, 01 Jun 1900. [CMB001]

13. Declaration of Intent for U.S. Citizenship by Hiram W.J. Bacon, Certificate #297, 07 Aug 1912. [BDL005]

14. 1920 U.S. Census of Minnesota, Polk County, Grove Park Township, Page 20, Lines 24-25, 13 Jan 1920. [CMB002]

15. Marriage Certificate of Hiram W.J. Bacon and Margaret Ronan, #198, 25 Mar 1882. [BDL004]

16. 1900 U.S. Census of Minnesota, Beltrami County, Copley Township, Page 218B, Line 89, 01 Jun 1900.

Modified Register for Joseph Bacon, Sr.

Second Generation - Susan

3. **Susan Bacon** was born[1] 05 May 1823 in Debden, Essexshire, England and was baptized[1] 03 Aug 1823 in Debden, Essexshire, England. She died[2,3] 10 May 1904 in Brant Township, Bruce County, Ontario and was buried[3] in Old Bethel Methodist/Prior Cemetery, Brant Township, Bruce County, Ontario.

Susan was enumerated in a census[4] in 1851 in Arthur Township, Wellington County, Canada West. She was enumerated in a census[5] in 1861 in Brant Township, Bruce County, Canada West. She was enumerated in a census[6] in 1871 in Brant Township, Bruce County, Ontario. She was enumerated in a census[7] in 1881 in Brant Township, Bruce County, Ontario. She received a Crown Patent[8] for Con 14, Lot 9 (102 acres) 22 Feb 1887 in Brant Township, Bruce County, Ontario. She sold[9] Con 14, Lot 9 (100 acres) 16 Mar 1887 in Brant Township, Bruce County, Ontario.

Susan married James Prior about 1839 in Upper Canada. James was born[10] 1815 in Essexshire, England. He died[11,12] 14 Mar 1879 in Brant Township, Bruce County, Ontario and was buried[11] in the Old Bethel Methodist/Prior Cemetery, Brant Township, Bruce County, Ontario.

James purchased land[13] Lot 18 EOSR, 4th Qtr (50 acrs) 01 Nov 1847 in Arthur Township, Waterloo County, Canada West. He purchased land[14] Lot 18, 3rd Div., EOSR (50 acres) 15 Feb 1856 in Arthur Township, Wellington County, Canada West. He pursued the occupation of farmer on Con 14, Lot 9 after about 1860 in Brant Township, Bruce County, Canada West.

Date of marriage computed as one year before the birth of first child.

James and Susan had the following children:

14 F i. **Elizabeth Anne Prior** was born[15,16] 12 Jul 1840 in Arthur Township, Wellington District, Canada West. She died[17] 25 Jun 1915 in Kincardine, Bruce County, Ontario and was buried[18] in Trout Creek Cemtery, South Himsworth Township, Parry Sound County, Ontario.

Elizabeth & Thomas had seven children, five boys and two girls, born between 1868 and 1880, all in Ontario.

Certificates: Death registration; Marriage photocopy.

Census-Records: 1851, 1861, 1871, 1881, 1901

Films:
C11756: Census 1851, Arthur Township, Wellington County, p 69, line 32
C1010: Census 1861, Bruce County, Brant Township, p 8, line 31
MS 248, Reel #5 . - Bruce County Marriage Register (1859 - 1869) p.88
C-9936: Census 1871, Bruce County, Sub-District H3, District No. 27, p65. photocopy provided by PAC, June 29 1978.
C13275: Census 1881, Brant Tp., Bruce Co., Dist 176, H2, p62, family #270
T6482/3: Census 1901, Himsworth Twp. N & S, t2, page 1, line 33, Hse 6, Family #6

Extant:
1851: Census (10 yrs.; BP Canada)
1861: Census (19 yrs.; BP U[pper] C[anada]
1871: Census (29 yrs.; Married)
1881: Census (40 yrs.)
1901: Census (widow, 58 yrs., BD 12 Jul 1843, Ont., Origin English)

Residence:
1851: Arthur Township, Wellington County - 1 story Log house
1861: Lot 9 Concession 14, Brant Tp., Bruce Co., Ont.

Religious-Affiliation:
1851, 1861: Church of England
1871: W. Methodist

Burial-Location:
Trout Creek United Cemetery, South Himsworth Township, Parry Sound District, Ontario.

Information:
Wesley Patterson, Kincardine, Ontario, 1975.
Researched and documented by Betty Allen, Langley, British Columbia, GEDCOM: Susan Bacon.ged, 3 Feb 2005 via email to Dean Wheaton, Clinton, OH, LLE004. Used by permission.

Elizabeth married[19,20] **Thomas Allen**, son of Thomas Allen and Jane McCallum, on 16 Jan 1867 in Walkerton, Bruce County, Canada West. Thomas was born[21,22,23] 1819 in Ireland. He died[24] 26 Sep 1899 in Trout Creek, South Himsworth Township, Parry Sound County, Ontario and was buried[24] in Trout Creek Cemetery, South Himsworth Township, Parry Sound County, Ontario.

Certificates: Marriages (2) - photocopies.

Census-Records: 1861, 1871, 1881

Films:
MS248 Reel #14, [1846] page 35 Simcoe County Marriage

Register (1842-1858)
C1073: Census 1861; Simcoe County, #382, Mono Township
MS 248, Reel #5. [1867] - Bruce County Marriage Register (1859 - 1869) p.88
C-9936: Census 1871: Bruce County, District 27, sub-district H3, p65, family #214.
C13275: Census 1881, Brant Tp., Bruce Co., Dist 176, H2, p62, family #270

Extant:
1861: Census (39 yrs., Lab.)
1867: Marriage reg'n - (age 40 yrs.)
1871: Census (45 yrs., BP Ireland, Married)
1881: Census (56 yrs., BP Ireland)
Occupation:
1881: Farm Laborer; Farmer at Mono Tp., Simcoe Co.; Brant Tp., Bruce Co. and S. Himsworth Tp.

Residences:
Lived in Mono Township Simcoe County (1861); Brant Township (1871) Bruce County (1881); South Himsworth Township (1899)

Religious-Affiliation:
1861: Methodist 1871: N C Methodist

Burial-Location:
Trout Creek Cemetery, South Himsworth Township, Parry Sound District, Ontario.

Information:
Birth: date from Trout Creek Cemetery Headstone, S. Himsworth Twp., Ont., 1975

Death: date from Index to Paisley Advocate Newspaper, Bruce County Gen. Soc., seen at S.L.C. Nov. 1992. Burial listed in "These Our Ancestors Were" page 119.
Married by: 1) Rev. Alexr. Lewis, Presbyterian.
2) Rev. Robert C. Moffatt, Canada Presbyterian.

Certificate:
Marrriage - Bruce County Marriage Register (1859-1869) MS 248, Reel #5, p. 88, Rev. Robert C. Moffatt, Canada Presbyterian, Witness: Henry Brown.
Researched and documented by Betty Allen, Langley, British Columbia, GEDCOM: Susan Bacon.ged, 3 Feb 2005 via email to Dean Wheaton, Clinton, OH, LLE004. Used by permission.

15 F   ii.   **Lucy Mimie Prior** was born[24,25] 07 Jul 1844 in Arthur Township, Wellington District, Canada West. She died[24,25,] 07 Dec 1884 in Brant Township, Bruce County, Ontario from liver complaint [of] 4 days and was buried[25] in Old Bethel Methodist/Prior Cemetery, Brant Township, Bruce County, Ontario.

Census-Records: 1851, 1861, 1871, 1881

Films:
C11756: Census 1851, Arthur Township, Wellington County, p 69, line 32
C1010: Census 1861, Bruce County, Brant Township, p 8, line 31
C9936: Census 1871, Bruce Co., H3 027 p87, line 14, Dwelling #287, Family #287
C13275: Census 1881, Brant Twp., Bruce Co., 176, H2, p82, line 11, Dwelling #350, Family #350

Extant:
1851: Census (7yrs., BP Canada, attending school)
1861: Census (17 yrs.; BP U[pper] C[anada]
1871: Census (27 yrs.)
1881: Census (36 yrs.)
1884: Death (40 yrs. 5 mos.) - Informant John Lee, Merchant, Walkerton.

Residence:
1851: Arthur Township, Wellington County - 1 story Log house
Lot 9 Concession 14, Brant Tp., Bruce Co., Ont.

Occupation:
1881: Dress Maker
Religious-Affiliation:
1851; 1861; 1871; 1881: Church of England

Burial-Location:
Old Bethel Methodist (Prior Family) Cemetery, Con. 1, N. D. R., Lot 12, Brant Township, Bruce County, Ontario (Johnson's Corner.)

Information:
Headstone transcribed by Dorothy Steckenreiter, 1976. Ontario death index - 12/07/84 - OVR#001924-84.
Died at home of Mr. John Lee, Merchant of Walkerton (Bruce Herald 11 Dec 1884, Vol 24 #22 page 3). Dorothy Steckenreiter letter, July 2003.
Researched and documented by Betty Allen, Langley, British Columbia, GEDCOM: Susan Bacon.ged, 3 Feb 2005 via email to Dean Wheaton, Clinton, OH, LLE004. Used by permission.
Lucy never married per Raymond Kalblfeisch, "The Bacon Family", Self published, Petoskey, Michigan, Abt 1980, The Collection of Dean Wheaton, Clinton, OH (KRW001, pg 4).

16 F iii.   **Susan Jane Prior**[26] was born[26,27] 01 Apr 1847 in Arthur Township, Wellington District, Canada West. She died[27] 1931 in Chesley, Bruce County, Ontario and was buried[27] in Chesley, Bruce County, Ontario.

Susan & Robert had nine children born from 1872 to 1888, four boys and five girls, all born in Bruce County.

Census-Records: 1851, 1861

Films:
C11756: Census 1851, Arthur Township, Wellington County, p 69, line 32
C1010: Census 1861, Bruce County, Brant Township, p 8, line 31
C13276: Census 1881, Elderslie, Bruce Co., Dist 177, M-1, p3, family #9

Extant:
1851: Census (5 yrs., BP Canada)
1861: Census (14 yrs.; BP U[pper] C[anada] - NB also listed with the Samuel Hoar family [Carrick Twp., Bruce Co.,E. Dist 2, p24, line 28.]
1881: Census (34 yrs.; BP Ontario, English)

Residence:
1851: Arthur Township, Wellington County - 1 story Log house
Lot 9 Concession 14, Brant Township, Bruce County, Ontario.
1881: Elderslie Twp., Bruce Co.

Religious-Affiliation:
1851: Church of England; 1881 - Presbyterian

Burial-Location:
Chesley Cemetery, Bruce County, Ontario.

Information:
BD - Harry Prior, 1976. year incorrect, Headstone in Chesley cemetery
shows 1847 - 1931. Publication of Bruce & Grey Co. branch, O.G.S.
Researched and documented by Betty Allen, Langley, British Columbia,
GEDCOM: Susan Bacon.ged, 3 Feb 2005 via email to Dean Wheaton,
Clinton, OH, LLE004. Used by permission.

Susan married[28,29] **Robert Fortune** on 28 Mar 1871 in Paisley,
Bruce County, Ontario. Robert was born[29] in Scotland. He
died[29] in Eldersley Twp, Bruce County, Ontario and was
buried[29] in Eldersley Twp, Bruce County, Ontario.

Census: 1901

Films:
C13276: 1881 Census, Elderslie, Bruce Co. N, Dist 177, M-1, p3, family
#9

Extant:
1881: Census (age 57 yrs., BP Scotland, Married)

Residence:
1881: Elderslie Twp., Bruce Co., Ont.
Religious-Affiliation:
1881: Presbyterian

Burial-Location:
Chesley Cemetery, Bruce County, Ontario.

Information:
!BD & DD - Raymond Harvie, April 2000.
MD - Married by Rev. McLean, Paisley, Ontario, Witnesses: Sarah Prior
and John Fortune - photocopy of marriage certificate from Family Bible,
received from Raymond Harvie, Apr 2000.
Researched and documented by Betty Allen, Langley, British Columbia,
GEDCOM: Susan Bacon.ged, 3 Feb 2005 via email to Dean Wheaton,
Clinton, OH, LLE004. Used by permission.

17 F   iv.   **Sarah Ann Prior** was born[30] about 1847 in Arthur Township,
Waterloo County, Canada West. She died[31] 1924 in Ontario and
was buried[31] in Walkerton, Bruce County, Ontario.

Sarah Ann & Archibold had four children, three boys and one
girl.

Census-Records: 1851, 1861

Films:
C11756: Census 1851, Arthur Township, Wellington County, p 69, line 32
C1010: Census 1861, Bruce County, Brant Township, p 8, line 31
C9936: Census 1871, Bruce Co., H3 027 p87, line 14, Dwelling #287, Family #287
#1,819,419: MS 932 - Reel 13; Ontario Marriage Register, OVR#002-132 - Surrey Public Library, July 2000.

Extant:
1851: Census (4 yrs., BP Canada)
1861: Census (12 yrs.; BP U[pper] C[anada]
1871: Census (25 yrs.)

Residence:
1851: Arthur Township, Wellington County - 1 story Log house
Lot 8 Concession 14, Brant Township, Bruce County, Ontario.

Religious-Affiliation:
1851; 1861; 1871: Church of England

Burial-Location:
Walkerton Protestant Cemetery, Bruce County, Ontario.

Information:
Birth & Death years, from headstone in Walkerton Protestant Cemetery, Bruce Co., Ont., from Bruce & Grey Branch, O. G. S. BP listed as "Upper Canada" 1851/2 census, Brant Twp.
Researched and documented by Betty Allen, Langley, British Columbia, GEDCOM: Susan Bacon.ged, 3 Feb 2005 via email to Dean Wheaton, Clinton, OH, LLE004. Used by permission.

Sarah married **Archibald McLeod** "Jim"[32,33] on 25 Aug 1874 in Paisley, Bruce County, Ontario. Jim was born[33] 1840 in Canada West. He died[33] 1902 in Ontario and was buried[33] in Walkerton, Bruce County, Ontario.

Certificates: Marriage registration photocopy.

Films:
Mfm MS 932 - Reel 13; Ontario Marriage Register, Surrey Public Library, July 2000.

Residence:
1874: Brant.

Religious-Affiliation:
1894: Disciples

Burial-Location:
Walkerton Protestant cemetery - Bruce & Grey Branch, OSG cemetery records.

Information:
Name - Ida Harvie, March 1976.
Researched and documented by Betty Allen, Langley, British Columbia, GEDCOM: Susan Bacon.ged, 3 Feb 2005 via email to Dean Wheaton, Clinton, OH, LLE004. Used by permission.

18 F   v.   **Mary Margaret Prior** was born[34] 1850 in Canada West. She died[35] about 1928.

Margaret and Thomas had nine children, seven boys and two girls.

Census-Records: 1851, 1861

Films:
C11756: Census 1851, Arthur Township, Wellington County, p 69, line 32
C1010: Census 1861, Bruce County, Brant Township, p 8, line 31

Extant:
1851: Census (2 yrs., BP Upper Canada)
1861: Census (11 yrs.; BP U[pper] C[anada]

Residence:
1851: Arthur Township, Wellington County - 1 story Log house
Lot 8 Concession 14, Brant Township, Bruce County, Ontario.

Religious-Affiliation:
1851: Church of England
1861: Church of England
Burial-Location:

Information:
Name from Harry Prior, 1975.
1851 & 1861 Ontario Census lists a "Mary" as "2 yrs." and "10 yrs." No 'Margaret' listed.
Researched and documented by Betty Allen, Langley, British Columbia, GEDCOM: Susan Bacon.ged, 3 Feb 2005 via email to Dean Wheaton, Clinton, OH, LLE004. Used by permission.

Mary married **Thomas Hill**[36] Thomas was born[36] 1848 in Canada West.

Films:
C13275: 1881 Census, Greenock, Bruce South, Ontario, Canada

Extant:
1881: Census - (age 33 yrs, BP Ontario, Origin Irish, Married)

Residence:
1880: residing in Brant Township when daughter Lucinda was born.
1881: residing in Greenock Township.

Burial-Location:
Location not found, possibly in Saskatchewan.

Information:
L/A of Thomas Henry Prior, Surrogate Court, Bruce Co., Ont.
First name from birth registration of daughter Lucinda, 24th April 1880, Bruce Co., Brant Tp., Ont.
Researched and documented by Betty Allen, Langley, British Columbia, GEDCOM: Susan Bacon.ged, 3 Feb 2005 via email to Dean Wheaton, Clinton, OH, LLE004. Used by permission.

19 F   vi.   **Jane Emma Prior** was born[37] 1852 in Canada West. She died[38] 1919 and was buried[38] in Walkerton, Bruce County, Ontario.

Jane and Austin had seven children, four boys and three girls.

Certificates: Marriage registration photocopy.
Census-Records: 1861, 1871

Films:
C1010: Census 1861, Bruce County, Brant Township, p 8, line 31
C9936: Census 1871, Bruce Co., H3 027 p87, line 14, Dwelling #287, Family #287
#102210-3: Ontario Marriage Register, MS 932 Reel 16, - Surrey Public Library, August 2000.
C13275: 1881 Census, Walkerton, Bruce South, Ontario, Dist 176, SubDist 1, p49, Family 237

Extant:
1861: Census (9 yrs.; BP U[pper] C[anada]
1871: Census (19 yrs.)

Residence:
Lot 9 Concession 14, Brant Tp., Bruce Co., Ont.
Religious-Affiliation:

1861; 1871: Church of England

Burial-Location:
Walkerton Protestant Cemetery, "1852 - 1919" headstone inscription - Bruce & Grey Br O.G.S. publication.
Information:
Jane Emma and "Irne E." on 1861 presumed to be same child.
Full name from Ontario Marriage Register Mfm.
Jane died prior to the probate of L/A of brother Thomas Henry Prior (1929).
Researched and documented by Betty Allen, Langley, British Columbia, GEDCOM: Susan Bacon.ged, 3 Feb 2005 via email to Dean Wheaton, Clinton, OH, LLE004. Used by permission.

Jane married[38] **Austin Holderness** on 29 Dec 1875 in Walkerton, Bruce County, Ontario. Austin was born[38] 1835. He died[38] 1919 and was buried[38] in Walkerton, Bruce County, Ontario.

Certificates: Marriage registration photocopy.

Census: 1881

Films:
#102,210-3; MS 932 Reel 16, Ont. Marriage Register, - Surrey Public Library, Aug. 2000.
C13275: Census 1881, Walkerton, Bruce Co., Dist 176, Subdist I, p 49, family #237

Extant:
1879: Informant for James Prior's death reg'n.
1881: Census (age 46 yrs.; BP England, Married)

Residence:
1881: Walkerton

Occupation:
1877- Farmer; 1878-Shoemaker/ Laborer; 1880-Bootmaker; 1881 - Bootmaker; 1887-Teamster

Religious-Affiliation:
1881-Methodist Canada
Burial-Location:
Walkerton Protestant Cemetery, dates in Bruce & Grey Br. O.G.S. publications.

Information:
First name appears to be "Ouston" or "Owston"! on marriage registration.
Name listed as "Owsten" on daughter Edith's, birth registration, [Mar 1880].

Researched and documented by Betty Allen, Langley, British Columbia, GEDCOM: Susan Bacon.ged, 3 Feb 2005 via email to Dean Wheaton, Clinton, OH, LLE004. Used by permission.

20 M vii.   **James Arthur Prior #1** was born[39] 24 Dec 1854 in Canada West. He died[39] 24 Mar 1866 in Bruce County, Canada West and was buried[39] in Old Bethel Methodist/Prior Cemetery, Brant Township, Bruce County, Canada West.

Census-Records: 1861

Films:
C1010: Census 1861, Bruce County, Brant Township, p 8, line 31

Extant:
1861: Census (7 yrs., BP U[per] C[anada])

Residence:
Lot 9 Concession 14, Brant Tp., Bruce Co., Ont.

Religious-Affiliation:
1861: Church of England

Burial-Location:
Old Bethel (Prior Family) Cemetery, Con. 1, N. D. R., Lot 12, Brant Township, Bruce County, Ontario (aka Johnson's Corner.)

Information:
Harry Prior 1975.
Researched and documented by Betty Allen, Langley, British Columbia, GEDCOM: Susan Bacon.ged, 3 Feb 2005 via email to Dean Wheaton, Clinton, OH, LLE004. Used by permission.

21 M viii.   **Elijah Prior** was born[40,41] 1855. He died[41] 27 Aug 1927 in Sundridge, Parry Sound County, Ontario and was buried[41] in Strong Community Cemetery, Sundridge, Parry Sound County, Ontario.

Elijah and Jean had one son born in 1880.

Certificates: Marriage registration photocopy.

Census-Records: 1861, 1881, 1891

Films:
C1010: Census 1861, Bruce County, Brant Township, p 8, line 31

C9936: Census 1871, Bruce Co., H3 027 p87, line 14, Dwelling #287, Family #287

No. 001351; MS 932, Reel 26, Ontario archives; read Sept. 2000.

C13244: Census 1881, Joly & Strong & Chapman, Muskoka, 131, V p65, family #300

T6355: Census 1891, Joly, Strong, Sundridge, Parry Sound, family #69

Extant:
1861: Census (5 yrs., BP U[pper] C[anada])
1871: Census (15 yrs.)
1881: Census (25 yrs., Married)
1891: Census (34 yrs.)

Occupation:
Farmer

Residence:
Lot 9 Concession 14, Brant Tp., Bruce Co., Ont.

Religious-Affiliation:
1861; 1871; 1891: Church of England

Burial-Location:
Strong Community Cemetery, Sundridge, Ont. "These Our Ancestors Were" p 306. Picture of headstone online at

Information:
Birthyear & Death date - from headstone,
Researched and documented by Betty Allen, Langley, British Columbia, GEDCOM: Susan Bacon.ged, 3 Feb 2005 via email to Dean Wheaton, Clinton, OH, LLE004. Used by permission.

Elijah & Jean grew up on adjacent farms in Bruce County, Ontario. (Email messages concerning the Prior Family exchanged between Gerry Adams (gadams@junctionnet. com) and Dean Wheaton, Dated 2 Feb - 1 Mar 1999, The Collection of Dean Wheaton, Clinton, OH, Mar 1999, NOTES: Includes a 5 generation descendancy of Elijah Prior (GBL001).)

Elijah married **Jean Minorgan**[41] daughter of John Minorgan, about 1879. Jean was born[41] about 1859 in Scotland. She was buried[41] in Strong Community Cemetery, Sundridge, Parry Sound County, Ontario.

Certificates: Marriage registration photocopy

Census: 1881, 1891

Films:
No. 001351; MS 932, Reel 26, Ontario archives; read Sept. 2000.
C13244: Census 1881, Joly & Strong & Chapman, Muskoka, 131, V p65, family #300
T6355: Census 1891, Joly, Strong, Sundridge, Parry Sound, family #69

Extant:
1881: Census (age 22 yrs., BP Scotland, Married)
1891: Census (age 32 yrs.)

Religious-Affiliation:
1881: Presbyterian; 1891 Church of England

Burial-Location:
Strong Community Cemetery, located at Sundridge, Lot 22, Con 11, Township of Strong, District of Parry Sound; "These Our Ancestors Were" - pp 304. Picture of headstone online at

Information:
First name from Harry Prior June 1976.
MD, Surname & Parents names from Marriage Registration, Sept. 2000.
Researched and documented by Betty Allen, Langley, British Columbia, GEDCOM: Susan Bacon.ged, 3 Feb 2005 via email to Dean Wheaton, Clinton, OH, LLE004. Used by permission.

Lorna, wife of Gordon Prior (Elijah's grandson), has Jean's Bible. Jean bought the Bible as a gift to her mother when she was a child. Lorna paid for it a few pence at a time and reclaimed it when her mother died.
(Email messages concerning the Prior Family exchanged between Gerry Adams (gadams@junctionnet.com) and Dean Wheaton, Dated 2 Feb - 1 Mar 1999, The Collection of Dean Wheaton, Clinton, OH, Mar 1999, NOTES: Includes a 5 generation descendancy of Elijah Prior (GBL001).)

22 M   ix.   **Thomas Henry Prior**[42] was born[43] 15 Sep 1856 in Canada West. He died[44] 07 Dec 1928 in Brant Township, Bruce County, Ontario and was buried[44] in Chesley Cemetery, Bruce County, Ontario.

Census-Records: 1861

Films:
C1010: Census 1861, Bruce County, Brant Township, p 8, line 31

C13275: Census 1881, Brant Twp., Bruce Co., 176, H2, p82, line 11, Dwelling #350, Family #350

Extant:
1861: Census (4 yrs., BP U[pper] C[anada])
1881: Census (23 yrs.)
1928: Died at home of his sister Susan Fortune who had taken him there when ill with pneumonia.

Residence:
Lot 8 Concession 14, Brant Tp., Bruce Co., Ont.

Occupation:
1881: Farmer

Religious-Affiliation:
1861; 1881: Church of England

Burial-Location:
Chesley Cemetery, Pt. Park Lot P, 2nd Str., Bruce County, Ontario

Information:
Birth & Death - from Surrogate Court Records, Bruce Co., Ont. March 1976. Value of Estate was $34,319.60 in 1929, a very successful farmer. Never married.
DP - Dorothy Steckenreiter letter, July 2003.
Researched and documented by Betty Allen, Langley, British Columbia, GEDCOM: Susan Bacon.ged, 3 Feb 2005 via email to Dean Wheaton, Clinton, OH, LLE004. Used by permission.

23 F   x.   **Charlotte S. Prior** was born[45] about 1859 in Canada West. She died[45,46] 06 Mar 1931 in Kelowna, British Columbia and was buried[46] Mar 1931 in Kelowna, British Columbia.

Charlotte and Edward had five children, four boys and one girl.

Certificates: Death registration photocopy

Census-Records: 1861, 1871

Films:
C1010: Census 1861, Bruce County, Brant Township, p 8, line 31
C9936: Census 1871, Bruce Co., H3 027 p87, line 14, Dwelling #287, Family #287
C13275: Census 1881, Brant Twp., Bruce Co., 176, H2, p82, line 11, Dwelling #350, Family #350
B13112: BC Death Registration, #1913-09-203161

Extant:
1861: Census (2 yrs., BP U[pper] C[anada])
1871: Census (11 [or 14] yrs.)
1881: Census (21 yrs.)

Residence:
Lot 9 Concession 14, Brant Tp., Bruce Co., Ont.

Religious-Affiliation:
1861; 1871; 1881: Church of England

Burial-Location:
Vernon, B. C.
Information:
Ida Harvie, March 1976; Harry Prior 1976;
Surrogate Court Records - L/A of Thomas Henry Prior, brother - 1976.
DD from an item in the Paisley Advocate newspaper on Mfm. from Paisley, Ontario Library. According to Death Reg'n, Charlotte had been in Ontario for "3 years", informant was "Chas Blain, Kelowna, BC".
Researched and documented by Betty Allen, Langley, British Columbia, GEDCOM: Susan Bacon.ged, 3 Feb 2005 via email to Dean Wheaton, Clinton, OH, LLE004. Used by permission.

Charlotte married **Edward Thomas Blaine**[47,48] Edward was buried[48] in Vernon, British Columbia.

Certificates: Death registration photocopy

Films:
B13110: B C Death Registration, #1909-09-197117

Extant:

Occupation:
1909: Rancher

Religious-Affiliation:
7th Day Adventist
Burial-Location:
Vernon, B. C.

Information:
name Thomas given by Ida Harvie, March 1976
name Edward listed in obit of Charlotte in Paisley Advocate March 1913.
Researched and documented by Betty Allen, Langley, British Columbia, GEDCOM: Susan Bacon.ged, 3 Feb 2005 via email to Dean Wheaton, Clinton, OH, LLE004. Used by permission.

24 F   xi.   **Phoebe Prior** was born[49] 20 Dec 1861 in Brant Township, Bruce County, Canada West. She died[49] 25 Dec 1861 and was buried[49] in Old Bethel Methodist/Prior Cemetery, Brant Twp, Bruce County, Canada West.

> Burial-Location:
> Old Bethel Methodist (Prior Family) Cemetery, Brant Tp., Bruce County, Ontario (Johnson's Corner, Walkerton).
>
> Information:
> Headstone, 1975. "age 5 ds. children of James and Susan Prior"
> Researched and documented by Betty Allen, Langley, British Columbia, GEDCOM: Susan Bacon.ged, 3 Feb 2005 via email to Dean Wheaton, Clinton, OH, LLE004. Used by permission.

25 M   xii.   **James Arthur Prior #2**[50] was born[50,51] 13 Feb 1863 in Bruce County, Canada West. He died[51] 07 Aug 1917 in Wolsley, Saskatchewan from cancer and was buried[51] in Wolsey Community Cemetery, Wolsey, Saskatchewan.

James and Mildred had six children, four boys and two girls born between 1889 and 1896. All were born in the Northwest Territories (Saskatchewan) except one daughter, Jemima, who was born in Muskoka County Ontario (Harth, Frankie).
James and Carolyn had four children, two boys and two girls born between 1907 and 1915.

> Census-Records: 1861, 1871, 1881, 1891
>
> Films:
> C1010: Census 1861, Bruce County, Brant Township, p8, line 31
> C9936: Census 1871, Bruce Co., H3 027 p87, line 14, Dwelling #287, Family #287
> C13275: Census 1881, Brant Twp., Bruce Co., 176, H2, p82, line 11, Dwelling #350, Family #350
> T6426: Census 1891, Assiniboia East, District No. 198, sub-district 37, page 9
>
> Extant:
> 1871: Census (8 yrs.; BP Ontario; English Origin)
> 1881: Census (18 yrs.)
> 1891: Census, (age 28 years, Married, parents both born in England)
> Occupation:
> 1881: Laborer
> 1891: Farmer

Residence:
1871: Lot 9 Concession 14, Brant Tp., Bruce Co., Ont.
Held patent for NE 1/2 Section 36, Twp 20, Range 10, West of 2nd Meridian, 23 Sept 1899, District of Assiniboia & South-East 1/4 Section 36, Twp 20, Rg 10, of Meridian. Entry for homestead 29 January 1896, Accepted 27 May 1899.

Religious-Affiliation:
1871; 1881: Church of England

Burial-Location:
Wolseley Community Cemetery, Saskatchewan - from SGS research, Sept. 2000.

Information:
Birth & Death - Harry Prior, Jan. & June 1976.
Homestead - Dorothy Steckenreiter letter, July 2003. (James would sleep walk and they would keep a tub of water in front of the door. He once hitched up the team and woke up when he put his foot on the cold hub of the wheel.
Dorothy Steckenreiter, visit May 24, 2004 - James had a terrible temper; was always clean shaven; made up poems in his head while working in the fields, would repeat them when in the house. Always wanted family to have the best. Named after his brother who died in 1866.
Researched and documented by Betty Allen, Langley, British Columbia, GEDCOM: Susan Bacon.ged, 3 Feb 2005 via email to Dean Wheaton, Clinton, OH, LLE004. Used by permission.

James married[51] (1) **Mildred Lillian Garrett**, daughter of Wallace Edgar Garrett and Nancy Jane Bryant, on 04 Mar 1889 in Kenlis Plains, Northwest Territories, Canada. The marriage ended in divorce. Mildred was born[52] 28 Jul 1875 in Ontario. She died[52] 21 May 1943 in Sardis, British Columbia.

Census: 1891

Films:
T6426: Census 1891, Assiniboia East, District No. 198, sub-district 37, page 9
Extant:
1891: Census (age 17 years, Married, both parents born in Ontario)
1896, January 21: left home of husband, James Arthur, went to the village of Grenfell, in the district of Assiniboia. (this date probably not correct as 6th child would have been only about 3 weeks old.)
1905, 16th May: Divorce decree granted to James Arthur, 1905 statues Ontario Courts.

Residence:

Religious-Affiliation:
1891: Methodist

Burial-Location:

Information:
BP from 1891 Census
Researched and documented by Betty Allen, Langley, British Columbia,
GEDCOM: Susan Bacon.ged, 3 Feb 2005 via email to Dean Wheaton,
Clinton, OH, LLE004. Used by permission.

James also married[52] (2) **Carolyn Alice Jane Theobald**[52] on 14
Nov 1905. Carolyn was born[52] 12 Feb 1883. She died[52] 29 Aug
1959 in Trenton, Ontario and was buried[52] 31 Aug 1959 in
Ontario.

Extant:
Residence:
Religious-Affiliation:

Burial-Location:
White's cemetery, Aug 31, 1959

Information:
Name from Harry Prior, 1976.
Dorothy Steckenreiter visit, 24 May 2004
Researched and documented by Betty Allen, Langley, British Columbia,
GEDCOM: Susan Bacon.ged, 3 Feb 2005 via email to Dean Wheaton,
Clinton, OH, LLE004. Used by permission.

26 M   xiii.   **George A. Prior** was born[53] about 12 Jan 1866 in Bruce County,
Canada West. He died[53] 12 Apr 1866 in Brant Township, Bruce
County, Canada West and was buried[53] in Old Bethel Methodist/
Prior Cemetery, Brant Twp, Bruce County, Canada West.

Extant:
1866: Death (aged 3 months)

Residence:
Lot 9 Concession 14, Brant Township, Bruce County, Ontario.

Religious-Affiliation:
Church of England

Burial-Location:
Old Bethel Methodist (Prior Family) Cemetery, Con. 1, N. D. R., Lot 12, Brant Township, Bruce County, Ontario.

Information:
Birth & Death - information copied from headstone, 1975. "aged 3 mo. children of James and Susan Prior"
Researched and documented by Betty Allen, Langley, British Columbia, GEDCOM: Susan Bacon.ged, 3 Feb 2005 via email to Dean Wheaton, Clinton, OH, LLE004. Used by permission.

27 F   xiv.   **Jemima Louise Prior** was born[53,54] 15 Dec 1871 in Brant Township, Bruce County, Canada West. She died[54,55,56] 09 Aug 1928 in Brant Township. Bruce County, Ontario and was buried[56] in Chesley, Bruce County, Ontario.

Census: 1871

Films:
C9936: Census 1871, Bruce Co., H3 027 p87, line 14, Dwelling #287, Family #287
C13275: Census 1881, Brant Twp., Bruce Co., 176, H2, p82, line 11, Dwelling #350, Family #350

Extant:
1871: Census (2 yrs.; BP Ontario; English Origin)
1881: Census (12 yrs.)

Residence:
1871: Lot 9 Concession 14, Brant Township, Bruce County, Ontario.
Occupation:
Seamstress in Chesley. Made her wedding dress but the man married someone else. (Dorothy Steckenreiter letter, July 2003.)

Religious-Affiliation:
1871; 1881: Church of England

Burial-Location:
Chesley Cemetery, Pt. Park Lot P 2nd Str., Bruce County, Ontario

Information:
Birth & Death - information from Harry Prior & Ida Harvie, 1976. Jemima never married, she kept house for brother Thomas Henry Prior.
Researched and documented by Betty Allen, Langley, British Columbia, GEDCOM: Susan Bacon.ged, 3 Feb 2005 via email to Dean Wheaton, Clinton, OH, LLE004. Used by permission.

Source References - Susan

1. Wilcock, Ruth, Report of Bacon Family Research in England, Debden Parish Registers, Essex, England, Unpublished, Nov 1982, Commissioned by Betty Allen, Langley, B.C., Line 30, The Collection of Dean Wheaton, 5976 Kungle Road, Clinton, OH 44216-9317. [BFR002]

2. *Bruce County Cemetery Gravestone Readings*, Old Bethel Methodist/Prior Cemetery, Page 2, #18 and #19, Bruce County Museum & Archives, 33 Victoria Street North, Southampton, Ontario N0H 2L0. "James Prior died March 14, 1879 aged 64 years; His wife Susan Bacon died May 10, 1904 aged 81 yrs 5 ds Natives of Essex England." Birth date of 5 May 1823 is consistent with her death date and age on gravestone. [OBC009]

3. Ontario Death Registrations, Film #1904, OVR #006053-04. Researched by Betty Allen.

4. 1851 Canadian Census of Wellington County, Arthur Township, C11756, PAge 69, Line 32, 1851, Library & Archives of Canada, 395 Wellington Street, Ottawa, Ontario, Canada K1A 0N4. Researched by Betty Allen. [LLE004]

5. 1861 Canada West Census of Bruce County, Brant Township, Researched by Betty Allen, Page 8, Lines 31-42, 1861, Library & Archives of Canada, 395 Wellington Street, Ottawa, Ontario, Canada K1A 0N4. "James, Age 45, Farmer, Church of England, 1 story log house; Susan, Age 37; Betsy, Age 19; Lucy, Age 17; Susan, Age 14; Sarah, Age 12; Mary, Age 11; Jane E., Age 9; James A. Age 7; Elijah, Age 5; Thomas, Age 4; Charlotte, Age 2." Mary Margaret is missing. [LLE003]

6. 1871 Canadian Census of Ontario, Bruce County, Brant Township, CNA C-9936, Page 87, Line 14, 1871. Researched by Betty Allen. [LLE004]

7. 1881 Canadian Census of Ontario, Bruce County, Brant Township, FHL #1375911, CNA C-13275, Page 82, Lines 11-16, 1881, FamilySearch Online, www.familysearch.org, Family History Library, Salt Lake City, Utah. "Susan, widow, age 57, farmer, Church of England; Lucy, age 36, dress maker; Thomas, age 23, farmer; Charlotte, age 21; James, age 18, Labourer; Jemmima, age 12." [WWD321]

8. Bruce County Registrar, Index of Land Instruments for Bruce County, Ontario, Microfilm A-3-9, , Walkerton Branch Library, 253 Durham Street East, Walkerton, Ontario N0G 2V0. [OBC002]

9. Bruce County Registrar, Index of Land Instruments for Bruce County, Ontario, Microfilm A-3-9, , 23 Mar 1887. "Grantee: Thomas H Prior, Reserving access to river for boats."

10. Allen, Betty, Prior, James & Susan, Family Goup Record, 21747 100th Avenue, Langley, British Columbia V1M 3V1, Page 1, Abt 1980, The Collection of Dean Wheaton, 5976 Kungle Road, Clinton, OH 44216-9317. [REV001, 66]

11. *Bruce County Cemetery Gravestone Readings*, Page 2, #18 & #19. "James Prior died March 14, 1879 aged 64 years."

12. Ontario Death Registrations, OVR #001-428-79.

13. Land Instruments of Arthur Township, Wellington District, Canada West, 25 Nov 1847, Wellington County Land Registry Office, 1 Stone Road West, Guelph, Ontario N1G 4Y2. Researched by Dorothy Steckenreiter via Betty Allen. [LLE004]

14. Land Instruments of Arthur Township, Wellington District, Canada West, 08 Mar 1856. "Price: 25 Pounds." Researched by Dorothy Steckenreiter via Betty Allen.

15. Allen, Betty, Allen, Thomas & Elizabeth, Family Group Record, 21747 100th Avenue, Langley, British Columbia V1M 3V1, Page 1, 1975, The Collection of Dean Wheaton, 5976 Kungle Road, Clinton, OH 44216-9317. Wife: Prior, Elizabeth Anne. Information from death certificate. [REV001, 67]

16. Allen, Betty, Mrs., GEDCOM: Prior.ged, James & Susan (Bacon) Prior Descendants, 21747 100th Avenue, Langley, British Columbia V1M 3V1, 604-888-7870 (21 Apr 1997), The Collection of Dean Wheaton, 5976 Kungle Road, Clinton, OH 44216-9317, LLE001. Has PoB as Arthur Twp.

17. Allen, Betty, Allen, Thomas & Elizabeth, Family Group Record, Page 1, 1975. Information from death certificate.

18. Allen, Betty, Allen, Thomas & Elizabeth, Family Group Record, Page 1, 1875.

19. Allen, Betty, Allen, Thomas & Elizabeth, Family Group Record, Page 1, 1975. "Robert C. Moffatt, Canada Presbyterian Church, Walkerton, Witness: Henry Brown, Walkerton." Information Source: Bruce County, Ontario Marriage Registers.

20. Allen, Betty, Mrs., GEDCOM: Prior.ged, James & Susan (Bacon) Prior Descendants. Information Source: Bruce County Marriage Register (1850-1869), pg. 88, Rev. Robert C. Moffatt, Canada Presbyterian.

21. Allen, Betty, Allen, Thomas & Elizabeth, Family Group Record, Page 1, 1975. Information from the Trout Creek Cemetery.

22. R. Allen, Betty, Allen, Thomas & Elizabeth, Family Goup Record, Page 1, 1975. Information Source: 1861 Census, Mono Twp., Simcoe Co., Canada West, PAC #1073.

23. Allen, Betty, Mrs., GEDCOM: Prior.ged, James & Susan (Bacon) Prior Descendants. Information Source: Trout Creek Cemetery headstone, South Himsworth Twp, Parry Sound County, Ontario.

24. Allen, Betty, GEDCOM: Susan Bacon Family (unpublished), 02 Feb 2005, The Collection of Dean Wheaton, 5976 Kungle Road, Clinton, OH 44216-9317, LLE004.

25. *Bruce County Cemetery Gravestone Readings*, Page 2, #9 & #18. "#9: Sacred to the Memory of Miss Lucy Prior died Dec 7, 1884 aged 40 years; #18: Lucy their daughter died Dec 7, 1884 aged 40 yrs 5 mos." Birth date computed from age (40y 5m) and death date.

26. Allen, Betty, Prior, James & Susan, Family Group Record, Page 1, Line 3, Abt 1980. Information Source: Surrogate Court, Bruce County, 1976.

27. Allen, Betty, Prior, James & Susan, Family Group Record, Page 1, Line 3, Abt 1980. Information Source: Harry Prior, Jan & Jun 1976.

28. Allen, Betty, Prior, James & Susan, Family Group Record, Page 1, Line 3, Abt 1980. Information Source: Ida Hovie, March 1976.

29. Allen, Betty, Mrs., GEDCOM: Prior.ged, James & Susan (Bacon) Prior Descendants.

30. Allen, Betty, Prior, James & Susan, Family Group Record, Page 1, Line 13, Abt 1980. Information Source: 1851 Census age is 4 yrs.

31. Allen, Betty, Prior, James & Susan, Family Group Record, Page 1, Line 13, Abt 1980.

32. Allen, Betty, Prior, James & Susan, Family Group Record, Page 1, Line 13, Abt 1980. Information Source: Ida Harvie, March 1976.

33. Allen, Betty, Prior, James & Susan, Family Group Record, Page 1, Line 13, Abt 1980. Information Source: Surrogate Court, Bruce County, March 1976.

34. Allen, Betty, Prior, James & Susan, Family Group Record, Page 1, Line 11, Abt 1980. Information Source: 1861 Census age is 2 yrs.

35. Allen, Betty, Prior, James & Susan, Family Group Record, Page 1, Line 11, Abt 1980.

36. Allen, Betty, Prior, James & Susan, Family Group Record, Page 1, Line 11, Abt 1908. Information Source: Surrogate Court, Bruce County, March 1976.

37. Harth, Frankie B., GEDCOM: Prior.ged, James & Susan Bacon Prior Descendants, harth@monarch.net, PO Box 51, Redcliff, Alberta, Canada T0J 2P0 , 403-548-7825, (514 Main Street SE), 27 Sep 1996, Person ID: #7, 1996. [HFB001]

38. Allen, Betty, Prior, James & Susan, Family Group Record, Page 1, Line 12, Abt 1980.

39. *Bruce County Cemetery Gravestone Readings*, Page 2, #18 & #19. "James A. died Mar 24, 1866 aged 12 yrs 3 mos." Birth computed from DoD (24 Mar 1866) and age (12y 3m).

40. Adams, Bonny L. (Goodhue), *Descendants of Elijah Prior*, gadams@junctionnet.com, 1 Mar 1999, Page 2, The Collection of Dean Wheaton, 5976 Kungle Road, Clinton, OH 44216-9317, GBL001. [GBL001]

41. Allen, Betty, Prior, James & Susan, Family Group Record, Page 1, Line 10, Abt 1980. Information Source: 1861 Census age is 5 yrs.

42. Allen, Betty, Prior, James & Susan, Family Group Record, Page 1, Line 5, Abt 1980. Information Source: Surrogate Court, Bruce County, March 1976.

43. Allen, Betty, Prior, James & Susan, Family Group Record, Page 1, Line 5, Abt 1980. Information Source: Harry Prior, Jan & Jun 1976.

44. Allen, Betty, Prior, James & Susan, Family Group Record, Page 1, Line 5, Abt 1980.

45. Allen, Betty, Prior, James & Susan, Family Group Record, Page 1, Line 14, Abt 1980. Information Source: 1861 Census age is infant.

46. Allen, Betty, Prior, James & Susan, Family Group Record, Page 2, Line 14, Abt 1980.

47. Allen, Betty, Prior, James & Susan, Family Group Record, Page 1, Line 14, Abt 1980. Information Sources: Surrogate Court, Bruce County, March 1976 and Ida Harvie, March 1976.

48. Allen, Betty, Mrs., GEDCOM: Prior.ged, James & Susan (Bacon) Prior Descendants. Name Edward was listed in obit of Charlotte in the Paisley Advocate, March 1913.

49. *Bruce County Cemetery Gravestone Readings*, Page 2, #18 & #19. "#18: Phoebe died Dec 25, 1861 aged 5 dys, #19: Feeby died Dec 25, 1866 aged 5 dys." DoB computed from DoD and age. Inscription #19 is from an original white stone, Inscription #18 is from a new (red) stone. The two transcriptions are each rendered correctly, see photographs 630-04 & 630-15 of the stones taken 15 Oct 2002 by Dean Wheaton. There is no compelling evidence for a DoB in either 1861 or 1866. There are other children born in both of these years.

50. Allen, Betty, Prior, James & Susan, Family Group Record, Page 1, Line 7, Abt 1980. Information Source: Harry Prior, Jan & Jun 1976.

51. Allen, Betty, Prior, James & Susan, Family Group Record, Page 1, Line 7, Abt 1980.

52. Harth, Frankie B., GEDCOM: Prior.ged, James & Susan Bacon Prior Descendants, Page 2.

53. *Bruce County Cemetery Gravestone Readings*, Page12, #18 & #19. "George A. died Apr 12, 1866 aged 3 mos." DoB computed from DoD and age.

54. Allen, Betty, Prior, James & Susan, Family Goup Record, Page 1, Line 9, Abt 1980. Information Source: Harry Prior, Jan & Jun 1976.

55. Allen, Betty, Prior, James & Susan, Family Goup Record, Page 1, Line 9, Abt 1980.

56. Harth, Frankie B., GEDCOM: Prior.ged, James & Susan Bacon Prior Descendants, Page

1, 19666. PoD.

Modified Register for Joseph Bacon, Sr

Second Generation - James

4. **James Bacon Sr** was born[1] 04 Mar 1825 in Debden, Essexshire, England and was baptized[1] 12 Jun 1825 in Debden, Essexshire, England. He died[2] 07 Oct 1906 in Bottineau, Bottineau County, North Dakota and was buried[2] in Bottineau, Bottineau County, North Dakota.

James was enumerated in a census[3] 1851 in Brant Township, Bruce County, Canada West. He received a Crown Patent[4] Con 1 SDR, Lot 17 (50 acres) 01 Oct 1857 in Brant Township, Bruce County, Canada West. He sold[5] Con 1 SDR, Lot 17 (50 acres) to Joseph Bacon, Jr. 28 Dec 1858 in Brant Township, Bruce County, Canada West.

James married[6] **Mary Norris** on 01 Feb 1847 in Wellington District, Canada West. Mary was born[7] 1827/1828 in Devonshire, England. She died[7] 03 Apr 1894 in Bottineau, Bottineau County, North Dakota and was buried[7] in Bottineau, Bottineau County, North Dakota.

They had the following children:

28 F   i.   **Mary Maud Bacon** was born[7] 1848 in Canada West. She died[7] 1856.

29 M   ii.   **James Bacon Jr.** was born[7] 15 Mar 1850 in Bruce County, Canada West. He died[7] Apr 1924 in Bottineau, Bottineau County, North Dakota.

James married[7] **Mary Ellen Smith** on 02 Dec 1885 in Crookston, Polk County, Minnesota. Mary was born[7] 08 Oct 1861 in Springvale, Wisconsin. She died[7] 04 Nov 1941 in Bottineau, Bottineau County, North Dakota.

James and Mary Ellen had nine children, all born in North Dakota, five boys and four girls. The first eight between 1886 and 1902.

30 M iii. **Joseph Henry Bacon** was born[7] 1853 in Canada West.

Joseph married[7] (1) **Unknown**.

Joseph and Wife #1 had two children, a boy born in 1877 and a girl born in 1888.

Joseph also married[7] (2) **Mary Ellen Kennedy**.

Joseph and Wife #2 (Mary Ellen) had nine children, six boys and three girls born between 1887 and 1903.

31 M iv. **Richard Bacon** was born[7] 1856 in Canada West.

Richard married[7] **Matilda**. Matilda was born[7] Sep 1858.

Richard and Matilda had six children, four boys and two girls. All were born in Minnesota between 1879 and 1898.

32 M v. **Benjamin Bacon** was born[7] Feb 1858 in Canada West.

Benjamin married[7] **Sarah** on 1882. Sarah was born Sep[7] 1859 in Canada West.

33 F vi. **Bethia Bacon** was born[8] 07 Apr 1859 in Bruce County, Canada West. She died[8] 21 Jun 1929 in Minneapolis, Minnesota and was buried[8] in Royalton, Minnesota.

Bethia married[8,9] **William Boyle**, son of James Boyle and Mary Porter, on 06 Nov 1876 in Elm Dale, Morrison County, Minnesota. William was born[9] 03 Oct 1840 in County Antrim, Ireland. He died[9,10] 21 Mar 1907 in Elm Dale, Morrison County, Minnesota and was buried[10] in Royalton, Minnesota.

Bethia made application for a widow's pension No. 866830 on the service of her husband William Boyle in Morrison County,

Minnesota on 11 Apr 1907. His pension certificate was No. 549214. On this date she claimed ownership of N 1/2 of the NE 1/4 of Sec 17 T127N R30W valued at $2,000 and the following property by will of her husband: SW 1/4 of the NE 1/4 of Sec 17 T127N R30W valued at $2,000; Lots 9-10-11-12-13 & N 1/2 of 14 in Block 4 Greens 1st addition to Royalton valued at $500; one house, no value; six cows worth $60, 3 young cattle, $24; one wagon worth $15; one sleigh worth $5; a seeder worth $40 for a total worth of $2844. Amount of mortgage $300; amount of debt due $150. Income from crops of 1906: wheat, 80 bu. worth $48.30 and oats, 81 bu. worth $27.30. Deceased husband had no life insurance [Pension file of Wm Boyle obtained by Larry Phillips].

William enlisted 10 Sep 1860 in Company C, 3rd Regiment, U.S. Infantry commanded by Henry W. Freedly and was discharged at Washington, DC on 14 Sep 1865. He was struck by a spent six pound canon shot in the groin at the Battle of Bull Run on 21 Jul 1861. He was judged 2/3 disabled and received a pension of $30/month.
William was 5' 9 1/2" tall, had a fair complexion, and grey eyes. He was a laborer at the time of his enlistment.

Bethia and William had fifteen children born between 1878 and 1899, five boys and ten girls.

Researched by Larry W Phillips, Winnipeg, Manitoba PLW001. Used by permission.

34 M vii. **George Bacon** was born[10] Feb 1866 in Canada West. He died[10] in Colfax, Washington.

George and Annie had six children, four boys and two girls born from 1892 to 1906.
In 1901 the family moved to Washington state.

George married[10] **Annie Edenore Mead** on 1890 in Crookston, Polk County, Minnesota. Annie was born[10] Mar 1868. She died[10] 1947 in Washington.

Annie is a half sister to Mary Ellen Smith (wife of James Bacon, Jr.).

35 M viii. **David Bacon** was born[11] 28 Jun 1869 in Canada West. He died[11] 14 Nov 1927.

David married[11] **Maria Bacon**, daughter of Elijah Bacon "Lige" and Maria McNeil, on 16 Jun 1900. The marriage ended in divorce. Maria was born[12] 05 Jul 1882 in Portage La Prairie, Manitoba. She died[13] 16 Apr 1967 in Jamestown, North Dakota and was buried[13] in Albert-Lea, Minnesota.

Maria and (1) David Bacon had three children born 1902-1907, two boys and one girl.
Maria and (2) David Clohessy had five children.

36 F ix. **Emily Louise Bacon** was born[13] 1870 in Canada West.

Emily married **Boyle**.

Source References - James

1. Wilcock, Ruth, Report of Bacon Family Research in England, Debden Parish Registers, Essex, England, Unpublished, Nov 1982, Commissioned by Betty Allen, Langley, B.C., Line 30, The Collection of Dean Wheaton, 5976 Kungle Road, Clinton, OH 44216-9317. [BFR002]

2. Goughnour, Constance (Morse), Bacon, James, Sr., Family Information Letter, Dated 9 Aug 1994, Page 5, The Collection of Dean Wheaton, 5976 Kungle Road, Clinton, OH 44216-9317. Lineage Chart. [MCC001]

3. 1851 Canada West Census of Bruce County, Brant Township, Reel #C-11715, Researched by Betty Allen, Langley, BC, Lines 26-29, 1851, Library & Archives of Canada, 395 Wellington Street, Ottawa, Ontario, Canada K1A 0N4. "James, Farmer, Age 28; Mary, Age 26; Mary, Age 4; James, Age 2." [LLE003]

4. Bruce County Registrar, Index of Land Instruments for Bruce County, Ontario, Microfilm A-3-9, Page 17, Walkerton Branch Library, 253 Durham Street East, Walkerton, Ontario N0G 2V0. [OBC002]

5. Bruce County Registrar, Index of Land Instruments for Bruce County, Ontario, Microfilm A-3-9, Page 17, Instr. #171, 03 Jan 1859.

6. Walker, Dan & Stratford-Devai, Fawne, Marriage Registers of Upper Canada/Canada West, Vol. 9: Part 1, Wellington District, 1840-1852, Wellington County Museum & Archives, RR #1, Fergus, Ontario N1M 2W3. "Both of Arthur." Marriages by Rev. John Simpson, New Connexion Methodist Minister #74. [MRW001]

7. Goughnour, Constance (Morse), Bacon, James, Sr., Family Information Letter, Pages 5-6.

8. Phillips, Larry W., GEDCOM: Phillips.ged, Descendants of Bethia Bacon, 1997 (Unpublished), The Collection of Dean Wheaton, 5976 Kungle Road, Clinton, OH 44216-9317. [PLW001]

9. U.S. Pension Agency, Civil War Pension File of William Boyle, Unpublished, Page H, U.S. National Archives and Records Administration, Washington, DC. Copy of Minnesota marriage registration. [PLW002]

10. U.S. Pension Agency, Civil War Pension File of William Boyle, Page D.

11. Goughnour, Constance (Morse), Bacon, James, Sr., Family Information Letter, #6.

12. Vital Statistics, Manitoba Finance Division of Consumer & Corporate Affairs Database, Reg, #1882-001166, Manitoba Finance, http://web2.gov.mb.ca/cca/vital/query.php. [GPM001]

13. Lilley, Lois, Compilation of Bacon Family Information , PO Box 175, Onanole. Manitoba R0J 1N0, Post marked 9 Aug 1994, Page 15, The Collection of Dean Wheaton, 5976 Kungle Road, Clinton, OH 44216-9317, LL_001. "Age 37 years." Maria died of complications at the birth of her daughter who was named Maria.

Modified Register for Joseph Bacon, Sr.

Second Generation - Charlotte

5. **Charlotte Bacon** was born[1] 31 Jul 1827 in Debden, Essexshire, England and was baptized[1] 06 Jan 1828 in Debden, Essexshire, England. She died[2] 31 Jan 1905 in Hill Hall, Saskatchewan and was buried[2] in Woodley-Cromar Cemetery, Hill-Hall, Saskatchewan.

Charlotte moved[3] about 1879 to Baconsville, Nelson County, North Dakota. She was enumerated in a census[4] 18 Jun 1900 in North Dakota, Bottineau County, Bottineau Township.

Charlotte married[5] (1) George Smith on 1845 in Hamilton, Canada West. George was born[5] 13 Mar 1814 in Ireland. He died[5,6] 02 Jul 1873 in Brant Township, Bruce County, Ontario and was buried[6] 02 Jul 1873 in Old Bethel Methodist/Prior Cemetery, Brant Township, Bruce County, Ontario.

They had the following children:

38 F   i.   **Mary Jane Smith** was born[7] 18 Feb 1846.

39 M   ii.   **William Smith** was born[8] 07 Oct 1848 in Arthur, Arthur Twp, Wellington County, Canada West.

William married[8] **Martha Mary Smith**, daughter of Bleakney Smith and Susanna Hilts, on 04 Feb 1871 in Culross Twp, Bruce County, Ontario. Martha was born[8] 23 Feb 1851 in Egremont Twp, Grey County, Canada West.

William & Martha had five boys and two girls born between 1872 and 1881 (GEDCOM 2226636.ged).

40 M   iii. **Samuel Smith** was born[9] 13 Dec 1859 in Canada East. He died[9] 20 Sep 1930 in Staraton, Ontario.

Samuel married[9] **Martha Jane Chesney**, daughter of Henry Chesney and E. Boden, on 28 Sep 1881 in St. Cloud, Steans

County, Minnesota. Martha was born[9] 13 Feb 1855 in Canada West. She died[10] 11 Mar 1902 in Pillager, Cass County, Minnesota.

Samuel & Martha had Five children, three boys and one girl, born between 1882 and 1892 (GEDCOM: 2226636.ged).

41 F iv.   **Susan Smith** was born[11] 27 Aug 1853. She died[11] in 1905.

Susan married[11] **Robert Chesney**. Robert was born[11] in 1846.

Robert and Susan had five children, three boys and two girls, before 1874 (GEDCOM: 2226636.ged).

42 F v.   **Sarah Smith** was born[12] 21 Sep 1855. She died[12] in 1906.

43 F vi.   **Emma Smith** was born[13] 20 Oct 1857. She died[13] in1915 in Oil Springs, Ontario.

Emma married[13] _____ **Hern**[14]

The Herns had three children, all girls (GEDCOM: 2226636. ged).

44 M vii.   **Gideon Smith** was born[15] 25 Sep 1859. He died[15] in 1927.

Gidion was a blacksmith and later a salesman for Shad, Bolton, and Boyal of Minneapolis. He visited his cousin Joe Bacon [3] in Petoskey several times (Kalbfleisch, "The Bacon Family," page 4).

9 F viii.   **Elizabeth Smith** was born[16] 23 Sep 1861. She died 18 Feb 1933 in Saskatoo, Saskatchewan.

Elizabeth married[16] **Arthur William Gordon** on 1878 in Ontario. Arthur was born[16] 02 Mar 1845. He died[16] in 1924.

Arthur and Elizabeth had nine children, five boys and four girls, between the years 1880 and 1901 (GEDCOM: 2226636. qed).

10 F ix. **Margaret Smith** was born[17] 02 Mar 1863. She died[17] in 1929.

Margaret married **Lankin**[17]

The Lankins had one child, a girl (GEDCOM:2226636.ged)

11 F x. **Maria Smith** was born[18] 23 May 1865 in Riversdale, Bruce County, Canada West. She died[18] 06 Feb 1894 in Cass County, Minnesota.

Maria had an illegitimate child by Leas. The child was named George Robert Cromar born 19 Jan 1880 in Riversdale, Bruce County (GEDCOM 2226636.ged)

Maria was not married[18] (1) to_____ **Leas**[18] in 1879.

Maria also married[18] (2) **David Henry Ridgley**, son of Jonathon Ridgley and Philena French, on 04 Jul 1881 in Little Falls, Morrison County, Minnesota. David was born[18] 05 May 1839 in Indiana. He died[18] 14 Dec 1907 in Hellensburg, Minnesota.

David and Maria had seven children, two boys and five girls, born 1882 to 1892, all in Minnesota (GEDCOM: 2226636. ged).
David was enumerated by the 1850 U.S. Census of Indiana, Pulaski County, Van Buren.

12 M xi. **Joseph Smith** was born[18] 10 Apr 1867. He died[18] 20 Apr 1870 in Brant Twp, Bruce County, Ontario and was buried[18] in Old Bethel Methodist/Prior Cemetery, Brant Twp, Bruce County, Ontario.

13 F xii. **Charlotte Smith** was born[19] 11 May 1869. She died[19] 04 Nov 1918 in Hill Hall, Saskatchewan and was buried[19] Nov 1918 in Woodley-Cormar Cemetery, Hill-Hall, Saskatchewan.

Charlotte married[19] **Thomas McPherson**. Thomas was born[19] in May 1869.

Thomas and Charlotte had five children, three boys and two girls between the years 1891 and Abt 1900 (GEDCOM 266636.ged).

14   xiii.   **Un-named Infant Smith** was buried[19] in Old Bethel Methodist/ Prior Cemetery, Brant Township, Bruce County, Ontario.

Charlotte also married[20] (2) **James Cromar** on 24 Oct 1878. James was born[20] about 1836 in Greenock, England. He died[20,21] 23 Dec 1907 in Hill Hall, Saskatchewan.

James was enumerated in a census[22] 1885 in Dakota Territory, Nelson County. He purchased land[22] Section 35, T154N R57W (5th PM) (160 acres) 29 Sep 1888 in Dahlen Township, Nelson County, Dakota Territory. He was naturalized[22] 27 Oct 1892 in Bottineau County, North Dakota. He filed a Declaration Intent to obtain U.S. Citizenship before 1894 in Polk County, Minnesota. He purchased land[23] W 1/2 NW 1/4 Sec 27 T163N R75W (5th PM) (80 acres) & NE 1/4 NE 1/4 Sec 28 T163N R75W (40 acres) & NW 1/4 of NE 1/4 Sec 28, T163N R75W (40 acres) 07 Dec 1897 in Bottineau County, North Dakota. He was enumerated in a census[24] 18 Jun 1900 in North Dakota, Bottineau County, Bottineau Township.

They had the following children:

15 M   xiv.   **George Cromar** was born[24] Jan 1880 in Canada.

Source References - Charlotte

1. Wilcock, Ruth, Report of Bacon Family Research in England, Debden Parish Registers, Essex, England, Unpublished, Nov 1982, Commissioned by Betty Allen, Langley, B.C., Line 30, The Collection of Dean Wheaton, 5976 Kungle Road, Clinton, OH 44216-9317. [BFR002]

2. Kephart, Billy Jo, GEDCOM: 222663.ged, George & Charlotte Bacon Smith Descendants, 23 Dec 2002, kephart@paulbunyan.net (Ancestry World Family Tree), FGR for Charlotte Bacon, 23 Dec 2002, Ancestry.com World Family Tree, www.ancestry.com. [KBJ001]

3. Kalbfleisch, Raymond W., The Bacon Family, Genealogist, Petoskey, Michigan, Self published, 8 pages, Page 4, The Collection of Dean Wheaton, 5976 Kungle Road, Clinton, OH 44216-9317, KRW001. Copied from Raymond's original by Dean Wheaton on 1 Aug 1994 at Petoskey, Michigan. [KRW001]

4. 1900 U.S. Census of North Dakota, Bottineau County, Bottineau Township, NA: T623, Roll 1226, Page 49, Lines 1-3, 18 Jun 1900, HeritageQuest Online, http://persi. heritagequestonline.com/hqoweb/library/do/census/. James & Charlotte are listed as having been married 24 years with a twenty year old son named George. Charlotte is also listed as having 0 (zero) children. [WWD316]

5. Kephart, Billy Jo, GEDCOM: 222663.ged, George & Charlotte Bacon Smith Descendants, 23 Dec 2002, Page 1, #1.

6. *Bruce County Cemetery Gravestone Readings,* Old Bethel Methodist/Prior Cemetery, Page 2, #3, Bruce County Museum & Archives, 33 Victoria Street North, Southampton, Ontario N0H 2L0. "George Smith died July 2, 1873 aged 59 years 3 mos & 22 days." This entry also mentions an Infant of Geo. & Charlotte Smith. Computed DoB = 11 Mar 1814. [OBC009]

7. Kephart, Billy Jo, GEDCOM: 222663.ged, George & Charlotte Bacon Smith Descendants, 23 Dec 2002, Page 1, #2.

8. Kephart, Billy Jo, GEDCOM: 222663.ged, George & Charlotte Bacon Smith Descendants, 23 Dec 2002, Page 2, #2.

9. Kephart, Billy Jo, GEDCOM: 222663.ged, George & Charlotte Bacon Smith Descendants, 23 Dec 2002, Page 3, #3.

10. Kephart, Billy Jo, GEDCOM: 222663.ged, George & Charlotte Bacon Smith Descendants, 23 Dec 2002, Page3, #3.

11. Kephart, Billy Jo, GEDCOM: 222663.ged, George & Charlotte Bacon Smith Descendants, 23 Dec 2002, Page 3, #4.

12. Kephart, Billy Jo, GEDCOM: 222663.ged, George & Charlotte Bacon Smith Descendants, 23 Dec 2002, Page 2.

13. Kephart, Billy Jo, GEDCOM: 222663.ged, George & Charlotte Bacon Smith Descendants, 23 Dec 2002, Page 3, #5.

14. Kephart, Billy Jo, GEDCOM: 222663.ged, George & Charlotte Bacon Smith Descendants, 23 Dec 2002.

15. Kephart, Billy Jo, GEDCOM: 222663.ged, George & Charlotte Bacon Smith Descendants, 23 Dec 2002, Page 2.

16. Kephart, Billy Jo, GEDCOM: 222663.ged, George & Charlotte Bacon Smith Descendants, 23 Dec 2002, Page 3, #6.

17. Kephart, Billy Jo, GEDCOM: 222663.ged, George & Charlotte Bacon Smith Descendants, 23 Dec 2002, Page 4, #7.

18. Kephart, Billy Jo, GEDCOM: 222663.ged, George & Charlotte Bacon Smith Descendants, 23 Dec 2002, Page 4, #8.

19. Kephart, Billy Jo, GEDCOM: 222663.ged, George & Charlotte Bacon Smith Descendants, 23 Dec 2002, Page 4, #9.

20. Kephart, Billy Jo, GEDCOM: 222663.ged, George & Charlotte Bacon Smith Descendants, 23 Dec 2002, GEDCOM.

21. Price, Wini, Family Data for James & Charlotte Bacon Cromar via Email, 14 Jan 2005, The Collection of Dean Wheaton, 5976 Kungle Road, Clinton, OH 44216-9317. James & Charlotte moved to the U.S. in the summer of 1880; James filled for U.S. Citizenship in Polk County, Minnesota and received his final papers in Bottineau County, North Dakota on 27 Oct 1894; they were enumerated by the 1885 Census of the Dakota Territory in Nelson County; They returned to Canada (Hill Hall, Saskatchewan) in 1902 where she died in 1905 and he in 1907. [PW_001]

22. North Dakota Land Records, Bureau of Land Management, General Land Records Office, Online Database, Cromar, James, 29 Sep 1888, Bureau of Land Management, http://www.glorecords.blm.gov/. [WWD318]

23. North Dakota Land Records, Bureau of Land Management, General Land Records Office, Online Database, James Cromar, 07 Dec 1897. Three adjoining parcels total 159.8 acres.

24. 1900 U.S. Census of North Dakota, Bottineau County, Bottineau Township, Page 49, Line 3, 18 Jun 1900. Charlotte is listed as having 0 (zero) children, James & Charlotte are listed as having been married 24 years and George as being age 20 years.

Modified Register for Joseph Bacon, Sr

Second Generation - John

7. **John Bacon** was born[1] 31 Dec 1831 in Debden, Essexshire, England and was baptized[1] 26 Aug 1832 in Debden, Essexshire, England. He died[2] 16 Feb 1914 in SE 36-12-25 w1, Near Crandall, Manitoba and was buried[3] in Kinsmore Cemetery, RM of Woodworth, Manitoba.

John received a Crown Patent[4] for Con 1 SDR, Lot 16 (50 acres) 17 May 1854 in Brant Township, Bruce County, Canada West. He gave a mortgage[5] on Con 1 SDR, Lot 16 (50 acres) for $1200 to the Trust & Loan Co. of Upper Canada 03 Jun 1859 in Brant Township, Bruce County, Canada West. He gave a mortgage[6] on Con 1 SDR, Lot 16 (50 acres) to the Huron & Erie Savings & Loan Society for $400 15 Jun 1864 in Brant Township, Bruce County, Canada West. He and his wife received a discharge of mortgage[7] on Con 1 SDR, Lot 16 (50 acres) from the Trust & Loan Co. of Upper Canada 27 Sep 1864 in Brant Township, Bruce County, Canada West. He gave a mortgage[8] on Con 1 SDR, Lot 16 to John Hunter for $600 on 05 Jun 1868 in Brant Township, Bruce County, Ontario. He gave a mortgage[9] on Con 1 SDR, Lot 16 (50 acres) to Edward Kilmer & John Hanks for $1375 on 01 Jul 1870 in Brant Township, Bruce County, Ontario. He and his wife received a discharge of mortgage[10] Con 1 SDR, Lot 16 (50 acres) from Huron & Erie Savings & Loan Society on 21 Jul 1870 in Brant Township, Bruce County, Ontario. He and his wife received a discharge of mortgage[11] on Con 1 SDR, Lot 16 (50 acres) from John Hunter on 29 Jul 1870 in Brant Township, Bruce County, Ontario. He was enumerated in a census[12] 1871 in Brant Township, Bruce County, Ontario. He sold[13] a small portion of Con 1 SDR, Lot 16 (1.08 acres) to the Wellington, Grey & Bruce Railroad for $100 on 20 Jul 1871 in Brant Township, Bruce County, Ontario. He gave a mortgage[14] on Con 1 SDR, Lot 16 (48.92 acres) to George Harvey for $1850 on 20 Feb 1876 in Brant Township, Bruce County, Ontario. He and his wife received a discharge of mortgage[15] on Con 1 SDR, Lot 16 (50 acres) from E. Kilmer & J. Hanks on 11 Mar 1876 in Brant Township, Bruce County, Ontario. He and his wife received a discharge of mortgage[16] Con 1 SDR, Lot 16 (50 acres) from George Harvey 01 Aug 1878 in Brant Township, Bruce County, Ontario. He gave a mortgage[17] on Con 1 SDR, Lot 17 (48.92 acres) to Robert Romanes for $1550 on 01 Aug 1878 in Brant Township, Bruce

County, Ontario. He gave a mortgage[18] on Con 1 SDR, Lot 16 (48.92 acres) to George Harvey for $52 on 01 Aug 1878 in Brant Township, Bruce County, Ontario. He sold[19] Con 1 SDR, Lot 16 (48.92 acres) to Duncan Kerr, Jr. On 03 Nov 1881 in Brant Township, Bruce County, Ontario. He and his wife received a discharge of mortgage[20] Con 1 SDR, Lot 16 (48.92 acres) from Mary & George Harvey 10 Nov 1881 in Brant Township, Bruce County, Ontario.

John married[20] **Elizabeth Hunter**, daughter of William Hunter and Agnes Hart, in 1856/1857. Elizabeth was born 1837 in Canada East. She died[20] 25 Mar 1919 in NW 28-12-24 W1, RM of Woodworth, Manitoba and was buried[21] in Kinsmore Cemetery, RM of Woodworth, Manitoba.

They had the following children:

51 F   i.   **Agnes Jane Bacon** was born[22] 1858. She died in 1937.

Agnes married[22] **David Bown**, son of Andrew Bown and Jane Haddow, on 26 Nov 1879 in Walkerton, Bruce County, Ontario. David was born[23] Apr 1858 in Galt, Canada West. He died[23] 04 Aug 1931 in Virden, Manitoba.

David and Agnes had five children, four boys and one girl (Taylor, "John and Elizabeth (Hunter) Bacon").

David grew up in the Galt, Ontario area. After he and Agnes married, they traveled to River Falls, Wisconsin near his mother and family.

In 1886 they set out for new territory - Arrow River, Manitoba. David eventually bought 640 acres of land and built a beautiful stone house similar to the many stone houses built much earlier in North Dumfries, Ontario. He continued his stone masonry. In 1906 he sold the farm to son Gerald. It was acquired by grandson Cecil and raised beautiful horses, showing them at local fairs until he retired to live in Kenton in 1974. The farm is still owned by his descendants.

Taylor, Elaine V., Bacon Family Information, 146 pages, Attachment to a Letter dated 18 May 1994, The Collection of Dean Wheaton, Clinton, OH, REV001.

52 F   ii.   **Alice Alivena Bacon** was born[24] 1860. She died[24] 1949 and was buried[24] in Kinsmore Cemetery, RM of Woodworth, Manitoba.

Alice married[25,26] **George Cox**[26] on 08 Oct 1879 in Brant Twp, Bruce County, Ontario. George was buried[26] in Kinsmore Cemetery, RM of Woodworth, Manitoba.
George and Alice had one child, a boy (Taylor, "John and Elizabeth (Hunter) Bacon").
George came from Cargill, Ontario in the fall of 1881 and filed his claim on NW 28-12-24 W1, RM of Woodsworth, Manitoba. Since he had no house, he returned to Ontario for the winter. Early in the spring he returned and married Alice in Portage La Prairie and brought her to the homestead. They later retired to Lenore, Manitoba. Both are buried in the Kinsmore Cemetery.
Taylor, Elaine V., Bacon Family Information, 146 pages, Attachment to a Letter dated 18 May 1994, The Collection of Dean Wheaton, Clinton, OH, REV001.

53 M   iii.   **Robert Hunter Bacon** was born[27,28] 1862 in Brant Twp, Bruce County, Canada West. He died[28] 04 Apr 1944 and was buried[28] in Scotia Cemetery, RM of Hamiota, Manitoba.

Robert and Mary had no children (Taylor, "John and Elizabeth (Hunter) Bacon").
Robert filed for his homestead on the same day as his father: Location = SW 12-36-25 W1, Name = Robert Hunter bacon, Grant and No. = H 20358, Entry Date = 13 Jun 1882, Patent Date = 31 Oct 1892.

Robert and Mary retired to Crandall, Manitoba. Both are buried in the Scotia Cemetery, SW 10-13-24 W1.

Robert married[29] **Mary Elizabeth McIntyre**, daughter of James McIntyre and Jeanette Hunter, on 02 Dec 1902 in Virden, Manitoba. Mary was born[29] in 1862. She died[29] 19 Aug 1941 and was buried[29] in Scotia Cemetery, RM of Hamiota, Manitoba.

54 F iv. **Sussanna Franklin Bacon** was born[30] 1864 in Brant Twp, Bruce County, Canada West. She died[30] in 1945 and was buried[30] in Ranger, Saskatchewan.

Sussanna married[30] **Robert David Flewelling** "Bob", son of James Morrice Flewelling and Jane Elmslie, on 04 Nov 1885 in Virden Manitoba. Bob was born[30] 16 Oct 1864 in Guelph, Canada West. He died[30] in 1942 and was buried[30] in Ranger, Saskatchewan.

Bob and Sussanna had eight children, three boys and five girls (Taylor, "John and Elizabeth (Hunter) Bacon").

Robert (Bob) and Sussanna farmed on SE 28-12-24 W1 while they were in the RM at Virden, Manitoba. In 1891 they moved to Carberry, Manitoba and in 1902 to the area of Saskatchewan know as Asquith. They later farmed near Ranger, Saskatchewan. Each of their children had large families.

Taylor, Elaine V., Bacon Family Information, 146 pages, Attachment to a Letter dated 18 May 1994, The Collection of Dean Wheaton, Clinton, OH, REV001.

55 F v. **Minnie Elizabeth Bacon** was born[31,32] 14 Sep 1867 in Bruce County, Ontario. She died[32] 02 Jan 1921 in NE 26-12-25 W1, RM of Woodworth, Manitoba and was buried[32] in Kinsmore Cemetery, RM of Woodworth, Manitoba.

Minnie married[32,33] **William Routledge**
"Bill", son of George Walton Routledge
and Ann Elizabeth Vaux, on 12 Dec 1888
in Wallace, Manitoba. Bill was born[33,] 14
Jun 1865 in Bruce County, Canada West.
He died[33,] 11 Oct 1936 and was buried[33] in
Kinsmore Cemetery, RM of Woodworth,
Manitoba.

William and Minnie had four children, three boys and one girl
(Taylor, *Our Routledge Heritage 1687-1992*).

William Routledge, better known as Bill, was born on June 6,
1865 in Bruce County, Ontario, most likely in the log house
on Con 7 Lot 2 of Brant Township where his parents lived
about five miles northwest of Walkerton. As a young man he
headed west to Canada's prairie provinces. He homesteaded
on a farm just north of Ravine School, north of Lenore,
Manitoba. He filed or obtained entry for his homestead: NE
26-12-25wl, No. 41 on October 12, 1886.

To understand the challenge facing our ancestors who had
pioneered in Canada and the United States, it is important
to understand the conditions and requirements that they had
to meet to obtain their homestead. William's homestead was
in the Dominion of Manitoba and these were the laws of
the land at that time. The land was divided into townships
consisted of 36 sections. Each section was divided into four
160 acres parcels or quarters. Certain quarters of land were set
aside for school development and railways. There were "free"
homesteads in each township, open for newcomers to claim
only if they met certain conditions.

To file for entry onto a homestead, the quarter had to be
vacant. The land William homesteaded had been occupied
by James Douglas but he had been absent since March 1885.
Mr. Douglas' date of entry had been May 4, 1883. He had
performed twelve months residence but had moved back to
Bruce County, Ontario. He had ten acres in crop in 1884,
twenty acres rented in crop in 1885 and the record indicates a
"Win. Rutledge" had four acres in barley(1). William then had
to complete an application stating that he had not previously

filed for a homestead. Entry bound him to certain conditions to be fulfilled before he could be granted his patent (deed or title).

William had to provide documentation to prove: when he obtained entry for this homestead; when he had built his house there; when he perfected his entry to the homestead by taking in his own personal possessions onto the land; when he began continuous residence and cultivation of the land; and, what portion of each year since first residence had he lived on the land. The Dominion government also needed to know: how much breaking had been done on his homestead in each year since William obtained entry; how many acres had he cultivated each year; how many horned cattle, horses, sheep and pigs he had each year; and, the size of his family and house.

Any additions to the house, new or expanded farm buildings and amount of land fenced were closely watched by the tax man for assessment of improvements. William was also required to report any indication of minerals or quarries on his land (there were none). If the meek were to inherit the earth, they weren't going get the mineral rights without a struggle. Further, if absent, William had to prove where he was, how far away, what he was doing and why(2). If, as in William's case, there had been improvements already made to the homestead, the new homesteader had to pay for them along with the $10 registration fee. These improvements included any land broken for crop and housing. The decision of the Lands Branch in Ottawa was final. Ottawa didn't make it easy for these early homesteaders.

William's claim was 120 acres of open prairie fit for cultivation, 20 acres of stubble land, hay land worth $2.75 per acre and a 12 by 16 frame house with a shingle roof. William paid $100 for the value of improvements to the land(3). According to his application for a Free Patent for Homestead, William lived on SE 2-13-25w1 with his sister Mary and Thomas Douglas from March 1887 to December 1887. He then lived on 36-12-25w1 from December 1887 to May 1888 and subsequently moved onto the homestead, NE 26-12-25wl, County of

Dennis, Province of Manitoba, in May 1888. He certified he had never been more than two miles away from the homestead at any time during the previous years.

In 1886, William had 30 acres broken(4) and added to the cleared land by breaking between three and 15 acres each year. By 1892, he was cropping 95 acres, had broken a further 15 acres and had six acres fallow. In 1887, he had two horses and by 1892, he had four horses and nine cattle. The main house was built before his entry in 1886. William doubled its original size by adding a 12 by 16 addition in 1888 for a cost of $100. By 1893, he had also built two stables: the first, 18 by 24 feet for $50; the second measured 20 by 20 feet and cost $25. A "granary" the same size as the second stable cost William fifty dollars. He had also fenced 20 acres in 1893 for a cost of $50

Ottawa took none of this on faith. In order for a homesteader to finally get title to the land he had slaved over, he had to file a fiat for an inspection of the land. A federal inspector checked to see if the previously mentioned improvements had been done and the rest of the conditions had been met. Once all the conditions were met, the settler received the patent to the land from the Dominion. "The patent was the first title to land issued by the government for some portion of the public domain(5)." William applied for a patent on January 14, 1893 and his application was approved by Ottawa five years later on March 27, 1898. His patent date was April 8, 1893, and his grant number was H.367426.

William married Minnie Bacon, fifth child of John and Elizabeth (Hunter) Bacon who was also from the Walkerton, Ontario area, on December 12, 1888. William and Minnie had five children: Henry (Harry), John (Jack), Robert (Bob) and Elizabeth (Annie) and a girl who died at birth. Minnie (Bacon) Routledge died on January 2, 1921 and William remarried Miss Mary Martin, formerly of Lucknow, Ontario, on June 26, 1922. It is this wife that the grandchildren remember as Grandma Routledge, although this woman was also an aunt to the mother of Harry's children.

Discussions of creating a school district began in 1897 because of an influx of more families. The Routledge children had to walk at least four and a half miles to the Palmerston school. On July 23, 1898, the first meeting was held at Penrith post office (28-12-25w1) which was also the home of Mr. and Mrs. John McKinnon. William Routledge was elected school chairman and trustee along with John Dryden and David Brown. Duncan McKinnon was voted in as a secretary-treasurer.

After much dispute over the location of a school, they chose a site at NE 1/4 of 23-12-25w1. It was near a crossing of a ravine running through the district and was named Ravine School. It opened with Miss Etta (Sadie) Scarth from Virden as the teacher on May 31, 1900. The opening of the new school was particularly good news for Annie and Harry who had previously had to walk to Palmerston(7). Later, all four children would attend Ravine School which was only a mile south of the farm. In the early years, school holidays were in January and February before being switched to the now conventional summer holidays(8). The Ravine School played an integral part in the lives of the Routledges and their neighbors because it was the centre of community activities. In later years, quite a few of William's and Minnie's grandchildren and even great-grandchildren would also attend Ravine before it closed in 1964.

William bought and sold cattle besides working the land. Harry farmed 25-12-24w1 and later moved down the road from the Ravine School to 24-12-25w1. In later years, Robert took over the home farm where he stayed until the fall of 1942 when he moved to the Hamiota, Manitoba area. Jack farmed across the road on 25-12-25w1 until 1941, then moved to the Scotia/Oakner District, Hamiota Municipality.

William died in October 1936 and was buried along side his first wife, Minnie, in the Kinsmore Cemetery, RM of Woodworth. Mary (Martin) Routledge died in September 1961, and was buried in the Virden Cemetery.

NOTES:

1) Letter of Agreement between Mr. James Douglas and William Routledge, dated August 26, 1886.

2) William Routledge's Application for Free Patent for Homestead, Ne of Section 26 Thp 12 Rge 25 of 1st Meridian Homestead No 41, January 14, 1893, County of Dennis, Province of Manitoba.

3) Letter of Agreement between Mr. James Douglas and William Routledge, dated August 26, 1886

4) Unlike Ontario where trees had to be cleared, the prairie of Manitoba had no trees but was covered by a thick, tough sod of tangled roots of prairie grasses which had to be broken up before crops could be planted in the rich soil.

5) Loveridge, D.M., "An Introduction to the Study of Land and Settlement Records," in Gerald Friesen, Bany Potyondli, Ed., "Guide to the Study of Manitoba Local History," (Winnipeg: University of Manitoba, 1981), page 123. This is the resource for the other definitions about land grants, refer to pages 119 and 120.

6) William Routledge's Application for Free Patent for Homestead.

7) Mrs. Dorothy Vipond, "Proudly We Speak: The History of Woodworth Municipality: 1878-1967," Woodworth Centennial Committee, Kenton, Manitoba, (Altona: D.W. Friesen & Sons Ltd., 1967), Pages 162 and 164.

8) Ibid, Vipond, Page 168.

Routledge, James W ., Researcher, Taylor, Elaine V. Routledge, Author, Taylor, Paul W., Ed., "Our Routledge Heritage: 1687-1992, George Walton and Ann (Vaux) Routledge Family," Pages 71-73, Copyright 1992, Routledge Family Research, The Collection of Dean Wheaton, Clinton, OH. Used by permission.

56 F   vi.   Mary Ellen Bacon "Nellie"[34] was born[34] in 1862. She died[34] in 1941 and was buried[34,] in the Kinsmore Cemetery, RM of Woodworth, Manitoba.

Nellie married[35] Robert Bacon "Bendie Bob"[35] son of Elijah Bacon "Lige" and Maria McNeil, on 21 Jan 1892 in Sifton, Manitoba. Bendie Bob was born[35] 1863. He died[35,36] 13 Jun 1925 in RM Of Miniota, Manitoba and was buried[36] in the Kinsmore Cemetery, RM of Woodworth, Manitoba.

Robert and Nellie had five children, four boy and one girl, born between 1892 and 1910 (Taylor, "Our Routledge Heritage, 1687-1992").

Robert was known as Bendie Bob because he was Bob from the bend area near Strathclair, Manitoba which was where his father had homesteaded.

Bob and Nellie lived on different farms in the Kinsmore, Ravine, and Palmerston areas of the RM of Woodsworth. They kept a lot of cattle over the years.

Bob, Nellie, and all of their children are buried in the Kinsmore Cemetery located near the farm the Boys last farmed.

None of their children married.

Taylor, Elaine V., Bacon Family Information, 146 pages, Attachment to a Letter dated 18 May 1994, The Collection of Dean Wheaton, Clinton, OH, REV001. Used by permission.

Source References - John

1. Wilcock, Ruth, Report of Bacon Family Research in England, Debden Parish Registers, Essex, England, Unpublished, Nov 1982, Commissioned by Betty Allen, Langley, B.C., Line 30, The Collection of Dean Wheaton, 5976 Kungle Road, Clinton, OH 44216-9317. [BFR002]

2. Taylor, Elaine V. (Routledge), *Bacon, John & Elizabeth (Hunter)*, Routledge Family Research, PO Box 28, Hamiota, Manitoba, Canada R0M 0T0, Page 1, The Collection of Dean Wheaton, 5976 Kungle Road, Clinton, OH 44216-9317. [REV001, 76]

3. Taylor, Elaine V. (Routledge), *Bacon, John & Elizabeth (Hunter)*, Page 1. John was originally buried in the Scotia Cemetery (RM of Hamiota, SW 10-13-24 w1) but he was reinterred in the Kinsmore Cemetery when it opened. The Kinsmore Cemetery is located five miles north and four miles west of Kenton on the NE 1/4-29-12-24 w1.

4. Bruce County Registrar, Index of Land Instruments for Bruce County, Ontario, Microfilm A-3-9, Page 16, Walkerton Branch Library, 253 Durham Street East, Walkerton, Ontario N0G 2V0. [OBC002]

5. Bruce County Registrar, Land Records of Bruce County, Ontario, Microfilm Series A, Instr. #205, 24 Jun 1859, Bruce County Registry Office, 203 Cayley Street, Walkerton, Ontario N0G 2V0. This mortgage was a combined one with his father Joseph, Sr. and brothers Isaac, Henry, Joseph, Jr. and Elijah for a total collateral of 300 acres. [OBC001]

6. Bruce County Registrar, Land Records of Bruce County, Ontario, Instr. #526, 28 Jul 1864.

7. Bruce County Registrar, Land Records of Bruce County, Ontario, Instr. # 255, 08 Oct 1864. Discharges Instr. #205 for $1200.

8. Bruce County Registrar, Land Records of Bruce County, Ontario, Instr. # 1042, 08 Jun 1868.

9. Bruce County Registrar, Land Records of Bruce County, Ontario, Instr. #1848, 29 Jul 1870.

10. Bruce County Registrar, Land Records of Bruce County, Ontario, Instr. #1846, 29 Jul 1870. Discharges Instr. #526 for $400.

11. Bruce County Registrar, Land Records of Bruce County, Ontario, Instr. #1847, 29 Jul 1870. Discharges Instr. #1042 for $600.

12. 1871 Census of Canada - Ontario: Searchable Database of Heads & Strays, http://db.library.queensu.ca/dbtw-wpd/exec/dbtwpub.dll, Dist . 27, Subdist H, Div 1, Pg 9, 1871,

Queen's University Libraries, 99 University Avenue, Kingston, Ontario K7L 3N6. "John, head, age 39, Wesleyan Methodist, farmer." [QUL001]

13. Bruce County Registrar, Land Records of Bruce County, Ontario, Instr. #2156, 13 Mar 1876. Right of way for the railroad.

14. Bruce County Registrar, Land Records of Bruce County, Ontario, Instr. #3647, 13 Mar 1876.

15. Bruce County Registrar, Land Records of Bruce County, Ontario, Instr. #3646, 13 Mar 1876. Discharges Instr. #1848 for $1375.

16. Bruce County Registrar, Land Records of Bruce County, Ontario, Instr. #4524, 01 Aug 1878. Discharges Instr. #3647 for $1850.

17. Bruce County Registrar, Land Records of Bruce County, Ontario, Instr. #4525, 01 Aug 1878.

18. Bruce County Registrar, Land Records of Bruce County, Ontario, Instr. #4526, 01 Aug 1878. Instr. #4927 assigned this mortgage from George Harvey to George Bridges on 1 Apr 1879, Instr. #4928 assigned this mortgage from George Bridges to Mary Harvey on 1 Apr 1879.

19. Bruce County Registrar, Land Records of Bruce County, Ontario, Instr. #6022, 19 Nov 1881. With the purchase of the land, Duncan Kerr assumed John Bacon's mortgage to Robert Romanes for $1550 (Instr. #4525) on 1 Aug 1878. Instr. #7279 discharges the mortgage of Instr. #4525 to Isabella Romanes by Duncan Kerr on 5 Dec 1885.

20. Bruce County Registrar, Land Records of Bruce County, Ontario, Instr. #6021, 19 Nov 1881. Discharges Instr. #4526 for $521.

21. Taylor, Elaine V. (Routledge), *Bacon, John & Elizabeth (Hunter)*, Page 1. The Kinsmore Cemetery is located five miles north and four miles west of Kenton on the NE 1/4-29-12-24 w1.

22. Taylor, Elaine V. (Routledge), *Bacon, John & Elizabeth (Hunter)*, Page 2.

23. Taylor, Elaine V. (Routledge), *Bacon, John & Elizabeth (Hunter)*, Page 2.

24. Taylor, Elaine V. (Routledge), *Bacon, John & Elizabeth (Hunter)*, Page 3.

25. Ontario Vital Records, Bruce County Marriages, Reg # 001365, Archives of Ontario, 77 Grenville Street, Unit 300, Toronto, Ontario, Canada, M5S 1B3, MS 932 Reel 29, Microfilm #102, 223-3. "Groom: George Cox, age 21, resident of Brant Twp, laborer, Parents: William & Betsy Cox; Bride: Alice Alwenna Bacon, age 19, resident of Brant Twp, Parents: John & Eliazabeth Bacon, Witnesses: Robt H Bacon & Mary J Cox, Methodist." Copy of registration from Betty Allen, 2001. [LLE002, 3]

26. Ontario District Marriages, Bruce County, Ontario, No page or Reg. #'s shown , Archives of Ontario, 77 Grenville Street, Unit 300, Toronto, Ontario, Canada, M5S 1B3, RG 8, Series 1-6-B, MS 248 Reel 5. "Groom: George Cox, age 21, resident of Brant, born Eramossa, Parents: William & Betsy Cox; Bride: Alice Alwenna Bacon, age 19, resident of Brant, born in Brant, Parents: John & Elizabeth Bacon; Witnesses: Robt H Bacon, Mary J Cox; date of marriage 8 Oct 1979 by license." [LLE002, 4]

27. Taylor, Elaine V. (Routledge), *Bacon, John & Elizabeth (Hunter)*, Pages 3-4.

28. Wheaton, Dean, Gravestone Photographs at Kinsmore Cemetery at Hamiota, Manitoba, 6 Jul 1996, Frame 11, The Collection of Dean Wheaton, 5976 Kungle Road, Clinton, OH 44216-9317, Roll 519. "Bacon: 1862 Robt. H. 1944; 1862 Mary E. 1941; At Rest." [519-11]

29. Vital Statistics, Manitoba Finance Division of Consumer & Corporate Affairs Database, Reg #1904-002138, Manitoba Finance, http://web2.gov.mb.ca/cca/vital/query.php.

30. Taylor, Elaine V. (Routledge), *Bacon, John & Elizabeth (Hunter)*, Pages 4-5.

31. Taylor, Elaine V. (Routledge), *Bacon, John & Elizabeth (Hunter)*, Pages 7-8.

32. Taylor, Elaine V. (Routledge), *Our Routledge Heritage 1687-1992: George Walton and Ann (Vaux) Routledge*, Routledge Family Research, PO Box 28, Hamiota, Manitoba R0M 0T0, 1992, Pages 71-73, The Collection of Dean Wheaton, 5976 Kungle Road, Clinton, OH 44216-9317.

33. Vital Statistics, Manitoba Finance Division of Consumer & Corporate Affairs Database, Reg. #1889-001091.

34. Taylor, Elaine V. (Routledge), *Bacon, John & Elizabeth (Hunter)*, Page 8.

35. Vital Statistics, Manitoba Finance Division of Consumer & Corporate Affairs Database, Reg. #1892-001079.

36. Vital Statistics, Manitoba Finance Division of Consumer & Corporate Affairs Database, Reg. #1925-027134. "Age 62 years."

Modified Register for Joseph Bacon, Sr.

Second Generation - Isaac

8. **Isaac Elisha Bacon** was born[1] 24 Sep 1833 in Debden, Essexshire, England and was baptized[1] 22 Oct 1833 in Debden, Essexshire, England. He died[2] 24 Jan 1895 in New Westminster, British Columbia and was buried[2,3] in British Columbia.

Isaac was enumerated in a census[4] in 1851 in Brant Township, Bruce County South, Canada West. He received a Crown Patent[5] Con 1 SDR, Lot 20 (50 acres) 17 May 1854 in Brant Township, Bruce Cunty, Canada West. He gave a mortgage[6] Con 1 SDR, Lot 20 (50 acres) to Trust & Loan Co. of Upper Canada for $1200 on 03 Jun 1859 in Brant Township, Bruce County, Canada West. He was enumerated in a census[7] in 1861 in Brant Township, Bruce County, Canada West. He and his wife received a discharge of mortgage[8] Con 1 SDR, Lot 20 (50 Acres) From Trust & Loan Co. of Upper Canada 27 Sep 1864 in Brant Township, Bruce County, Canada West. He sold[9] Con 1 SDR, Lot 20 (50 acres) to Andrew Thompson for $1000 on 25 Feb 1865 in Brant Township, Bruce County, Canada West. He was enumerated in a census[10] in 1871 in Brant Township, Bruce County, Canada West. He was enumerated in a census[11] in1881 in Little Sasketchewan, Manitoba.

Isaac is the twin of Elijah.

Certificates: Death registration photocopy

Census-Records: 1851, 1861, 1871, 1881

Films:
C11715: Census 1851, Bruce county, Brant Township, p9, line 8
C1010: Census 1861, Bruce County, Brant Township, District #1, p6, line 47
349,154: Census 1871, Brant Tp., page 9, read at S. L. C.
C13284: Census 1881, Little Saskatchewan, Western Extension, Manitoba, Dist. 186 E5 p38, #263
B13088: B C Death registration, Reg'n # 1895-09-78675, SPL July 2000.

Extant:
1851: Census (20 yrs., BP England)
1861: Census (28 yrs.; Married; living in 1 story Log House.)

1881: Census (48 yrs.; English origin)
1895: Died at Essondale Asylam, New Westminster, B. C.
Residence:
Crown Patent - Lot 20 Con 1 S. D. R. 50 acres, May 17, 1854, Brant Tp.,
Bruce Co., Ont.
Farmed NE 31-16-21 near Strathclair, Manitoba.
1883: "Moved to the Springbend area, just north of Enderby [BC] in 1883."
1899 Grant for Tp. 19, Range 9, West of the 6th Meridan, British Columbia.
SW 1/4 14.

Occupation:
1851, 1861, 1881: Farmer

Religious-Affiliation:
1851: Episcopalian;   1861: Census - P[rimitive] M[ethodist]; 1881 -
Methodist

Burial-Location:
Most likely in cemetery at Essondale, Coquitlam, BC [not confirmed yet]
Researched and documented by Betty Allen, Langley, British Columbia,
GEDCOM: Isaac Bacon.ged.paf, 19 Feb 2005 via email to Dean Wheaton,
Clinton, OH, LLE005. Used by permission.

Isaac married **Mary Margaret Watson** about 1854.
Mary was born[11] about 1836 in England. She was
buried[12,13] in Lansdowne Cemetery, Enderby, British
Columbia.

Census-Records:1861, 1871

Films:
C1010: Census 1861, Bruce County, Brant Township, District #1, p6, line
47
349,154: Census 1871, Brant Tp., page 9, read at S. L. C.
C13284: Census 1881, Little Saskatchewan, Western Extension, Manitoba,
Dist. 186 E5 p38, #263

Extant:
1861: Census (24 yrs.; BP England; Married; living in 1 story Log House.)
1881: Census (45 yrs., Origin English)

Residence:
Crown Patent - Lot 20 Con 1 S. D. R., May 17, 1854, Brant Tp., Bruce Co.,
Ont.
Farmed NE 31-16-21 near Strathclair, Manitoba.
1899: Tp. 19, Range 9, West of the 6th Meridian, British Columbia. SW 1/4
14.

Religious-Affiliation:
1861: Census - P[rimitive] M[ethodist]

Information:
Name from Land Records, Brant Tp., Bruce Co., Ont. & Earl Bacon (1982).
Researched and documented by Betty Allen, Langley, British Columbia,
GEDCOM: Isaac Bacon.ged.paf, 19 Feb 2005 via email to Dean Wheaton,
Clinton, OH, LLE005. Used by permission.

57 M i. **John William Bacon** was born[13,14] 1855 in Canada West.

John and Mary had two children, one boy and one girl born
about 1877 and 1879.

Census-Records:1861, 1871, 1881
Films:
C1010: Census 1861, Bruce County, Brant Township, District #1, p6, line
47
349,154: Census 1871, Brant Tp., page 9, read at S. L. C.
C13282: Census 1881, Winnipeg, Selkirk, Manitoba, Dist 183, C5, pg 24,
Family #79.

Extant:
1861: Census (6 yrs.; BP U[pper] Canada; living in 1 story Log House.)
1881: Census (age 28 yrs., Origin English, BP England)

Residence:
Crown Patent - Lot 20 Con 1 S. D. R., May 17, 1854, Brant Tp., Bruce
Co., Ont.
Farmed NE 31-16-21 near Strathclair, Manitoba.
1899 Grant for Tp. 19, Range 9, West of the 6th Meridan, British Columbia.
SW 1/4 14.

Occupation:
Farmer
Religious-Affiliation:
1861: Census - P[rimitive] M[ethodist]

Information:
Full name from marriage registration of sister Husley, [1889] read August
2000, Surrey Public Library.
1881 census BP states England, sb Ontario, if this is correct John. BA
Researched and documented by Betty Allen, Langley, British Columbia,
GEDCOM: Isaac Bacon.ged.paf, 19 Feb 2005 via email to Dean Wheaton,
Clinton, OH, LLE005. Used by permission.

John married **Mary ?**[14] Mary was born[14] about 1855 in England.

Information:
Name from 1881 Census, Winnipeg, Selkirk, Manitoba.
Researched and documented by Betty Allen, Langley, British Columbia, GEDCOM: Isaac Bacon.ged.paf, 19 Feb 2005 via email to Dean Wheaton, Clinton, OH, LLE005. Used by permission.

58 F ii. **Elizabeth Bacon** was born[14,15,16] 1856 in Canada West.

Census-Records:1861, 1871

Films:
C1010: Census 1861, Bruce County, Brant Township, District #1, p6, line 47
349,154: Census 1871, Brant Tp., page 9, read at S. L. C.
MS 248 Reel 5 R G 8 Series 1 - 6 - B - Ontario Marriage Registers; Brant Mission, Primitive Methodist Church, Bruce County, Ontario, p 2.

Extant:
1861: Census (5 yrs.; BP U[pper] Canada; living in 1 story Log House.)

Residence:
Crown Patent - Lot 20 Con 1 S. D. R., May 17, 1854, Brant Tp., Bruce Co., Ont.
Farmed NE 31-16-21 near Strathclair, Manitoba.
1899 Grant for Tp. 19, Range 9, West of the 6th Meridian, British Columbia. SW 1/4 14.

Religious-Affiliation:
1861: Census - P[rimitive] M[ethodist]
Researched and documented by Betty Allen, Langley, British Columbia, GEDCOM: Isaac Bacon.ged.paf, 19 Feb 2005 via email to Dean Wheaton, Clinton, OH, LLE005. Used by permission.

Elizabeth married[16] **Stephen Gooding**, son of James Gooding and Emma ?, on 25 Oct 1876 in Brant Township, Bruce County, Canada West. Stephen was born about 1859 in Canada West.

MR: Date of Marriage 25 Sep 187? His birth about 1850

Information:Name, age - Ontario Marriage Register, MS 248 Reel 5 R G 8 Series 1 - 6 - B; Brant Mission, Primitive Methodist Church, Bruce County, Ontario - p 2.
Researched and documented by Betty Allen, Langley, British Columbia, GEDCOM: Isaac Bacon.ged.paf, 19 Feb 2005 via email to Dean Wheaton, Clinton, OH, LLE005. Used by permission.

59 F   iii.   **Ruth Rebecca Bacon** was born[16,17] in 1858 in Canada.

> Certificates: Marriage
> Census-Records: 1861, 1871
> Films:
> C1010: Census 1861, Bruce County, Brant Township, District #1, p6, line 47
> 349,154: Census 1871, Brant Tp., page 9, read at S. L. C.
> MS 248 Reel 5 - R G 8 Series 1 - 6 - B - Ontario Marriage Register; Brant Mission, Primitive Methodist Church, Bruce County, Ontario.
> Extant:
> 1861: Census (3 yrs.; BP U[pper] Canada; living in 1 story Log House.)
> Residence:
> Crown Patent - Lot 20 Con 1 S. D. R., May 17, 1854, Brant Tp., Bruce Co., Ont.
> Farmed NE 31-16-21 near Strathclair, Manitoba.
> 1899 Grant for Tp. 19, Range 9, West of the 6th Meridian, British Columbia. SW 1/4 14.
> Religious-Affiliation:
> 1861: Census - P[rimitive] M[ethodist]
> Information:
> Full name - Ontario Marriage Register, Brant Mission, Primitive Methodist Church, Bruce County, Ontario - p 2, MS 248 Reel 5 R G 8 Series 1 - 6 - B.
> Researched and documented by Betty Allen, Langley, British Columbia, GEDCOM: Isaac Bacon.ged.paf, 19 Feb 2005 via email to Dean Wheaton, Clinton, OH, LLE005. Used by permission.

Ruth married[17] **William Fleet**, son of George Fleet and Mary, on 25 Sep 1876 in Walkerton, Bruce County, Ontario. William was born[17] about 1855 in Canada.

> Information:
> Name, age, BP - Ontario Marriage Register, MS 248 Reel 5 R G 8 Series 1 - 6 - B; Brant Mission, Primitive Methodist Church, Bruce County, Ontario, p 2.
> Note: There is a "William FLEAT age 25, in 1881 Census, Listowell, Perth North, Ontario, Dist 172, Subdist H, Div 1, p51, Family #257, Mfm. #C13272 - wife Rebeca age 23 and children Charlott 4 yrs, Mary 2 yrs, and Iva 1 yr., also a Mary Bacon age 19 yrs." Could this be our family and name misspelled?
> Researched and documented by Betty Allen, Langley, British Columbia, GEDCOM: Isaac Bacon.ged.paf, 19 Feb 2005 via email to Dean Wheaton, Clinton, OH, LLE005. Used by permission.

60 M   iv.   **Isaac Elisha Bacon** was born[17] 26 Jan 1860 in Brant Township, Bruce County, Canada West. He died[17,18] 10 Dec 1864 in Brant Township, Bruce County, Canada West and was buried[18,] in Old Bethel Methodist/Prior Cemetery, Brant Township, Bruce County, Canada West.

61 F   v.   **Susanna Bacon** was born[19] 11 Nov 1863 in Brant Township, Bruce County, Canada West. She died[19] 25 Nov 1863 in Brant Township, Bruce County, Canada West and was buried[19] in Old Bethel Methodist/Prior Cemetery, Brant Twp, Bruce County, Canada West.

> Extant:
> 1863: Death - 14 days old. - headstone in Old Bethel Cemetery.
> Residence:
> Lot 20 Con 1 S. D. R. 50 acres, May 17, 1854, Brant Tp., Bruce Co., Ont.
> Burial-Location:
> Old Bethel (Prior Family) Cemetery, Con. 1, N. D. R., Lot 12, Brant Township, Bruce County, Ontario.
> "Susanna dau of Isaac & Margaret Bacon died 25th Nov 1863 aged 14 days"
>
> Information:
> Name, & BD, DD - Prior Family Cemetery, transcribed by Dorothy Steckenreiter & publication of Bruce & Grey Branch, OGS.
> Researched and documented by Betty Allen, Langley, British Columbia, GEDCOM: Isaac Bacon.ged.paf, 19 Feb 2005 via email to Dean Wheaton, Clinton, OH, LLE005. Used by permission.

62 F   vi.   **Husley Hannah Bacon** was born[19] 11 Nov 1863 in Brant Township, Bruce County, Canada West. She died[19] 17 Mar 1945 in Armstrong, British Columbia from terminal pneumonia, auricular fibrillation, chronic myocarditis and was buried[19] 20 Mar 1945 in Armstrong-Spallumcheen Cemetery, Armstrong, British Columbia.

> Husley has the same date of birth as Susanna. Therefore they must be twins which means Husley was also born in Brant Township.
> Husley and Moses had three girls born 1889 to 1897. Husley and ___ Denny has one child, a boy.
>
> Certificates: [2nd] Marriage registration to Moses Levar photocopy

Films:
C13284: Census 1881, Little Saskatchewan, Western Extension, Manitoba, Dist. 186 E5 p38, #263
B11387: B C Marriages, reg'n # 1889-09-167634, SPL 2000.
B13186: B. C. Death Registration No. 1945-09-658777; Surrey Public Library, July, 2000.

Extant:
1881: Census (age 18 yrs., BP Ontario, Origin English; name listed as "Hulda K")
1889: B. C. Marriage Registration - "age 25, residence Lansdowne, BP Walkerton, Ontario, Widow, religion Methodist.

Religious-Affiliation:
1889: Methodist
Burial-Location:
Armstrong-Spallumcheen Cemetery, Armstrong, B. C., from B. C. G. S. card file.
Cause of death - "Terminal Pneumonia; Auricular Fibrillation; Chronic Myocarditis."

Information:
Name from Enderby & District Museum, letter to James Routledge, Feb. 1989.
Married twice - 1st to Mr. Denny, unable to read microfilm, entry too faint.

Researched and documented by Betty Allen, Langley, British Columbia, GEDCOM: Isaac Bacon.ged.paf, 19 Feb 2005 via email to Dean Wheaton, Clinton, OH, LLE005. Used by permission.

Husley married[19] (1) **Moses Robinson Levar**[19] son of Benjamin Levar and Margaret Reid, on 06 May 1889 in Lansdowne, British Columbia. Moses was born[19] 20 Jun 1849 in Leverville, New Brunswick, Canada West. He died[19] 20 May 1920 in Armstrong, British Columbia and was buried[19] 23 May 1920 in Armstrong, British Columbia.

Films:
B13117: B. C. Death registration No. 1920-09-264870, B. C. Archives, read Dec. 2000.

Extant:
1889: B. C. Marriage Registration - "age 39, residence Lansdowne, BP St. Stephens, N. B., Bachelor, Rancher, religion Baptist." read August 2000, Surrey Public Library.

Residence:
1889: Lansdowne area in Vernon district, B. C.

Religious-Affiliation:
1889: Baptist

Burial-Location:
Armstrong-Spallumcheen Cemetery, Armstrong, B. C., from B. C. G. S. card file.

Information:
Name from Enderby & District Museum, letter to James Routledge, Feb. 1989.
Place of Birth - B.C. Death Certificate for daughter Olive Izetta Levar.
Birthyear - " Forty-fifth Report Okanagan Historical Society", page 168.
Researched and documented by Betty Allen, Langley, British Columbia, GEDCOM: Isaac Bacon.ged.paf, 19 Feb 2005 via email to Dean Wheaton, Clinton, OH, LLE005. Used by permission.

Husley also married (2) **Denny**[19]

Information:
Married - unable to read microfilm, entry too faint.
Surname from article "Forty Fifth Report Okanagan Historical Society", page 168.
Researched and documented by Betty Allen, Langley, British Columbia, GEDCOM: Isaac Bacon.ged.paf, 19 Feb 2005 via email to Dean Wheaton, Clinton, OH, LLE005. Used by permission.

63 F   vii. **Margaret Bacon** was born[14] about 1866 in Canada West.

Census: 1881

Films:
C13284: Census 1881, Little Saskatchewan, Western Extension, Manitoba, Dist. 186 E5 p38, #263

Extant:
1881: Census (15 yrs., BP Ontario, English origin)
Researched and documented by Betty Allen, Langley, British Columbia, GEDCOM: Isaac Bacon.ged.paf, 19 Feb 2005 via email to Dean Wheaton, Clinton, OH, LLE005. Used by permission.

64 M viii. **Isaac Elisha Bacon** was born[14] 17 Jul 1874 in Brant Township, Bruce County, Ontario.

Isaac served in the military[19] 17th Troop AD SAC S.A. to fight in the Boer War in South Africa. He pursued the occupation[205] of policeman 25 Jul 1908 - 12 Aug 1915 in Pretoria, South Africa.

Isaac and Wilhelmina had four children. Isaac and Jacoba had three children.

Isaac went to Africa with the 17 Troop AD SAC S.A. to fight in the Boer War. After the war he joined the police in Pretoria, South Africa on 25 Jul 1908.

He left the police in 1925 with a very good and efficient records (a copy is on pages 29-30 of Lois's letter). According the record, Isaac was 5 ft 6 1/5 in, Brown hair, Brown eyes, fair complexion, a Methodist, born 17 Jul 1874 in Ontario, Canada, and divorced on 6 Jan 1917.

Certificates: B C Land Grant

Census-Records: 1881

Films:
C13284: Census 1881, Little Saskatchewan, Western Extension, Manitoba, Dist. 186 E5 p38, #263

Extant:
1881: Census (7 yrs., BP Ontario, English origin)

Residence:
1899 Grant for Tp. 19, Range 9, West of the 6th Meridian, British Columbia. SW 1/4 14.

Information:
Name from Enderby & District Museum to James Routledge, Feb. 1989. Isaac fought in the Boer War and married there afterwards, & raised a family.
Marius Bacon, grandson, S. Africa, June 2000 researching this family.
Researched and documented by Betty Allen, Langley, British Columbia, GEDCOM: Isaac Bacon.ged.paf, 19 Feb 2005 via email to Dean Wheaton, Clinton, OH, LLE005. Used by permission.

Isaac married[21] (1) **Wilhelmina Francina Pretorius** on 1904. The marriage ended in divorce. Wilhelmina died[21] 1874.

Isaac also married[21] (2) **Jacoba Dorothea Johanna** on 1921. Jacoba died[21] 1948.

65 F   ix.   **Caroline Bacon**[21] was born[21] about 1876 in Ontario.

       Census: 1881

       Films:
       C13284: Census 1881, Little Saskatchewan, Western Extension, Manitoba, Dist. 186 E5 p38, #263

       Extant:
       1881: Census (5 yrs., BP Ontario, English origin)

       Information:
       Name from Enderby & District Museum to James Routledge, Feb. 1989. Researched and documented by Betty Allen, Langley, British Columbia, GEDCOM: Isaac Bacon.ged.paf, 19 Feb 2005 via email to Dean Wheaton, Clinton, OH, LLE005. Used by permission.

Source References - Isaac

1. Wilcock, Ruth, Report of Bacon Family Research in England, Debden Parish Registers, Essex, England, Unpublished, Nov 1982, Commissioned by Betty Allen, Langley, B.C., Line 30, The Collection of Dean Wheaton, 5976 Kungle Road, Clinton, OH 44216-9317. [BFR002]

2. Allen, Betty, Isaac Bacon Three Generation Descendancy PAF Database, Unpublished, The Collection of Dean Wheaton, 5976 Kungle Road, Clinton, OH 44216-9317. [LLE005]

3. Death Registration of British Columbia for Isaac Bacon, Reg. # 1895-09-78675, SPL Jul 2000. Researched by Betty Allen. [LLE005]

4. 1851 Canada West Census of Bruce County, Brant Township, Reel #C-11715, Researched by Betty Allen, Langley, BC, Lines 7-8, 1851, Library & Archives of Canada, 395 Wellington Street, Ottawa, Ontario, Canada K1A 0N4. "Elijah, Age 23 Farmer, Episcopalian; Isaac, Age 20, Farmer." [LLE003]

5. Bruce County Registrar, Index of Land Instruments for Bruce County, Ontario, Microfilm A-3-9, Page 20, Walkerton Branch Library, 253 Durham Street East, Walkerton, Ontario N0G 2V0. [OBC002]

6. Bruce County Registrar, Index of Land Instruments for Bruce County, Ontario, Microfilm A-3-9, Page 20, Instr. #205, 24 Jun 1859. This mortgage was a combined one with his father Joseph, Sr. and brothers James, Henry, Joseph, Jr. and Elijah for a total collateral of 300 acres.

7. 1861 Canada West Census of Bruce County, Brant Township, Researched by Betty Allen, C1010, District #1, Page 6, Line 47, Library & Archives of Canada, 395 Wellington Street, Ottawa, Ontario, Canada K1A 0N4. [LLE005]

8. Bruce County Registrar, Index of Land Instruments for Bruce County, Ontario, Microfilm A-3-9, Page 20, Instr. #255, 08 Oct 1864.

9. Bruce County Registrar, Land Records of Bruce County, Ontario, Microfilm Series A, Reel A-61, Insrt. #579, 01 Mar 1865, Bruce County Registry Office, 203 Cayley Street, Walkerton, Ontario N0G 2V0. [OBC002]

10. 1871 Canadian Census of Ontario, Bruce County, Brant Township, FHL #349154, Page 9. Researched by Betty Allen at Salt Lake City. [LLE]

11. 1881 Census of Canada, Manitoba, Little Saskatchewan, Household #263, Page 38, 1881, FamilySearch Online, www.familysearch.org, Family History Library, Salt Lake City, Utah. FHL Film #1375920, NA C-13284. "Isaac, age 48; Margaret, age 45; Hulda K., age 18; Margaret, age 15; Isaac, age 7; Caroline, age 5; family is Methodist." Margaret's birth: 1881 - 45 = Abt 1836. [WWD315]

12. Lilley, Lois, Bacon, Isaac and Margaret (Lilley), Family Information, Unpublished, Page 1, The Collection of Dean Wheaton, 5976 Kungle Road, Clinton, OH 44216-9317, LLE002. No other place information than Lansdowne Cemetery is given. [LL_004, 27]

13. Allen, Betty, Isaac Bacon Three Generation Descendancy PAF Database. Has town and province only (Enderby, BC).

14. Lilley, Lois, Bacon, Isaac and Margaret (Lilley), Family Information, Page 1.

15. Ontario District Marriages, Bruce County, Ontario, No Page or Rec. #'s shown (Gooding), Archives of Ontario, 77 Grenville Street, Unit 300, Toronto, Ontario, Canada, M5S 1B3, RG 8, Series 1-6-B, MS 248 Reel 5. "Groom: Stephen Gooding, age 26, resident of Welsley, born in Ontario, Parents: James & Emma Gooding; Bride: Elizabeth Bacon, age 21 , resident of Walkerton, born in Ontario, Parents: Isaac & Margaret Bacon; Witnesses: Mary Ann Bacon & J Reinhardt; married by C Mattersley, 25 Oct 1876." Copy of the registration received from Betty Allen. [LLE002, 8]

16. Allen, Betty, Isaac Bacon Three Generation Descendancy PAF Database. Gives year and place.

17. Ontario District Marriages, Bruce County, Ontario, No Page or Rec. #'s shown (Fleet). "Groom: William Fleet, age 21, resident of Maryborough, born in Canada, Parents: George & Mary Fleet; Bride: Ruth Rebecca Bacon, age 17, resident of Walkerton, born in Canada, Parents: Isaac & Margaret Bacon; Witnesses: Elizabeth Bacon & James McL??, married by LG Scott, 25 Sep 1976." Copy of the registration from Betty Allen.

18. Lilley, Lois, Bacon, Isaac and Margaret (Lilley), Family Information, Page 1. "Died at age 4y 10m 5d."

19. Lilley, Lois, Bacon, Isaac and Margaret (Lilley), Family Information, Page 1. "Died at age 14 days."

20. Petoria, South Africa Police Department, Employment Record of Isaac Elisha Bacon, Emp #3220, The Collection of Dean Wheaton, 5976 Kungle Road, Clinton, OH 44216-9317, LL_004, 29-30. "Religion: Methodist; Hair: brown; Eyes: brown; Complexion: fair; Birth: Jul 17, 1874 Ontario, Canada; Marital Status: married crossed out then divorced 6 Jan 1917; Next of kin: crossed out then George Edward 11 Nov 1913; Stationed: Potchefstroom, Dist. #41, 20 Aug 1908; Reason for Discharge: Purchased." Copy of record from Lois Lilley Dec 2001. [LLE002, 29]

21. Lilley, Lois, Bacon, Isaac and Margaret (Lilley), Family Information, Page 1. "Marriage ended in divorce on 6 Jan 1917."

Modified Register for Joseph Bacon, Sr.

Second Generation - Elijah

9.   **Elijah Bacon** "Lige" was born[1] 24 Sep 1833 in Debden, Essexshire, England and was baptized[1] 22 Oct 1833 in Debden, Essexshire, England. He died[2] about 1907 in Pope, RM of Hamiota, Manitoba and was buried[2] in Scotia Cemetery, RM of Hamiota, Manitoba.

Lige was enumerated in a census[3] 1851 in Brant Township, Bruce County, Canada West. He received a Crown Patent[4] Con 1 SDR, Lot 19 (50 acres) 17 May 1854 in Brant Township, Bruce County, Canada West. He gave a mortgage[4] Con 1 SDR, Lot 19 (50 acres) to Trust & Loan Co. of Upper Canada for $1200 on 03 Jun 1859 in Brant Township, Bruce County, Canada West. He gave a mortgage[5] Con 1 SDR, Lot 19 (50 acres) to Huron & Erie Savings & Loan Society for $400 on 15 Jun 1864 in Brant Township, Bruce County, Canada West. He and his wife received a discharge of mortgage[6] Con 1 SDR, Lot 19 (50 acres) from Trust & Loan Co. of Upper Canada on 27 Sep 1864 in Brant Township, Bruce County, Canada West. He sold[7] Con 1 SDR, Lot 19 (50 acres) to Alex McCarter for $1325 on 01 Mar 1867 in Brant Township, Bruce County, Canada West. He was enumerated in a census[8] in 1871 in Brant Township, Bruce County, Ontario.

Elijah was the twin of Isaac.

Lige married[9] **Maria McNeil**, daughter of Jno. McNeil and Mary, on 27 Jan 1863 in Brant Twp, Bruce County, Ontario. Maria was born[9] 1844 in Carrick Twp, Bruce County, Ontario. She died[10,11] 05 Jul 1882 in Portage La Prairie, Manitoba and was buried[11] in Portage Hillside Cemetery, Portage La Prairie, Manitoba.

> Maria was buried in an unmarked gave in the northwest corner of the Hillside Cemetery. The records for that part of the cemetery were lost or destroyed many years ago (Lilley, LL_001).
> Daughter Lucy took over after her mother's death and raised the family (Lilley, LL_001).

They had the following children:

66 M   i.   **Robert Bacon** "Bendie Bob"[12] was born[12] 1863. He died[12,13]13 Jun 1925 in RM Of Miniota, Manitoba and was buried in Kinsmore Cemetery, RM of Woodworth, Manitoba.

Bendie Bob married[14] **Mary Ellen Bacon** "Nellie"[14] daughter of John Bacon and Elizabeth Hunter, on 21 Jan 1892 in Sifton, Manitoba. Nellie was born[15] 1862. She died[15] 1941 and was buried[15] in the Kinsmore Cemetery, RM of Woodworth, Manitoba.

> Robert and Nellie had five children, four boys and one girl, born between 1892 and 1910 (Taylor, *Our Routledge Heritage, 1687-1992*).

> Robert was known as Bendie Bob because he was Bob from the bend area near Strathclair, Manitoba which was where his father had homesteaded.
> Bob and Nellie lived on different farms in the Kinsmore, Ravine, and Palmerston areas of the RM of Woodsworth. They kept a lot of cattle over the years.
> Bob, Nellie, and all of their children are buried in the Kinsmore Cemetery located near the farm the Boys last farmed.
> None of their children married.

> Taylor, Elaine V., Bacon Family Information, 146 pages, Attachment to a Letter dated 18 May 1994, The Collection of Dean Wheaton, Clinton, OH, REV001. Used by permission.

67 F   ii.   **Agnes Bacon** was born[15] in1866.

> Agnes married[16] **Thomas Atkins** "Tommy".

> Tommy & Agnes went to British Columbia in early 1900s (Lilley, LL_006)

68 F iii. **Lucy Bacon** was born[17] in 1867 in Brant Township, Bruce County, Canada West. She died[17] 03 Jan 1951 in Strathclair, Manitoba.

Lucy married[17,18] (1) **Alexander Morrison** on 01 Dec 1886 in Strathclair, Manitoba. Alexander was born[18] in 1857 in Owen Sound, Canada West. He died[18] in 1896 in Strathclair, Manitoba.

Lucy and Alexander had six children, three boys and three girls, born between 1887 and 1896 in Strathclair, Manitoba (Allen, LL_004).

Lucy also married[18] (2) **Donald Morrison**, brother of Alexander, in 1899. Donald was born[18] in 1871 in Owen Sound, Ontario. He died[18] in 1964 in Strathclair, Manitoba.

Lucy and Donald also had six children, two boys and four girls, all born after 1900 in Strathclair (Allen, LL_004).

69 M iv. **James Bacon** was born[19] 29 Oct 1870. He died[19] 08 Jul 1871 in Ontario and was buried[19] in the Old Bethel Methodist/Prior Cemetery, Brant Township, Bruce County, Canada West.

70 M v. **James A Bacon** was born[20] 1871 in Ontario. He died[20] 1951 in Manitoba.

James never married (Lilley, LL_001).

71 F vi. **Eliza Jane Bacon** was born[20] 15 Sep 1872 in Brant Township, Bruce County, Ontario. She died[20] 20 May 1936 in Strathclair, Manitoba and was buried[20] in Strathclair, Manitoba.

Eliza Jane and John had ten children, five boys and five girls, born 1892-1915 all in Strathclair, Manitoba (Allen, LL_004, page 4).

Eliza married[21] **John McPhee Morrison**, brother of Alexander and Donald, on 26 Apr 1890 in Strathclair, Manitoba. John was born[21] 1882 in Owen Sound, Ontario. He died[21] 1948 in Strathclair, Manitoba and was buried[21] in Strathclair, Manitoba.

Johnny came to Strathclair, Manitoba in 1880 with brother's Alex and Peter. Their parents arrived later.
Johnny was well known for his skill in treating sick animals. When others thought it best to destroy the animals, he was often able to bring them to a full recovery. He was especially good during the sleeping sickness epidemic.
He farmed until his wife passed away. He then rented the land out and moved into Strathclair into his mother's house across from the Post Office.

72 F　vii.　**Susan Bacon** was born[22] 09 Apr 1875.
Susan immigrated[22] 25 Apr 1920 to the United States through Buffalo, New York.

Susan & Jim lived in the USA 1920-1944 (possibly later). They had five children. (Lilley, LL_006)

Susan married[23] **James Porter** on 09 Mar 1894 in Winnipeg, Manitoba.

73 M　viii.　**Joseph Bacon** was born[23] in 1880.

Joseph married[23] **Rose Viola Welch** in 1902. Rose was born[23] in 1883. She died[23] in 1928.

74 F　ix.　**Maria Bacon** was born[24] 05 Jul 1882 in Portage La Prairie, Manitoba. She died[24] 16 Apr 1967 in Jamestown, North Dakota and was buried[24] in Albert-Lea, Minnesota.

Maria married[25] (1) **David Bacon**, son of James Bacon Sr and Mary Norris, on 16 Jun 1900. The marriage ended in divorce. David was born[25] 28 Jun 1869 in Canada West. He died[25] 14 Nov 1927.

David Bacon and Maria had three children, two boys and a girl, born 1902-1904 (Goughnour, page 6).
Maria also married[26] (2) **David Clohessy**[26]

David Clohessy and Maria had five children.

Source References - Elijah

1. Wilcock, Ruth, Report of Bacon Family Research in England, Debden Parish Registers, Essex, England, Unpublished, Nov 1982, Commissioned by Betty Allen, Langley, B.C., Line 30, The Collection of Dean Wheaton, 5976 Kungle Road, Clinton, OH 44216-9317. [BFR002]

2. Lilley, Lois, Compilation of Bacon Family Information , PO Box 175, Onanole. Manitoba R0J 1N0, Post marked 9 Aug 1994, Page 3, 1991, The Collection of Dean Wheaton, 5976 Kungle Road, Clinton, OH 44216-9317, LL_001.

3. 1851 Canada West Census of Bruce County, Brant Township, Reel #C-11715, Researched by Betty Allen, Langley, BC, Lines 7-8, 1851, Library & Archives of Canada, 395 Wellington Street, Ottawa, Ontario, Canada K1A 0N4. "Elijah, Age 23 Farmer, Episcopalian; Isaac, Age 20, Farmer." [LLE003]

4. Bruce County Registrar, Index of Land Instruments for Bruce County, Ontario, Microfilm A-3-9, Page 19, Walkerton Branch Library, 253 Durham Street East, Walkerton, Ontario N0G 2V0. This mortgage was a combined one with his father Joseph, Sr. and brothers Isaac, Henry, Joseph, Jr. and James for a total collateral of 300 acres. [OBC002]

5. Bruce County Registrar, Index of Land Instruments for Bruce County, Ontario, Microfilm A-3-9, Page 19, Instr. 527, 28 Jul 1864.

6. Bruce County Registrar, Index of Land Instruments for Bruce County, Ontario, Microfilm A-3-9, Page 19, Instr. #255, 08 Oct 1864.

7. Bruce County Registrar, Land Records of Bruce County, Ontario, Microfilm Series A, Reel A-62, Instr. 790, 02 Mar 1867, Bruce County Registry Office, 203 Cayley Street, Walkerton, Ontario N0G 2V0. An Agreement (Instr. 780) dated 15 Feb 1867 and registered 18 Feb 1867 was granted by Eljjah to Alex McCarter. [OBC001]

8. 1871 Census of Canada - Ontario: Searchable Database of Heads & Strays, http://db.library. queensu.ca/dbtw-wpd/exec/dbtwpub.dll, Dist. 27, Subdist H, Div 1, Pg 40, 1871, Queen's University Libraries, 99 University Avenue, Kingston, Ontario K7L 3N6. "Elijah, Head, age 35, Primitive Methodist, farmer." [QUL001]

9. Lilley, Lois, Compliation of Bacon Family Information (Lilley), Page 14. "Rev. Thos. Reid, Canadian Wesleyan Methodist New Connexion Church. Witness: Thos. McNeil."

10. Lilley, Lois, Compliation of Bacon Family Information (Lilley), Page 15. "Age 37 years." Maria died of complications at the birth of her daughter who was named Maria.

11. Vital Statistics, Manitoba Finance Division of Consumer & Corporate Affairs Database, Reg. #1882-001284, Manitoba Finance, http://web2.gov.mb.ca/cca/vital/query.php. [GPM001]

12. Taylor, Elaine V. (Routledge), *Bacon, John & Elizabeth (Hunter)*, Routledge Family Research, PO Box 28, Hamiota, Manitoba, Canada R0M 0T0, Page 8, The Collection of Dean Wheaton, 5976 Kungle Road, Clinton, OH 44216-9317. [REV001, 83]

13. Vital Statistics, Manitoba Finance Division of Consumer & Corporate Affairs Database, Reg. #1925-027134. "Age 62 years."

14. Vital Statistics, Manitoba Finance Division of Consumer & Corporate Affairs Database, Reg. #1892-001079.

15. Wheaton, Dean, Gravestone Photographs at Kinsmore Cemetery at Hamiota, Manitoba, 6 Jul 1996, Frame 11, The Collection of Dean Wheaton, 5976 Kungle Road, Clinton, OH 44216-9317, Roll 519. "Bacon: 1862 Robt. H. 1944; 1862 Mary E. 1941; At Rest." [519-11]

16. Lilley, Lois, *Bacon, Isaac & Elijah, Family Information*, In a letter to Dean Wheaton dated 20 Sep 1996 (Unpublished), Page 1, The Collection of Dean Wheaton, 5976 Kungle Road, Clinton, OH 44216-9317. [LL_006]

17. Allen, Betty, Bacon, Elijah, Descendants, Via letter dated 27 Feb 1996, Unpublished, Page 20, The Collection of Dean Wheaton, 5976 Kungle Road, Clinton, OH 44216-9317. [LL_004]

18. Vital Statistics, Manitoba Finance Division of Consumer & Corporate Affairs Database, Reg. #1886-001081.

19. *Bruce County Cemetery Gravestone Readings*, Old Bethel Methodist/Prior Cemetery, Page 2, #6, Bruce County Museum & Archives, 33 Victoria Street North, Southampton, Ontario N0H 2L0. "James son of Elijah & Mariah Bacon died July 8, 1871 aged 8 mos & 10 days." Compute DoB = DoD - Age = 29 Oct 1870. [OBC009]

20. Allen, Betty, Bacon, Elijah, Descendants, Page 4.

21. Vital Statistics, Manitoba Finance Division of Consumer & Corporate Affairs Database, Reg. #1892-001076.

22. U.S. Dept. of Labor, Immigration & Natrualization Service, Certificate of Arrival of Susan Bacon Porter, Cert. #14-46678, 10 Jun 1940, The Collection of Dean Wheaton, 5976 Kungle Road, Clinton, OH 44216-9317. Contained in a letter from Lois Lilley to Dean Wheaton received 15 Aug 1994 (LL_001, page 13). "Arrival via the Michigan Central Railway." Cert. issued by the District Court, Bottineau, North Dakota, 10 Jun 1940.

23. Vital Statistics, Manitoba Finance Division of Consumer & Corporate Affairs Database, Reg. #1894-001276.

24. Vital Statistics, Manitoba Finance Division of Consumer & Corporate Affairs Database, Reg, #1882-001166.

25. Goughnour, Constance (Morse), *Bacon, James, Sr., Family Information Letter*, Dated 9 Aug 1994, #6, The Collection of Dean Wheaton, 5976 Kungle Road, Clinton, OH 44216-9317.

26. Goughnour, Constance (Morse), Bacon, James, Sr., Family Information Letter, Pages 5-6.

Modified Register for Joseph Bacon, Sr.

Second Generation - Emma Jane

10. **Emma Jane Bacon** "Jane" was born[1,2] 17 Jul 1836 in Buffalo, New York. She died[3,4] 27 Oct 1907 in Petoskey, Emmet County, Michigan from bright's disease and was buried[5,6] in the Bliss Township Cemetery, Bliss, Emmet County, Michigan.

Jane was enumerated in a census[7] 05 Jun 1884 in Bliss Township, Emmet County, Michigan. She was enumerated in a census[8] 1900 in Bliss Township, Emmet County, Michigan.

Jane married[9] (1) **Samuel John Hoar Sr.**, son of Samuel Hoar and Elizabeth Bunsell, in Bruce County, Ontario. Samuel was born[10] 02 Nov 1832 in Boston, Lincolnshire, England. He died[10] 22 Sep 1883 in Levering, Emmet County, Michigan and was buried[10] in the Bliss Township Cemetery, Emmet County, Michigan.

Samuel pursued the occupation[11] of farmer in 1880 in Bliss Twp, Emmet County, Michigan. He was enumerated in a census[11] 03 Jun 1884 in Bliss Township, Emmet County, Michigan.

They had the following children:

75 F   i.   **Jennie Hoar** was born[12] in Canada West. She died[12] in Canada West.

76 F   ii.   **Carrie Hoar** was born[12] in Canada West. She died[12] in Canada West.

77 F   iii.   **Lucy Hoar** was born[12] in Canada West. She died[12] in Canada West.

78 F   iv.   **Mary Hoar** was born[13] 21 Jan 1855 in Bruce County, Canada West. She died[13,14] 26 Jan 1926 in Levering, Emmet County, Michigan from chronic nephritis and was buried[15] in the Carp Lake Township Cemetery, Emmet County, Michigan.

Mary married[15] **George Louis Carlton** on 25 Sep 1872 in Walkerton, Bruce County, Canada West. George was born[15] 14 Feb 1853 in Toronto, Canada West. He died[15] 23 Jan 1925 in Levering, Emmet County, Michigan and was buried[15] in the Carp Lake Township Cemetery, Emmet County, Michigan.

George has biography information in the Notes[16] (1) about Michigan and North Dakota. He owned land[17] T38N R4W, Sec 33, E1/2 of NE 1/4 (80 acres) 1902 in Carp Lake Twp, Emmet County, Michigan. He was enumerated in a census[18] 17 Jan 1902 in Carp Lake Twp, Emmet County, Michigan. He owned land[19] in Sec 33 (160 acres) with an assessed value of $1,800 in 1903 in Carp Lake Twp, Emmet County, Michigan.

(1) George and Mary came to Levering, Emmet County, Michigan in 1879 from Ontario. In 1882 he went to the Fargo, North Dakota, took up a homestead, and returned to Levering for his family. Returning westward they were delayed by bad weather and arrived after the deadline for occupying homesteads. Someone else had taken their claim. They returned to levering in 1887 to a 160 acre farm in Section 33 of Carp Lake Township, Emmet County, Michigan (the 1902 plat Book of Emmet Co shows him owning only 80 acres, E 1/2 of NE 1/4 Sec 33). George was aligned with the Republican Party and held several local governmental offices: Supervisor of Carp Lake Township from 1892-1904 when he resigned to become Emmet County Treasurer to which he was elected on November 8 of that year. The Carleton's were members of the Methodist Episcopal Church. George was affiliated with the Free and Accepted Masons and the Knights of the Maccabees.

George and Jane had eight children, three boys and five girls, born between about 1872 and 1895.

79 F v. **Susanna Hoar** "Susan" was born[20] 02 Aug 1856 in Carrick Township, Bruce County, Canada West. She died[20,21] 23 Dec 1937 in Levering, Emmet County, Michigan and was buried[21] in the Carp Lake Township Cemetery, Emmet County, Michigan.

Susan has biography information in the Notes[22] (1) about traveling from Southampton, Ontario to Cheboygan, Michigan.

(1) Susanna and her family came from Southampton to Cheboygan by steamship in 1881 with her brother John.

Susan married[22] **William John Reed** on 17 Jan 1877 in Walkerton, Bruce County, Canada West. William was born[22] 15 Mar 1855 in Eden Grove, Canada West. He died[22] 04 Oct 1938 in Levering, Emmet County, Michigan.

William and Susan had two children, a boy born 1877 and a girl born 1879.

80 M vi.   **John Hoar** was born[23] 26 Feb 1858 in Carrick Township, Bruce County, Canada West. He died[23,24] 01 Apr 1917 in Levering, Emmet County, Michigan from internal tumor and was buried[25] in the Carp Lake Township Cemetery, Emmet County, Michigan.

John was enumerated in a census[26] 27 Jun 1900 in Carp Lake Township, Emmet County, Michigan. He owned land[26] in T38N R4W, Sec 33, SE 1/4 & W 1/2 of NE 1/4 (240 acres) in 1902 in Carp Lake Township, Emmet County, Michigan. He owned land[27] in Sec 33 (240 acres) valued at $3,900 in 1903 in Carp Lake Township, Emmet County, Michigan. He was enumerated in a census[28] 22 Apr 1910 in Carp Lake Township, Emmet County, Michigan. He has biography information in the Notes[29] (1) about traveling from Southampton, Ontario to Cheboygan, Michigan.

(1) John came to the port of Cheboygan, Michigan in 1881 by steamship with his sister Susan and her family from Southampton, Ontario.
John & Jennie had four children, two boys and two girls, born between 1889 and 1896 in Carp Lake Township, Emmet County, Michigan.

John married[29] **Jane Ellen Galloway** "Jennie", daughter of David Galloway and Mary Anne Couch, on 26 Jun 1888 in Petoskey, Emmet County, Michigan. Jennie was born[29] 15 Oct 1859 in Walkerton, Bruce County, Canada West. She died[29] 21 Sep 1930 in Ann Arbor, Washtenaw County, Michigan and was buried[29] in the Carp Lake Township Cemetery, Emmet County, Michigan.

Jennie is the daughter of Mary Ann (Couch) Galloway and the granddaughter of Christopher Couch.

81 F   vii.   **Elizabeth Jane Hoar** was born[30,31] 03 Jan 1862 in Canada West. She died[31] 12 Nov 1899 in Levering, Emmet County, Michigan.

Elizabeth married[32] **Levi A. Prout**, son of John Prout and Jane Rathburn, on 02 Jul 1890 in Harbor Springs, Emmet County, Michigan. Levi was born about 1862 in Canada West.

Levi and Elizabeth had one child, John, born in 1892.

82 M   viii.   **Samuel John Hoar Jr.** was born[33] 01 Nov 1864 in Carrick Township, Bruce County, Canada West. He died[34] 07 Aug 1933 in Levering, Emmet County, Michigan from paralysis agitaus and was buried[35] in the Bliss Township Cemetery, Emmet County, Michigan.

Samuel was enumerated in a census[36] 16 Jun 1894 in Bliss Township, Emmet County, Michigan. He pursued the occupation[36] of farmer in 1894 in Bliss Township, Emmet County, Michigan. He was enumerated in a census[37] 09 Jun 1900 in Bliss Township, Emmet County, Michigan. He pursued the occupation[38] of farmer in 1900 in Bliss Township, Emmet County, Michigan. He owned land[39] in T38N R5W, Sec 25, W 1/2 of SE 1/4 (80 acres) in 1902 in Bliss Township, Emmet County, Michigan. He owned land[40] in T38N R5W, Sec 25, W1/2 of SE 1/4 (80 acres) valued at $1,960 in 1903 in Bliss Township, Emmet County, Michigan. He pursued the occupation[41] of butcher in a slaughterhouse in 1910 in McKinley Township, Emmet County, Michigan. He was enumerated in a census[42] 09 May 1910 in McKinley Township, Emmet County, Michigan. He was enumerated in a census[275] 1920 in McKinley Township, Emmet County, Michigan. He pursued the occupation[43] of auto salesman in 1920 in McKinley Township, Emmet County, Michigan.

Samuel married[44] **Lucy Lucinda Crandall**, daughter of Merrill C. Crandall and Sarah Harkness, on 21 Nov 1893 in Readmond, Emmet County, Michigan. Lucy was born[45] 23 May 1871 in Ross Twp, Kalamazoo County, Michigan. She died[45] 06 Feb 1949 in Cheboygan, Cheboygan County, Michigan from cerebal thrombosis and was buried[45,46] 21 Apr 1949 in the Bliss Township Cemetery, Bliss, Emmet County, Michigan.

83 M   ix. **Joseph Hoar** was born[47] 25 Apr 1868 in Brant Township, Bruce County, Canada West. He died[47] 25 Apr 1919 in Brockton, Montana.

Joseph has biography information in the Notes[47] (1) about Michigan, Idaho, Saskatchewan and Montana.

(1) The family went from Michigan to Idaho, returned to Michigan, and then went to Saskatchewan where their home burned. They returned for a second time to Levering and subsequently settled in Brockton, Montana.

Joseph and Lillie had six children, one boy and five girls, between 1894 and 1912.

Joseph married[48] **Lillie Mae Shrock**, daughter of Peter Shrock and Fanny Carber, on 02 Nov 1893 in Brutus, Emmet County, Michigan. Lillie was born[48] 28 Apr 1875 in Goshen, Indiana. She died[48] 05 Sep 1955 in Artesia, California.

84 M   x. **Esell H. Hoar** was born[48] about 1869 in Canada.

Jane also married[49] (2) **David B. Hoar**, son of Samuel Hoar and Elizabeth Bunsell, on 29 Mar 1894 in Bliss, Emmet, Michigan. David was born[48] 01

Apr 1844 in England. He died[50] 21 Jan 1908 in Levering, Emmet County, Michigan.

David was enumerated in a census[51] 27 Jun 1894 in Bliss Township, Emmet County, Michigan. He owned land[52] in T38N R5W, Sec 35, SE 1/4 of SW 1/4 (40 acres) in about 1900 in Bliss Township, Emmet County, Michigan. He was enumerated in a census[52] 02 Jun 1900 in Bliss Township, Emmet County, Michigan. He owned land[52] in T38N R5W, Sec 35, SE 1/4 of SW 1/4 (40 acres) in 1902 in Bliss Township, Emmet County, Michigan. He owned land[53] in Sec 35 (40 acres) with an assessed value of $580 in 1903 in Bliss Township, Emmet County, Michigan.

> David and (1) Emma (Wakefield) had three children, all boys, between 1869 and 1871.
>
> David and (2) Mary Ann (Kennedy) had three children, two boys and one girl.
>
> David and (3) Emma Jane (Bacon) had no children.

Source References - Emma Jane

1. Kalbfleisch, Raymond W., *The Bacon Family*, Genealogist, Petoskey, Michigan, Self published, 8 pages, Page 5, The Collection of Dean Wheaton, 5976 Kungle Road, Clinton, OH 44216-9317, KRW001. Copied from Raymond's original by Dean Wheaton on 1 Aug 1994 at Petoskey, Michigan.

2. County Clerk, Death Records of Emmet County, Michigan 1907-1920, Vol: 1907-1920, Rec. #131, 11 Nov 19907, Family History Library, 35 North West Temple, Salt Lake City, Utah 84150, Microfilm #0966504. "Age: 71y 3m 10d, DoD: 27 Oct 1907." Computed DoB = DoD - Age = 17 Jul 1836. [WWD103, 10]

3. County Clerk, Death Records of Emmet County, Michigan 1907-1920, Vol: 1907-1920, Record #131, 11 Nov 1907. "Occupation: Housewife, Age: 71y 3m 10d, Deceased name: Jane Emily, Parents: Joseph Bacon and Susanna Franklin."

4. Kalbfleisch, Raymond W., *The Hoar Family Record*, Self published before 1994, Page 7, The Collection of Dean Wheaton, 5976 Kungle Road, Clinton, OH 44216-9317, KRW002. Jane died at the Lockwood Hospital in Petoskey, Michigan.

5. Greenwood Cemetery, Greenwood Cemetery Records, 111 Greenwood Street, Petoskey, Michigan 49770, Hoar Extract, Seq #17183, The Collection of Dean Wheaton, 5976 Kungle Road, Clinton, OH 44216-9317. "Funeral: 29 Oct 1907, Funeral Home: Stone Funeral Home, Petoskey, Michigan." [GGC054, 3]

6. Wheaton, Dean, *Bliss Township Cemetery, Transcription of Notes Recorded from Headstones, Bliss, Michigan*, Tape #28B, 228-339, 16 Sep 1995, #6, 16 Sep 1995, The Collection of Dean Wheaton, 5976 Kungle Road, Clinton, OH 44216-9317, WWD167. "Hoar: Samuel J. 1832-1883 Father, Jane E. 1836-1907 Mother." [WWD167]

7. 1884 Michigan Census of Emmet County, Bliss Township, Genealogical Society of Utah, Page 166, Lines 7-10, 05 Jun 1884, Family History Library, 35 North West Temple, Salt Lake City, Utah 84150, Microfilm #0927462. "Hoar: Jane E., wife, widow, age 48; John, son, age 26; Samuel J, son, age 20; Esell H., son, age 15." There is some question as to the spelling of son Esell's name on the microfilm. [WWD140, 2]

8. 1900 U.S. Census of Michigan, Emmet County, Bliss Township, U.S. National Archives, Page 26, Lines 48-51, 1900, Western Reserve Historical Society Library, Cleveland, Ohio, Microfilm M593, Roll #710. "Hoar, David B, head, born Apr 1844, married 6 yrs; Jane E, wife, born Jul 1835; dau., Jessie M., born Feb 1881; Walter, son, born Oct 1886." [WWD070]

9. Kalbfleisch, Raymond W., *The Hoar Family Record*, Page 7.

10. Kalbfleisch, Raymond W., *The Hoar Family Record*, Page 6.

11. 1884 Michigan Census of Emmet County, Bliss Township, Page 361, Lines 28-33, 03 Jun 1880. "Hoar, Samuel J., head, farmer, age 47; Jane E., wife, age 43; Elizabeth, dau., age 23; Samuel, son, age 16; Joseph, son, age 12; Carlton, Carrie, gdau., age 4."

12. Kalbfleisch, Raymond W., *The Hoar Family Record*, Page 7. Died as a child.

13. Kalbfleisch, Raymond W., *The Hoar Family Record*, Page 8.

14. County Clerk, Death Records of Emmet County, Michigan 1921-1930, Microfilmed by The Genealogical Society of Utah, Vol: 1921-1930, Rec. #20, Family History Library, 35 North West Temple, Salt Lake City, Utah 84150, Microfilm #0966504. [WWD104, 6]

15. Wheaton, Dean, *Carp Lake Township Cemetery: Transcription of Notes Recorded from Headstones, Levering, Michigan*, Tape #28B, 228-339, 16 Sep 1995, The Collection of Dean Wheaton, 5976 Kungle Road, Clinton, OH 44216-9317, WWD166. "On a large Carlton Family Stone: Carl C. 1895-1918, George 1853-1925, Mary 1855-1926, Mary E. 1891-1892."

16. *Biographical History of Northern Michigan Containing Biographies of Prominent Citizens* (BF Bowen & Company, 1905), Pages 844-845, Boyne District Library, 342 North Lake Street, Boyne City, Michigan 49712. [FN_001, 11]

17. P.A. & J.W. Myers, Surveyors and Draughtsmen, *1902 Plat Book of Emmet County Michigan* (The Consolidated Publishing Company, 610 Boston Block, Minneapolis, Minnesota, E.P. Noll & Co., Map Publishers, No. 9 North 6th Street, Philadelphia, Pennsylvania, 1902), Pages 28-29, The Collection of Dean Wheaton, 5976 Kungle Road, Clinton, OH 44216-9317. Republished as *Grandfather's Land*, PO Box 8, Hemlock, Michigan 48626, 1973 in 8.5" X 11" paperback format without attribution to the original.

18. 1920 U.S. Census of Michigan, Emmet County, Carp Lake Township, Page 20, Lines 8587, 17 Jan 1920, Family History Library, 35 North West Temple, Salt Lake City, Utah 84150, Microfilm #1820763. "Carlton, George Louis, head, age 66, immigrated 1879, naturalized 19098, farmer; Mary, wife, age 64, immigrated 1879, naturalized 1908; Cecil, dau., age 32." [WWD190, 25]

19. *Directory, Petoskey City & Emmet County* (R.L. Polk & Company, 68-70-72 Griswold Street, Detroit, Michigan, 1973), Vol. 1903, Page 276, Petoskey Public Library, 451 East Mitchell Street, Petoskey, Michigan 49770. "Supervisor of Carp Lake Township."

20. Kalbfleisch, Raymond W., *The Hoar Family Record*, Pages 7 & 9.

21. Greenwood Cemetery, Greenwood Cemetery Records, Reed Extract 12 Dec 1994, Seq # 19574.

22. Kalbfleisch, Raymond W., *The Hoar Family Record*, Page 9.

23. Kalbfleisch, Raymond W., *The Hoar Family Record*, Page 10.

24. County Clerk, Death Records of Emmet County, Michigan 1907-1920, Rec. #124.

25. Wheaton, Dean, *Carp Lake Township Cemetery, Transcription of Notes Recorded from Headstones, Levering, Michigan*, #1, 16 Sep 1995. "Hoar John 1858-1917, Jennie E. 1869-1930." There is a small "Mother" stone on the right and a "Father" stone on the left of the large stone.

26. 1900 U.S. Census of Michigan, Emmet County, Carp Lake Township, National Archives, MS593, Reel 710, Page 38, Lines 44-50, 27 Jun 1900, Western Reserve Historical Society Library, Cleveland, Ohio. Family History Library microfilm #1249710. "Hoar, John, head, age 42; Jennie, wife, age 32; Bina, dau., age 11; Levi, son, age 9; Samuel H., son, age 7; Susan V., dau., age 4; Unreadable, servant, farm laborer." [WWD178, 28]

27. *Directory, Petoskey City & Emmet County*, Page 300.

28. 1910 U.S. Census of Michigan, Emmet County, Carp Lake Township, Page 90, Lines 18-22, 22 Apr 1910, Family History Library, 35 North West Temple, Salt Lake City, Utah 84150, Microfilm #1374658. "Hoar, John, head, age 52; Jennie E., wife, age 40; Levi J., son, age 19; Samuel D., son, age 17." [WWD189, 42]

29. Kalbfleisch, Raymond W., *The Hoar Family Record*, Pages 10 & 11.

30. Greenwood Cemetery, Greenwood Cemetery Records, Prout Extract, Seq #19459. "Age: 37y 10m 9d, Death: 11/12/1899, Funeral: 11/14/1899." Funeral Home Record, Stone Funeral Home, Petoskey, Michigan. Computer DoB from DoD - Age = 3 Jan 1862.

31. Kalbfleisch, Raymond W., *The Hoar Family Record*, Page 12. This source has DoB as 1860.

32. County Clerk, Marriage Records of Emmet County Michigam 1887-1899, Vol. 2, Page 15, Rec. #214, Family History Library, 35 North West Temple, Salt Lake City, Utah 84150, Microfilm #0966507. [WWD040, 10]

33. Kalbfleisch, Raymond W., *The Hoar Family Record*, Page 7 & 13.

34. County Clerk, Death Records of Emmet County, Michigan 1931-1956, Surnames A-K, Page 65, Rec. #188, 10 Oct 1933, Family History Library, 35 North West Temple, Salt Lake City, Utah 84150, Microfilm #09660505. "Death 7 Aug 1933 McKinley Twp, Age 69y 8m 6d, married, retired, Parents; Samuel Hoar & Emma Bacon." [WWD105, 28]

35. Wheaton, Dean, *Bliss Township Cemetery, Transcription of Notes Recorded from Headstones, Bliss, Michigan*, #35. "Hoar Family Stone with six individual stones: Andrew 1870-1965, Grace A. 1873-1951, Marjorie 1900-1973, Crandall 1908-1942, Lucy L. 1871-1949, Samuel J. 1863-1933."

36. 1894 Michigan Census of Emmet County, Bliss Township, Schedule 3, Page 84, Line 5, 16 Jun 1894, Family History Library, 35 North West Temple, Salt Lake City, Utah 84150,

Microfilm #0915306. "Agricultural Census, owns 40 acres; land, fences & buildings value = $1,000; Farm implements & machinery value = $1,200, Live stock value = $300, 1893 farm produce value = $200." [WWD149, 14]

37. 1900 U.S. Census of Michigan, Emmet County, Bliss Township, Page 29, Lines 69-72, 09 Jun 1900. "Hoar, Samuel J., head, age 36; Lucy L., wife, age 29; Gertrude J., dau., age 1; Sammores, Ruby R., servant, age 16."

38. 1900 U.S. Census of Michigan, Emmet County, Bliss Township, Page 29, Line 6, 09 Jun 1900.

39. P.A. & J.W. Myers, Surveyors and Draughtsmen, *1902 Plat Book of Emmet County Michigan*, Page 33.

40. P.A. & J.W. Myers, Surveyors and Draughtsmen, *1902 Plat Book of Emmet County Michigan*, Page 300.

41. 1910 U.S. Census of Michigan, Emmet County, McKinley Township, Page 69, Line 6, 09 May 1910, Family History Library, 35 North West Temple, Salt Lake City, Utah 84150, Microfilm #1374658. [WWD180, 69]

42. 1910 U.S. Census of Michigan, Emmet County, McKinley Township, Page 214, Lines 6-9, 09 May 1910. "Hoar, Samuel, head, age 45; Lucy L., wife, age 39; Gertrude, dau., age 11; Marga E., dau., age 9."

43. 1920 U.S. Census of Michigan, Emmet County, McKinley Township, Page 90, Lines 7-10, Family History Library, 35 North West Temple, Salt Lake City, Utah 84150, Microfilm #1820763. "Hoar, Samuel J., head, age 57, immigration 1877, auto salesman; Lucy, wife, age 48; Marjorie, dau., age 19, saleslady in grocery store; Crandall, son, age 11." [WWD190, 57]

44. County Clerk, Marriage Records of Emmet County Michigan 1887-1899, Vol. 2, Page 39, Rec. #86. "FB Tripp, Clergyman, Witnesses: BW Walker, Levering and Grace Crandall, Readmond."

45. County Clerk, Death Records of Emmet County, Michigan 1931-1956, Surnames E-K, Page 66D, Rec. #121, 07 Feb 1949. "Housewife, widow of Samuel, Parents: Merrill Crandall & Sarah Harkness, Age 77y 8m 13d, Undertaker: Quinton Stone, Petoskey." Death registration gives place of burial as Levering on 9 Feb 1949. Greenwood Cemetery records give it as Bliss Township Cemetery on 21 Apr 1949 and her gravestone is in the Bliss Twp Cemetery.

46. Greenwood Cemetery, Greenwood Cemetery Records, Hoar Extract: Seq #17185. "Bliss Township, Age 77y 8 m 13d, Death 6 Feb 1949, Funeral 9 Feb 1949, Birth 23 May 1871, Burial 21 Apr 1949, Stone Funeral Home, Petoskey."

47. Kalbfleisch, Raymond W., *The Hoar Family Record*, Page 14.

48. County Clerk, Marriage Records of Emmet County Michigam 1887-1899, Vol. 2, Page 38, Rec. #78.

49. County Clerk, Marriage Records of Emmet County Michigam 1887-1899, Vol. 2, Page 40, Rec. #115. "Groom: David Hoar, age 48, resides in Bliss, born england, farmer, parents: Samuel Hoar & Elizabeth Bunsell; Bride: Emogene Hoar (Emogene Bacon), age 50, resides in Bliss, born in New York, farmer, parents: Joseph Bacon & Susanna Franklin; both married once previous, FB Tripp, Clergyman; witnesses: Joseph H Hoar & Lillie Hoad." Emogene is a mis-communication of Emma Jane. Note that Jane is listed with an occupation of farmer - she has been operating her first husband's farm. David's statement of one previous marriage is wrong - he was married twice previously.

50. Kalbfleisch, Raymond W., *The Hoar Family Record*, Page 20.

51. 1894 Michigan Census of Emmet County, Bliss Township, Schedule 3, Page 57, Line 4, 27 Jun 1894. "Hoar, David: owner, 40 acres total, 27 acres improved, 13 acres woodland, value of land bldgs & fences = $1,000, value of implements & machinery = $35, value of livestock = #400, farm production 1893 = $363."

52. Lee, Elnora Fay, *A Century of Bliss* (Self published, 1976), Page 12, Petoskey Public Library, 451 East Mitchell Street, Petoskey, Michigan 49770, MICH 977.488 LEE. [FE_001, 12]

53. *Directory, Petoskey City & Emmet County*, Vol 1903, Page 300.

Modified Register for Joseph Bacon, Sr.

Second Generation - Henry

11. **Henry B. Bacon** was born[1] 11 Oct 1839 in Hamilton, Upper Canada. He died[1,2] 12 Sep 1916 in Resort Township, Emmet County, Michigan from gangrene and was buried[1] 14 Sep 1916 in Greenwood Cemetery, Petoskey, Emmet County, Michigan.

Henry received a Crown Patent[3] Con 1 NDR, Lot 15 (50 acres) 01 Oct 1857 in Brant Township, Bruce County, Canada West. He gave a mortgage[4] Con 1 NDR, Lot 15 (50 acres) to Trust & Loan Co. of Upper Canada for $1200 on 03 Jun 1859 in Brant Township, Bruce County, Canada West. He gave a mortgage[5] Con 1 NDR, Lot 15 (50 acres) to Huron & Erie Savings & Loan Society for $350 on 11 Jun 1864 in Brant Township, Bruce County, Canada West. He and his wife received a discharge of mortgage[6] Con 1 NDR, Lot 15 (50 acres) from Trust & Loan Co. of Upper Canada 27 Sep 1864 in Brant Township, Bruce County, Canada West. He gave a mortgage[7] Con 1 NDR, Lot 15 (50 acres) to Joshua Jamieson for $303 on 18 Jun 1867 in Brant Township, Bruce County, Canada West. He and his wife received a discharge of mortgage[8] Con 1 NDR, Lot 15 (50 acres) from Matthew Pinkerton 22 Apr 1868 in Brant Township, Bruce County, Ontario. He gave a mortgage[9] Con 1 NDR, Lot 15 (50 acres) to Patrick Godfrey for $678 on 22 Apr 1868 in Brant Township, Bruce County, Ontario. He and his wife received a discharge of mortgage[10] Con 1 NDR, Lot 15 (50 acres) 28 Apr 1868 in Brant Township, Bruce County, Ontario. He was enumerated in a census[11] in 1871 in Brant Township, Bruce County, Ontario. He gave a mortgage[12] Con 1 NDR, Lot 15 (50 acres) to Canada L. Cr. Co. for $1000 on 10 Mar 1871 in Brant Township, Bruce County, Ontario. He and his wife received a discharge of mortgage[13] Con 1 NDR, Lot 15 (50 acres) from Patrick Godfrey 04 May 1871 in Brant Township, Bruce County, Ontario. He sold[14] Con 1 NDR, Lot 15 (50 acres) to Uriah Roswell for $1050 on 05 Aug 1871 in Brant Township, Bruce County, Ontario. He and his wife received a discharge of mortgage[15] Con 1 NDR, Lot 15 (50 acres) from Can. L. Cr. Co. 14 Mar 1876 in Brant Township, Bruce County, Ontario. He was enumerated in a census[16] 24 Jun 1880 in Bear Lake Township, Charlevoix County, Michigan. He was enumerated in a census[17] 10 Jul 1900 in Resort Township, Emmet County, Michigan. He owned land[18] in T33N, R6W, Sec 2 (66 acres) valued at $1,900 in 1903 in Resort Township, Emmet County, Michigan. He was enumerated in a census[19] 18 May 1910 in Resort Township, Emmet County, Michigan. He had an obituary published[20] in "The Petoskey Evening News and Daily Resorter" on 13 Sep 1916 in Petoskey, Emmet County, Michigan. He has biography information published[21] in the article "The Bacon Family" with a photograph taken about 1930 in 1992 in Petoskey, Emmet County, Michigan. He has biography information published[22] in an untitled article by Dean Wheaton (5th Grade) in 1952 in Petoskey, Emmet County, Michigan. He has unpublished biographical information[23] about the Morford, Bacon, and Couch Families in Resort Township, Emmet County, Michigan. He has unpublished biographical information[24] in an interview with Ruth Bacon Bates 20 Jul 1994.

Henry married[25] **Elizabeth Franklin Couch**, daughter of Christopher Couch and Mary Ann Tighe, on 27 Jan 1863 in Walkerton, Bruce County, Canada West. Elizabeth was born[26,27] 16 Aug 1843 in Douro Township, Peterborough County, Canada West and was baptized[27] 30 Jun 1848 in Peterborough, Peterborough County, Canada West. She died[27,28] 20 Jun 1916 in Petoskey, Emmet County, Michigan and was buried[28] 22 Jun 1916 in Greenwood Cemetery, Petoskey, Emmet County, Michigan.

Elizabeth had an obituary published[29] in "The Petoskey Evening News and Daily Resorter" on 20 Jun 1916 in Petoskey, Emmet County, Michigan.

They had the following children:

85 F   i.   **Mary Ann Bacon** was born[30] 29 Nov 1863 in Brant Township, Bruce County, Canada West. She died[30] 02 Jan 1864 in Brant Township, Bruce County, Canada West and was buried[31] in the Old Bethel Methodist/Prior Cemetery, Brant Township, Bruce County, Canada West.

86 M ii. **Isaac Bacon** was born[32,33] 08 Dec 1864 in Brant Township, Bruce County, Canada West. He died[33] 17 Apr 1900 in Hayes Township, Charlevoix County, Michigan and was buried[34,35] 19 Apr 1900 in Greenwood Cemetery, Petoskey, Emmet County, Michigan.
Isaac has biography information in the Notes[36] (1) about Resort Township, Emmet County, Michigan.

Note (1) While working for his Uncle Josiah Couch clearing land in 1885, a flying stick struck Isaac on the side of the head. This accident was blamed for his death due to a tumor of the brain some 15 years later. Soon after Isaac and Mary married they adopted Milton Fish who was then less than a year old.

Isaac married[37] **Mary Shannon**, daughter of Henry Shannon and Mary Armstrong, on 25 Dec 1897 in Ivy, Michigan. Mary was born[38] Jun 1873 in New York.

Mary has biography information in the Notes[38] (1) about Resort Township, Emmet County, Michigan. She was enumerated in a census[38] 21 Jun 1900 in Hayes Township, Charlevoix County, Michigan.

Note (1) Mary was a school teacher. After Isaac died, Mary moved to the Bay City-Saginaw, Michigan area, remarried, and had a daughter.

87 M   iii.   **Albert Edward Bacon** was born[39,40] 25 Feb 1867 in Brant Township, Bruce County, Canada West. He died[40] 10 Jan 1961 in East Jordan, Charlevoix County, Michigan and was buried[41] 13 Jan 1961 in Maple Lawn Cemetery, Boyne City, Charlevoix County, Michigan.

Albert was enumerated in a census[42] 19 Jun 1900 in Wilson Township, Charlevoix County, Michigan. He was enumerated in a census[43] 29 Jan 1920 in Boyne City, Charlevoix County, Michigan. He has biography information in the Notes[43] (1) about Boyne City, Charlevoix County, Michigan. He has biography information in the Notes[44] (2) about Northern Michigan.

(2) His chief occupation was teamster and lumberman. At one point he, with brothers Isaac and Joe, started a livery stable in Boyne City, Michigan. After a year and a half the stable caught fire burning eight horses and the buggies and harness. Much of his work with horses was in the woods lumbering. With the decline of lumbering, this work became scarce and he returned

to the old farm homestead at Walloon Lake in 1920. After a five year stay he moved to the Tubbs Farm [Sec 36, SW 1/4 of NW 1/4, 40 acres, two miles north of the homestead] for three years. He lived the last years of his life in Boyne City. Although Albert was married three times, he had no children.

Albert married[45] (1) **Bernice Grace Newville**, daughter of John A. Newville and Anna Patience Demming, on 29 Sep 1892 in Boyne City, Charlevoix County, Michigan. The marriage ended in divorce. Bernice was born[45] Mar 1873 in Boyne City, Charlevoix County, Michigan. She died[45] about 1916 in Boyne City, Charlevoix County, Michigan.

(1) Albert's first wife, Bernice, became pregnant by their hired man, Bill Ralston, who boarded with them. Bernice asked Albert for a divorce which he didn't contest. They had been married about eighteen years.

Albert also married[46] (2) **Ella Fanan**, daughter of James Fanan, on 30 Nov 1911 in Boyne City, Charlevoix County, Michigan. Ella was born about[46] 1873 in Michigan.

Albert also married[47] (3) **Sarah Louise Newville** "Sadie", daughter of Frank Newville and Clara Miller, on 30 Aug 1919 in Charlevoix, Charlevoix County, Michigan. Sadie was born[48] 19 Jun 1878 in Michigan. She died[48] 25 Jan 1952 in Boyne City, Charlevoix County, Michigan from cerebral hemorrhage & arteriosclerosis and was buried[48,49] 22 Apr 1952 in Maple Lawn Cemetery, Boyne City, Charlevoix County, Michigan.

Sadie has biography information in the Notes[50] (1) about Petoskey, Emmet County, Michigan.

(1) Sarah was known as Sadie. Sadie always brought two molasses cakes to the Bacon-Morford-Wheaton Reunion held annually at Magnus Park in Petoskey, Michigan in the mid 1900s. Avis (Pagel) Cushing [granddaughter of Emma

(Bacon) Pagel] remembers that the teenagers would always fight over them - they had the best carmel frosting.

88 M iv. **Joseph Elias Bacon** "Joe" was born[51] 31 Mar 1870 in Brant Township, Bruce County, Ontario. He died[52] 28 Sep 1972 in Little Traverse Hospital, Petoskey, Emmet County, Michigan and was buried[53,54] 30 Sep 1972 in Maple Lawn Cemetery, Boyne City, Charlevoix County, Michigan.

Joe was enumerated in a census[55] 21 Jun 1900 in Hayes Township, Charlevoix County, Michigan. He was enumerated in a census[56] 28 Apr 1910 in Boyne City, Charlevoix County, Michigan. He was enumerated in a census[57] 02 Jan 1920 in Resort Township, Emmet County, Michigan. He owned land[58] in Sec 11 & 14 (159 acres) valued at $6,300 in 1924 in Resort Township, Emmet County, Michigan. He has biography information published[58] in the article "The Bacon Family" including a photograph taken about 1930 in 1992 in Resort Township, Emmet County, Michigan. He has unpublished biographical information[59] in the Bacon-Morford-Wheaton Reunion Notes in 1963 in Magnus Park, Petoskey, Emmet County, Michigan. He has biography information published[60] in the story "Joe Bacon Plans on Becoming a Centenarian" with a photograph in Mar 1969 in Petoskey, Emmet County, Michigan. He has biography information published[61] in a story "Hemingway Pal Browses Through the Vintage Past" in Mar 1970 in Petoskey, Emmet County, Michigan. He had an obituary published[62] in the Petoskey News-Review on 29 Sep 1972 in Petoskey, Emmet County, Michigan. He has unpublished biographical information[63] in a college class term paper written in 1993. He has unpublished biographical information[64] 20 Jul 1994 in Kentwood, Kent County, Michigan.

Joe and Sarah had eight children, five boys and three girls. Two of the boys died in infancy.

Joe married[65] (1) **Sarah A. Brown**, daughter of John Brown and Thankful Lewis, on 22 Oct 1894 in Petoskey, Emmet County, Michigan. Sarah was born[67] 20 Aug 1877. She died[67] 02 Jan 1936 and was buried[66,67] 04 Jan 1936 in Maple Lawn Cemetery, Boyne City, Charlevoix County, Michigan.

Joe also married[68] (2) **Sara Nelson**, daughter of Joseph Steel and Hattie _____, on 27 Jan 1952 in Oakland County, Michigan.

89 F   v.   **Jane Algerina Bacon** "Jennie" was born[69] 11 Dec 1872 in Brant Township, Bruce County, Ontario. She died[70] 10 May 1956 in Mansfield, Richland County, Ohio and was buried[71] 13 May 1956 in Greenwood Cemetery, Petoskey, Emmet County, Michigan.

Jennie married[72] **Edwin Alfred Morford**, son of William Lane Morford and Francis Louise Dickerson, on 23 Nov 1891 in Resort Twp, Emmet County, Michigan. Edwin was born[73] 14 Oct 1866 in Rutland Township, Barry County, Michigan. He died[74] 21 Feb 1947 in Flint, Genesee County, Michigan and was buried[74,75] 06 Aug 1956 in Greenwood Cemetery, Petoskey, Emmet County, Michigan.

Edwin was enumerated in a census[76] 12 Jun 1900 in Petoskey, Emmet County, Michigan. He was enumerated in a census[77] 18 May 1910 in Resort Township, Emmet County, Michigan. He has unpublished biographical information[78] in a manuscript with two photos about his and Jennie's life in Ontario, Michigan & Ohio. He has biography information published[79] in an article "The Morford Family" with a photo taken on his & Jennie's 50th wedding anniversary. He has biography information published[80] in an article "Boarding Houses & Hotels". He has biography information published[81] in a monograph by his son, Wm H. Morford, about life on the farm 1900/1914 in Resort Township,

Emmet County, Michigan. He had an obituary published[82] in "The Flint Journal" on 22 Feb 1947 in Flint, Genesee County, Michigan.

Edwin and Louella had one child. Louella and the child died at the child's birth in 1889.

Edwin and Jennie had seven children between 1893-1902, three died in infancy, two boys and two girls lived to adulthood.

90 M   vi. **Theodore Huston Bacon** was born[83] 11 Oct 1875 in Brant Township, Bruce County, Ontario. He died[84] 19 Oct 1959 in Petoskey, Emmet County, Michigan and was buried[85] in greenwood Cemetery, Petoskey, Emmet County, Michigan.

Theodore was enumerated in a census[86] 02 Jan 1920 in Resort Township, Emmet County, Michigan.

Huston never married and had no children.

91 F   vii. **Lillie Mary Hope Bacon** was born[87] 10 May 1878 in Brant Township, Bruce County, Ontario. She died[88] 13 Jan 1960 in Little Traverse Hospital, Petoskey, Emmet County, Michigan and was buried[89] 20 Apr 1960 in Greenwood Cemetery, Petoskey, Emmet County, Michigan.

Lillie married[90] **Walter Rhynear Wheaton**, son of Andrew Wheaton and Eliza Jane Benway, on 15 Jun 1904 in Resort Township, Emmet County, Michigan. Walter was born[91] 18 Apr 1875 in Norwood Township, Charlevoix County, Michigan. He died[92] 28 Apr 1945 in Petoskey, Emmet County, Michigan from coronary thrombosis and was buried[93,94] 01 May 1945 in Greenwood Cemetery, Petoskey, Emmet County, Michigan.

Walter owned land[95] T33N R6W, Sec 1, N 3/8 of E 1/2 of NE 1/4 (30 acres) in 1902 in Resort Township, Emmet County, Michigan. He owned land[96] Sec 1 (31 acres) with an assessed value of $325 in 1903 in Resort Township, Emmet County, Michigan. He owned land[97] Sec 19 (40 acres) with an assessed value of $500 in 1909 in Bear Creek Township, Emmet County, Michigan. He was enumerated in a census[98] 20 Apr 1910 in Boyne City, Charlevoix County, Michigan. He has unpublished biographical information[99] about a trip to Manitoba to visit an uncle in Aug 1912. He owned land[100] Sec 26 (60 acres) with an assessed value of $800 in 1919 in Friendship Township, Emmet County, Michigan. He was enumerated in a census[101] 20 Jan 1920 in Friendship Township, Emmet County, Michigan. He owned land[102] two parcels in Sec 26 of 60 acres each valued at $800 & $300 in 1925 in Friendship Township, Emmet County, Michigan. He owned land[103] Sec 26 (120 acres) assessed at $800 in 1925 in Friendship Township, Emmet County, Michigan.

92 F viii. **Dollie Mabel Bacon** was born 30 Apr 1881 in Resort Township, Charlevoix County, Michigan. She died[104] 16 Jun 1945 in Traverse City State Hospital, Traverse City, Grand Traverse County, Michigan from chronic myocarditis and was buried[105] 19 Jun 1945 in Greenwood Cemetery, Petoskey, Emmet County, Michigan.

Dollie was committed[106] to the Traverse City State Hospital on 26 Nov 1918 in Traverse City, Grand Traverse County, Michigan. She suffered illness[107] due to tuberculosis in Traverse City State Hospital, Traverse City, Grand Traverse County, Michigan.

Dollie never married and had no children.

93 F ix. **Emma Alice Franklin Bacon** was born[108,109] 07 Sep 1883 in Resort Township, Emmet County, Michigan. She died[110] 25 Nov 1974 in Petoskey, Emmet County, Michigan and

was buried[110] 27 Nov 1974 in Greenwood Cemetery, Petoskey, Emmet County, Michigan.

Emma married[111] **Henry C. Pagel**, son of Christian Pagels and Marie Bull, on 22 Nov 1905 in Emmet County, Michigan. Henry was born[112,113] 06 Jul 1882 in Petoskey, Emmet County, Michigan. He died[114] 15 Mar 1972 and was buried[114] 18 Mar 1972 in Greenwood Cemetery, Petoskey, Emmet County, Michigan.

Henry purchased land[115] T34N R5W, Sec 19, NE 1/4 of SW 1/4 for $800 on 12 Mar 1904 in Bear Creek Township, Emmet County, Michigan. He was enumerated in a census[116] 25 Apr 1910 in Resort Township, Emmet County, Michigan. He sold[117] T34N R5W, Sec 19, NE 1/4 of SW 1/4 (40 acres) for $800 on 03 Jun 1919 in Bear Creek Township, Emmet County, Michigan. He was enumerated in a census[118] 02 Jan 1920 in Resort Township, Charlevoix County, Michigan. He has unpublished biographical information[119] in the Bacon-Morford-Wheaton Reunion notes "Henry & Emma (Bacon) Pagel" in Michigan & Florida. He has biography information published[120] in a story with photograph taken in November 1969 in 19 Nov 1969 in Petoskey, Emmet County, Michigan.

Henry & Emma had five children, two boys and three girls, between 1908 and 1929. One girl died in childhood.

94 F x. **Lucy Violet Bacon** was born[121] 30 Jan 1886 in Resort Township, Charlevoix County, Michigan. She died[122] 30 Aug 1939 in Little Traverse Hospital, Petoskey, Emmet County, Michigan from coronary thrombosis and was buried[123,124] 02 Sep 1939 in Greenwood Cemetery, Petoskey, Emmet County, Michigan.

Lucy married[125] **Warner Abner Wheaton** , son of Andrew Wheaton and Eliza Jane Benway, on 31 Oct 1906 in Resort Township, Emmet County,

Michigan. Warner was born[126,127] 12 Apr 1885 in Norwood Township, Charlevoix County, Michigan. He died[128] 28 Apr 1967 in Harbor Springs, Emmet County, Michigan and was buried[129] 01 May 1967 in Greenwood Cemetery, Petoskey, Emmet County, Michigan.

Warner pursued the occupation[129] of farmer 1906 - 1907 in Resort Township, Emmet County, Michigan. He resided[130] 18 Jun 1907 in Boyne City, Charlevoix County, Michigan. He pursued the occupation[130] of laborer in a chemical plant in 1907 in Boyne City, Charlevoix County, Michigan. He was enumerated in a census[131] 22 Apr 1910 in 508 North Park Street, Boyne City, Charlevoix County, Michigan. He purchased land[133] T34N R5W, Sec 19, NE 1/4 of SW 1/4 (40 acres) for $800 on 03 Jun 1919 in Bear Creek Township, Emmet County, Michigan. He purchased land[133] T34N R5W, Sec 19, E 1/2 of NW 1/4 of SW 1/4 (20 acres) for $700 on 05 Jun 1919 in Bear Creek Township, Emmet County, Michigan. He gave a mortgage[134] T34N R5W, Sec 19, E 3/4 of N 1/2 of SW 1/4 (60 acres) for $1050 on 05 Jun 1919 in Bear Creek Ownership, Emmet County, Michigan. He was enumerated in a census[135] 02 Jan 1920 in Resort Township, Emmet County, Michigan. He pursued the occupation[135] of farmer in 1920 in Resort Township, Emmet County, Michigan. He owned land[136] Sec 19 [T34N R5W, NE 1/4 of SW 1/4] (40 acres) with an assessed value of $1,000 in 1925 in Bear Creek Township, Emmet County, Michigan. He pursued the occupation of carpenter in 1925 to about 1950 in Petoskey, Emmet County, Michigan. He sold[137] 2.472 acres along the east edge of NE 1/4 of SW 1/4, Sec 19 T34N R5W for M-131 Right of Way for $130 on 03 Feb 1933 in Bear Creek Township, Emmet County, Michigan. He gave a mortgage[138] on a Massey-Harris Cultivator for $67.00 on 25 Aug 1934 in Bear Creek Township, Emmet County, Michigan. He gave a mortgage[139] T34N R5W, Sec 19, E 3/4 of N 1/2 of NE 1/4 (60 acres) for $1,000 on 01 Nov 1934 in Bear Creek Township, Emmet County, Michigan. He purchased land[140] Lot #210, Glen Haven Subdivision for $1 19 Nov 1934 in Flint Township, Genesee County, Michigan. He and his wife received a discharge of mortgage[141] T34N R5W, Sec 19, E 3/4 of N 1/2 of NE 1/4 (60 acres) on 01 Feb 1935 in Bear Creek Township, Emmet County, Michigan. He and his wife received a discharge of mortgage[142] T34N R5W, Sec 19, E 3/4 of N 1/2 of SW 1/4 (60 acres) for $1,000 on 24 Oct 1946 in Bear Creek Township, Emmet County, Michigan. He sold[143] T34N R5W, Sec 19, E 3/4 of N 1/2 of SW 1/4 (60 acres) for $4,000 on 25 Oct 1948 in Bear Creek Township, Emmet County, Michigan.

Warner registered for the World War I Selective Service in Emmet County, Michigan on 12 Sep 1918. He was a self-employed farmer at RFD #1, Petoskey, Michigan. Local Board for Emmet Co., State of Michigan, Registration #C21-6-4. He was never called to serve. Ancestry.com searchable records (WDE001).

Warner and Lucy had three boys born between 1915 and 1922. The middle child died in infancy.

Source References - Henry

1. Greenwood Cemetery, Greenwood Cemetery Records, 111 Greenwood Street, Petoskey, Michigan 49770, Bacon Extract, Seq #1374-4, The Collection of Dean Wheaton, 5976 Kungle Road, Clinton, OH 44216-9317. "Age 76y 11m 1d, DoD 12 Sep 1916, Funeral 14 Sep 1916, Burial 14 Sep 1916, Stone Funeral Home, Petoskey, Grave location Sec F, Blk 84, Lot 10." DoB computed from DoD and age is 11 Oct 1839. [GGC002]

2. County Clerk, Death Records of Emmet County, Michigan 1907-1920, Vol 1907-1920, Rec. #184, 25 Oct 1916, Family History Library, 35 North West Temple, Salt Lake City, Utah 84150, Microfilm #0966504. "Died 12 Sep 1916 Resort Twp, widower, age 76y 11m 1d, farmer, born in Canada, Parents: Joseph Bacon and Susanna Franklin." [WWD103, 5]

3. Bruce County Registrar, Index of Land Instruments for Bruce County, Ontario, Microfilm A-3-9, Page 249, Walkerton Branch Library, 253 Durham Street East, Walkerton, Ontario N0G 2V0. [OBC002]

4. Bruce County Registrar, Land Records of Bruce County, Ontario, Microfilm Series A, Microfilm A-60, Instr. #205, 24 Jun 1859, Bruce County Registry Office, 203 Cayley Street, Walkerton, Ontario N0G 2V0. This mortgage was a combined one with his father Joseph, Sr. and brothers Isaac, James, Joseph, Jr. and Elijah for a total collateral of 300 acres. [OBC001]

5. Bruce County Registrar, Index of Land Instruments for Bruce County, Ontario, Microfilm A-3-9, Page 249, Instr. #524, 28 Jul 1864.

6. Bruce County Registrar, Index of Land Instruments for Bruce County, Ontario, Microfilm A-3-9, Page 249, Instr. 255, 08 Oct 1864. Discharges mortgage of Instr. #205.

7. Bruce County Registrar, Index of Land Instruments for Bruce County, Ontario, Microfilm A-3-9, Page 249, Instr. #861, 19 Jun 1867. This mortgage was a assigned by grantee Joshua Jamieson to a new grantee Matt Pinkerton on 19 Jun 1867 in Instr. #862.

8. Bruce County Registrar, Index of Land Instruments for Bruce County, Ontario, Microfilm A-3-9, Page 249, Instr. 1012, 23 Apr 1868. Discharges mortgage of Instr. 861.

9. Bruce County Registrar, Index of Land Instruments for Bruce County, Ontario, Microfilm A-3-9, Page 249, Instr. 1013, 23 Apr 1868.

10. Bruce County Registrar, Index of Land Instruments for Bruce County, Ontario, Microfilm A-3-9, Page 249, Instr. #1015, 04 May 1868. Discharges mortgage of Instr. 524.

11. 1871 Census of Canada - Ontario: Searchable Database of Heads & Strays, http://db.library.queensu.ca/dbtw-wpd/exec/dbtwpub.dll, Dist. 27, Subdist H, Div 1, Pg 9, 1871, Queen's University Libraries, 99 University Avenue, Kingston, Ontario K7L 3N6. "Henry, head, age 31, Primitive Methodist, farmer." [QUL001]

12. Bruce County Registrar, Index of Land Instruments for Bruce County, Ontario, Microfilm A-3-9, Page 249, Instr. 2058, 5 Par 1871.

13. Bruce County Registrar, Index of Land Instruments for Bruce County, Ontario, Microfilm A-3-9, Page 249, Instr. #2172, 15 Aug 1871. Discharges mortgage of Instr. #1013.

14. Bruce County Registrar, Land Records of Bruce County, Ontario, Reel A-65, Instr. #2173, 10 Aug 1871.

15. Bruce County Registrar, Index of Land Instruments for Bruce County, Ontario, Microfilm A-3-9, Page 249, Instr. #3658, 16 Mar 1876. Discharges mortgage of Instr. #2085.

16. 1880 U.S. Census of Michigan, Charlevoix County, Bear Lake Township, Page 17, Lines 34-41, 24 Jun 180, Family History Library, 35 North West Temple, Salt Lake City, Utah 84150, Microfilm #1254576. "Bacon, Henry, head, age 40, farmer; Elizabeth, wife, age 36; Isaac, son, age 15; Albert E., son, age 13; Joseph, son, age 10; Jane, dau., age 7; Theodore, son, age 4; Lillie, dau., age 2." Bear Lake Twp, Charlevoix County, was absorbed into Resort Twp, Charlevoix County in Aug 1880. Resort Twp was moved from Charlevoix County to Emmet County on 6 Apr 1896. [WWD144, 29-31]

17. 1900 U.S. Census of Michigan, Emmet County, Resort Township, National Archives T623, Roll #710, Page 17, Lines 86-93, 10 Jul 1900, Detroit Public Library, 5201 Woodward Avenue, Detroit, Michigan 48202. Family History Library microfilm #1240710. "Bacon, Henry, head, age 60, born Oct 1839, farmer; Elizabeth, wife, born Aug 1844, age 56; Huston T., son, born Oct 1875, age 24; Lillie M.H., dau., born May 1878, age 22; Dollie M., dau., born Apr 1887, age 19; Allace M., dau., born Sep 1883, age 16; Lucy V., dau., born Jan 1886 age 14." [WWD002, 5]

18. *Directory, Petoskey City & Emmet County* (R.L. Polk & Company, 68-70-72 Griswold Street, Detroit, Michigan, 1973), Page 268, 1903, Petoskey Public Library, 451 East Mitchell Street, Petoskey, Michigan 49770. [WWD109, 1]

19. 1910 U.S. Census of Michigan, Emmet County, Resort Township, Page 285, Lines 66-70, 18 May 1910, Family History Library, 35 North West Temple, Salt Lake City, Utah 84150, Microfilm #1374658. "Bacon, Henry, head, age 70; Elizabeth, wife, age 66, Huston T., son, age 34; Dolly M., dau., age 29; Couch, Alfred, nephew, age 8." Alfred is the son of Edward and Harriet Couch. Edward is Elizabeth's brother. [WWD180, 106-107]

20. *The Petoskey Evening News and Daily Resorter*, Wednesday, September 13, 1916, 13 Sep 1916, The Collection of Dean Wheaton, 5976 Kungle Road, Clinton, OH 44216-9317. [ODD001, 38]

21. Rehkopf, Mildred, Ed., *Resort Township Remembers*, Printed by Mitchell Graphics, Petoskey, Michigan (Resort Township, 1992), Page 12, 1992, The Collection of Dean Wheaton, 5976 Kungle Road, Clinton, OH 44216-9317.

22. Petoskey Public Schools Students, *Many Moons* (Petoskey High School, 1952), Page 31, The Collection of Dean Wheaton, 5976 Kungle Road, Clinton, OH 44216-9317. Family history stories by students on the occasion of the Petoskey Centennial.

23. Olmstead, David D., Genealogical Information on the Morford, Bacon and Couch Families, Unpublished, 1995, The Collection of Dean Wheaton, 5976 Kungle Road, Clinton, OH 44216-9317, ODD001.

24. Wheaton, Dean, Interview with Ruth Bacon Bates, Conducted 20 Jul 1994 in Kentwood, Michigan, Unpublished , The Collection of Dean Wheaton, 5976 Kungle Road, Clinton, OH 44216-9317, WWD079.

25. LDS Church, *International Genealogical Index: Ontario*, Mar 1992, Microfiche P0028, Page 282, Family History Library, 35 North West Temple, Salt Lake City, Utah 84150. "Bacon, Henry, Elizabeth McCouch M 27 Jan 1863, Bruce." Bride's surname should be Couch not McCouch. [IGI005, 1]

26. Greenwood Cemetery, Greenwood Cemetery Records, Bacon Extract, Seq # 1374-3. "Age 72y 10m 4d, DoD 20 Jun 1916, Funeral 22 Jun 1916, Burial 22 Jun 1916, Stone Funeral Home, Petoskey." DoB computed from DoD and age is 18 Aug 1843.

27. St. John's Anglican Church, Parish Registers of St. John's Anglican Church, Peterborough, Ontario, Sec. 3, 1842-1849, Trent Valley Archives, 567 Carnegie Avenue, Peterborough, Ontario K9L 1N1. [TVA001]

28. County Clerk, Death Records of Emmet County, Michigan 1907-1920, Vol. 1907-1920, Rec. #133, 07 Aug 1917. "DoD 20 Jun 1916, Married, age 72y 10m 4d, PoD Petoskey, PoB Canada, Parents: Chris Couch and Mary A. Tie."

29. *The Petoskey Evening News and Daily Resorter*, 20 Jun 1916.

30. Bacon, Henry, et al, *Bacon, Henry Family Bible*, A typed copy of the Bible family pages by Laetha Alldread (Unpublished), The Collection of Dean Wheaton, 5976 Kungle Road, Clinton, OH 44216-9317, DB0010.

31. *Bruce County Cemetery Gravestone Readings*, Old Bethel Methodist/Prior Cemetery, Page 2, #7, Bruce County Museum & Archives, 33 Victoria Street North, Southampton, Ontario N0H 2L0. "Bacon: Gone to Soon Mary Ann daughter of Henry & Elizabeth Bacon died 2nd Jan 1864 ages 1 month 4 days." DoB computed from DoD - age = 29 Nov 1863. [OBC009]

32. County Clerk, Death Records of Charlevoix County, Michigan 1868-1913, Genealogical Society of Utah, Vol. I, Page 98, Rec. #388, Family History Library, 35 North West Temple, Salt Lake City, Utah 84150, Microfilm #0965393. Microfilm label has dates of 1868-1905 but records are on the film as late as 1913. "Death 17 Apr 1900 in Hayes Twp of a cerebral tumor, married, age 35y 7m 9d, PoB Canada, farmer, parents: Henry Bacon & Elizabeth Couch." DoB computed from DoD and age = 8 Sep 1864; this conflicts with most other secondary sources which have 8 Dec 1864. [WWD127, 28]

33. Bacon, Elizabeth, *Bacon (Henry & Elizabeth) Family Bible Births*, 08 Dec 1864, The Collection of Dean Wheaton, 5976 Kungle Road, Clinton, OH 44216-9317, DB0011. Photographic copy of the births page from the Bible, 2 Nov 1945.

34. Greenwood Cemetery, Greenwood Cemetery Records, Bacon Extract: Seq #1374-1. "Bacon, Isaac; age 35y 7m 9d; Sec F, Blk 84, Grave 10; DoD 17 Apr 1900; Funeral & Burial 19 Apr 1900 Stone Funeral Home, Petoskey; marker on his grave." DoB computed from DoD and age = 8 Sep 1864.

35. Wheaton, Dean, Gravestone Photographs at Greenwood Cemetery, Unpublished, Roll 591, Frames 02 & 04, 07 Jun 1999, The Collection of Dean Wheaton, 5976 Kungle Road, Clinton, OH 44216-9317. 591-02: five individual & family stones; 591-04: right-most two individual stones Huston 1875-1959 and Isaac 1864-1900; Sec F, Blk 84.

36. Kalbfleisch, Raymond W., *The Bacon Family*, Genealogist, Petoskey, Michigan, Self published, 8 pages, Page 6, The Collection of Dean Wheaton, 5976 Kungle Road, Clinton, OH 44216-9317, KRW001. Copied from Raymond's original by Dean Wheaton on 1 Aug 1994 at Petoskey, Michigan. [KRW002, 6]

37. County Clerk, Marriage Records of Emmet County Michigam 1887-1899, Vol. 2, Page 71, Rec. #114, Family History Library, 35 North West Temple, Salt Lake City, Utah 84150, Microfilm #0966507. "Groom: age 23, resident of Resort Twp, born in Canada, farmer, parents: Henry Bacon & Elizabeth Couch; Bride age 25, resident Resort Twp, born in New York, housekeeper, parents: Henry Shannon & Mary Armstrong; neither married before; Richard Yost, clergyman." [WWD040, 7]

38. 1900 U.S. Census of Michigan, Charlevoix County, Hayes Township, Page 14, Lines 15-18, 21 Jun 1900, Family History Library, 35 North West Temple, Salt Lake City, Utah 84150, Microfilm #1240706. "Shannon, Henry, head, born May 1830 in New York, age 70; Mary, wife, born Jul 1832 in Canada, age 67; Bacon, Mary, dau., born Jun 1873 in New York, age 27, widow; Fish, Milton, boarder, born Jun 1899, age 11/12 in Michigan." Mary is living with her parents two months after husband Isaac's death. [WWD163, 9]

39. *Bacon, Henry, Family Bible Records (Ruth Bate's Copy)*, The Collection of Dean Wheaton, 5976 Kungle Road, Clinton, OH 44216-9317, WWD055, 16. Copy of hand-written page, received from Ruth Bacon Bates, 10 Apr 1994, Kentwood, Michigan.

40. Bacon, Elizabeth, *Bacon (Henry & Elizabeth) Family Bible Births*, 25 Feb 1967.

41. *Burial Records, Maple Lawn Cemetery, Boyne City, Michigan*, Lot 15, Grave 7, Clerk's Office Boyne City, Michigan, 319 North Lake Street, Boyne City, Michigan 49712. "Albert Bacon (vault), date of burial Jan 13, 1961, grave 7." [GBC001, 10]

42. 1900 U.S. Census of Michigan, Charlevoix County, Wilson Township, Page 29, Sht 15, Lines 56-57, 19 Jun 1900, Family History Library, 35 North West Temple, Salt Lake City, Utah 84150, Microfilm # 1240706. "Bacon, Albert, head, born Feb 1867 in Canada, age 33, married 7; Bernice, wife, born Mar 1873 in Michigan, age 27." [WWD007, 3]

43. 1920 U.S. Census of Michigan, Charlevoix County, Boyne City Village, Page 149, Lines 52-54, 20 Jan 1920, Family History Library, 35 North West Temple, Salt Lake City, Utah 84150, Microfilm #1820758. "Bacon, Albert, head, age 52, laborer at factory; Sarah L., wife, age 40; Aldread, Jenevieve, step-dau., age 15; living on Marel Street in a rented house." [WWD189, 9]

44. Morford, William H., *Albert Edward Bacon: Son of Henry & Elizabeth Bacon* (Unpublished, 1963), The Collection of Dean Wheaton, 5976 Kungle Road, Clinton, OH 44216-9317, WMH001, 2. Written for the 1963 Bacon-Morford-Wheaton Reunion held at Magnus Park in Petoskey, Michigan.

45. County Clerk, Marriage Records of Charlevoix County, Michigan 1868-1925, Vol., 2, Page 212, Rec. #159, Family History Library, 35 North West Temple, Salt Lake City, Utah 84150, Microfilm #0965392. "William: age 37, resides in Boyne City, born in Canada, laborer, Parents: not given & Jennie Ruth; Bernice Bacon/Bernice Newville: age 38, resides in Boyne City, born in Michigan, housewife, Parents: John Newville & not given; both married once previous, Jay M. Gleason Minister, Witnesses: Harle & Mrs Harle Wilson." [WWD054, 17]

46. County Clerk, Marriage Records of Charlevoix County, Michigan 1868-1925, Vol. 2, Page 213, Rec. #178. "Albert: age 25, resides in Boyne City, born in Canada, farmer, Parents: Henry Bacon & Elizabeth Couch; Ella: Poequette nee Fanan, age 38, resides in Boyne City, born in Michigan; housekeeper; Parents: James & not given; JA Bready, minister, both married once previous; witnesses: Joseph E Bacon & Sarah A Bacon."

47. County Clerk, Marriage Records of Charlevoix County, Michigan 1868-1925, Vol. 2, Page 298, Rec. 82. "Albert: age 51, resides in Boyne City, born in Canada, farmer, Parents: Henry Bacon & Elizabeth Couch, married twice previous; Sarah Alldred, Sarah Newville (divorced), age 40, resides in Boyne City, born in Michigan, domestic, Parents: Frank Newville, married once previous; Rev. Henry Candler, Clergyman, Witnesses: Bessie & Emily Candler, Charlevoix."

48. Boyne City Registrar, Certificate of Death for Sarah L. (Newville) Bacon, Unpublished, Local File #1, The Collection of Dean Wheaton, 5976 Kungle Road, Clinton, OH 44216-9317, GBC002, 1. "Deceased: Sarah Louise Bacon, 529 E. Main, Boyne CIty; DoD: 25 Jan 1952; married, DoB: 19 Jun 1878; age 73; housewife; Parents: John Newville, Clara ?; Informant: Albert Bacon; Cause of Death: cerebral hemorrhage (6 days) arterio sclerosis (2 yrs); AF Litzenburger, MD; Burial: 29 Jan 1952, Maple Lawn, Stackus [Funeral Home], Boyne City."

49. *Burial Records, Maple Lawn Cemetery, Boyne City, Michigan*, Lot 15, Grave 6. "Sarah L. Bacon (Died 1/25/62), age 37, Burial April 22, 1952." Date of death clearly should be "1952" instead of "1962".

50. Cushing, Avis (Pagel), Family Records: Cushing, Avis to Wheaton, Dean, Letter dated 13 Sep 1995, Page 11, 13 Sep 1995, The Collection of Dean Wheaton, 5976 Kungle Road, Clinton, OH 44216-9317, PAE001. [PAE001, 11]

51. Bacon, Henry, *Family Bible Records (Ruth Bate's Copy)*, 31 Mar 1870.

52. Vital Records Inquiry, Emmet County, Michigan Deaths, Bacon, Printed 30 Aug 1994, Unpublished, The Collection of Dean Wheaton, 5976 Kungle Road, Clinton, OH 44216-9317. Screen prints by the County Clerk. "Bacon, Joseph, death 28 Sep 1972 in Petoskey, Lib/Fol: 72/P216." [GEM003, 7]

53. Burial Records, Maple Lawn Cemetery, Boyne City, Michigan, Lot 218, Grave 5. "Joseph Bacon, age 102, burial Sept. 30, 1952." The year of burial clearly should be 1972; Lot 218, Grave 5.

54. Wheaton, Dean, Gravestone Photographs at Maple Lawn Cemetery, Boyne City, Michigan, Unpublished, Roll 443, Frame 34, 25 Jul 1994, The Collection of Dean Wheaton, 5976 Kungle Road, Clinton, OH 44216-9317. "Joseph E. Bacon Mar. 31, 1870, Sept. 28, 1972."

55. 1900 U.S. Census of Michigan, Charlevoix County, Hayes Township, Page 14, Lines 4-8, 21 Jun 1900. "Bacon, Joseph E., head, born Mar 1871in Canada, age 29, married 6 yrs, blacksmith, renting; Sarah H., wife, born Aug 1876 in Canada, age 23; Esther, dau., born Oct 1895 in Michigan; Carl, son, born May 1898 in Michigan, Casady, Leslie, boarder, born Jun 1881 in Michigan, age 18, blacksmith."

56. 1920 U.S. Census of Michigan, Charlevoix County, Boyne City Village, Page 277, Lines 69-76, 28 Apr 1910. "Bacon, Joseph E., head, State Street, age 40, married 15 yrs, blacksmith in owned shop; Sarah A., wife, age 31, 7 children 6 living; Esther J., dau., age 14; Carl J., son, age 11; Ruth S., dau., age 9; Earl F., son, age 7; Nina, dau., age 3; Ernest C., son, age 0/12."

57. 1920 U.S. Census of Michigan, Emmet County, Resort Township, Page 163, Lines 79 84, 02 Jan 1902, Family History Library, 35 North West Temple, Salt Lake City, Utah 84150, Microfilm #1820763. Also NARA T625, Reel 763. "Bacon, Joseph E., head, age 49, farmer; Sarah A., wife, age 41; Carl J., son, age 21; Earl F., son, age 16; Nina M., dau., age 12; John H., son, age 7; also living in the home: Schuler, Esther J., head, age 24, Lucille, B., dau., age 4." Esther Schuler is the widowed daughter of Joseph & Sarah Bacon. [WWD190, 95]

58. *Directory, Petoskey City & Emmet County*, Vol. 1924-1925, Page 283, 1924.

59. Morford, William H., *Joseph Elias Bacon: Son of Henry & Elizabeth Bacon* (Unpublished, 1963), The Collection of Dean Wheaton, 5976 Kungle Road, Clinton, OH 44216-9317, WMH001, 1. Written for the 1963 Bacon-Morford-Wheaton Reunion.

60. *Joe Bacon Plans on Becoming Centenarian* (Petoskey News-Review, Petoskey, Michigan), Page ?, Mar 1969, The Collection of Dean Wheaton, 5976 Kungle Road, Clinton, OH 44216-9317. On the occasion of Joe's 99th birthday. [DB0007]

61. Dammann, Tom, *Hemingway Pal Browses Through the Vintage Past* (Petoskey News-Review, Petoskey, Michigan), Page ?, Mar 1970, The Collection of Dean Wheaton, 5976 Kungle Road, Clinton, OH 44216-9317. On the occasion of Joe's 100th birthday. [DB0005]

62. *Joe Bacon, Emmet Resident for 94 Years Dies at 102* (Petoskey News-Review), Page 1, 29 Sep 1972, The Collection of Dean Wheaton, 5976 Kungle Road, Clinton, OH 44216-9317. [DB0013]

63. Brown, Michael C., *Family Economic History*, Pages 4-6, 20 Apr 1993, The Collection of Dean Wheaton, 5976 Kungle Road, Clinton, OH 44216-9317, BMC001. A paper submitted as a requirement for a college course. Obtained from Michael's grandmother, Bessie (Pop) Bacon, wife of John [4], 30 Jul 1994. [BMC001]

64. Wheaton, Dean, Interview with Ruth Bacon Bates, Page 1, 20 Jul 1994. "Dad was all business, all farm stock (cows, pigs, dog, etc.) were all registered."

65. County Clerk, Marriage Records of Charlevoix County, Michigan 1868-1925, Vol. 2, Page 43, Rec. #349. "Joseph: age 24, resides in Resort Twp, born in Canada, farmer, parents: Henry Bacon, Elizabeth Couch; Sarah: age 17, resides in Hayes Twp, born Canada, housemaid, parents: John Brown & Thankful Lewis; neither previously married, Fayettte Thompson, Minister of the Gospel, witnesses: Geo Brown & Lillie MH Bacon."

66. Burial Records, Maple Lawn Cemetery, Boyne City, Michigan, Lot 218, Grave 3. "Mrs. Joe Bacon, burial Jan 4, 1936, grave 3."

67. Wheaton, Dean, Gravestone Photographs at Maple Lawn Cemetery, Boyne City, Michigan, Roll 443, Frame 35, 25 Jul 1994. "Sarah A. Bacon, Born Aug. 20, 1877, Died 2 Jan 1936." Lot 218, Grave 3.

68. County Clerk, Marriage Records of Emmet County, Michigan 1932-1956, Vol. A-K, Page 12-C, Rec. #3, Family History Library, 35 North West Temple, Salt Lake City, Utah 84150, Microfilm #0966508. "Joseph: age 81, resides Petoskey RFD, born in Canada, retired, married previously once, parents: Henry Bacon & Elizabeth Couch; Sara: age 76, resides in Petoskey, born in Michigan, married previously twice, parents: Joseph & Hattie Steel; Wm Morford, Minister; witnesses: Earl Bacon & Margaret Frost both of Detroit." Wm Morford is Joe's nephew, son of sister Jennie. [WWD134, 4]

69. Bacon, Elizabeth, *Bacon (Henry & Elizabeth) Family Bible Births*, 11 Dec 1872.

70. Bacon, Henry, et al, *Bacon, Henry Family Bible.*

71. Greenwood Cemetery, Greenwood Cemetery Records, Morford Extract, Seq #2722-1. "Sec H, Blk 168, Lot 3, Pos. NW 1/4, Grave 1; age 83y 4m 29d; DoD 5/10/56; Funeral 5/14/56; Burial 5/13/56; Stone Funeral Home, Petoskey."

72. County Clerk, Marriage Records of Charlevoix County, Michigan 1868-1925, Vol. 2, Page 24, Rec. #71. "Edwin: age 25, resides in Resort Twp, farmer, Parents: WL Morford & Francis Dickerson; Jennie: age 18, resides in Resort Twp, housemaid, Parents: Henry Bacon & Lizzie Couch; David Engle, Minister of the Gospel, Witnesses: Fred Wooden & Abbie Brown, both of Resort Twp."

73. Olmstead, David D., Morford, Thomas & Bacon Families, Unpublished, Page 6, The Collection of Dean Wheaton, 5976 Kungle Road, Clinton, OH 44216-9317, ODD001. Received via letter postmarked 9 May 1994.

74. Olmstead, David D., Morford, Thomas & Bacon Families, Page 11. Edwin was originally buried in the North Bay Cemetery, Sec. 20, Bay Twp, Charlevoix Co. beside his first wife, Luella Hunt, in Feb 1947 at second wife Jennie's insistance. Son William had his father reinterred in Greenwood Cemetery on 6 Aug 1956 beside his mother, Jennie, because North Bay Cemetery did not have perpetual care.

75. Greenwood Cemetery, Greenwood Cemetery Records, Morford Extract, Seq #2722-2. "Sec H, Blk 168, Lot 3, Pos. NW 1/4, Grave 2; age 80y 4m 7d; DoD 21 Feb 1947; Funeral 25 Feb 1947; Burial 6 Aug 1956; Stone Funeral Home."

76. 1900 U.S. Census of Michigan, Emmet County, Petoskey City, Page 2, Lines 71-75, 12 Jun 1900, Family History Library, 35 North West Temple, Salt Lake City, Utah 84150, Microfilm #1240710. "Morford, Edwin, head, living on Emmet Street, age 33, carpenter; Jane A, wife, age 27, 6 children 3 living; Hazel, dau., age 4; William H, son, age 4; Aaron E., son, age 1/12." [WWD178, 41]

77. 1910 U.S. Census of Michigan, Emmet County, Resort Township, Page 285, Lines 71-76, 18 May 1910. "Morford, Edward A., head, age 43, carpenter & farmer; Jennie A., wife, age 37, 7 children 4 living; Hazel M., dau., age 14; William H., son, age 13; Chalmers Z., son, age 10; Bernice, dau., age 7."

78. Olmstead, David D., Morford, Thomas & Bacon Families, Pages 6-12.

79. Rehkopf, Mildred, Ed., *Resort Township Remembers*, Page 11-12, 15, 1992.

80. Krenich, Dorothy Munson, *Muhqua Nebis: A Compilation of Legends of Walloon* (Walloon Trust, 1984), Page 13, The Collection of Dean Wheaton, 5976 Kungle Road, Clinton, OH 44216-9317. While Ed & Jennie are not specifically mention, other sections describe other aspects of Resort Twp and Walloon Lake.

81. Morford, William Henry, *Memories: Growing up on a Northern Michigan Farm 1900-1914* (PineCone Genealogy, Clinton, Ohio, 1994), The Collection of Dean Wheaton, 5976 Kungle Road, Clinton, OH 44216-9317.

82. *Obituary of Edwin Alfred Morford* (The Flint Journal, Flint, Michigan), The Collection of Dean Wheaton, 5976 Kungle Road, Clinton, OH 44216-9317. A copy of the obituary is contained in "The Morford-Thomas-Bacon Families", Olmstead, David D. (ODD001, 11).

83. Bacon, Elizabeth, *Bacon (Henry & Elizabeth) Family Bible Births*, 11 Oct 1875.

84. Vital Records Inquiry, Emmet County, Michigan Deaths, Bacon, Lib/Fol: 59/215.

85. Greenwood Cemetery, Greenwood Cemetery Records, Bacon Extract, Seq # 1374-2. "Bacon, Theodore Huston, age 84y 0m 8d, Sec G, Blk 84, Lot 10, Grave 2, marker, DoD 19 Oct 1959, Funeral 22 Oct 1959, burial 22 Oct 1959, Stone Funeral Home, Petoskey."

86. 1920 U.S. Census of Michigan, Emmet County, Resort Township, Page 163, Lines 63-67, 02 Jan 1920. "Wheaton, Harlow, head, age 54, farmer; Mary E., wife, age 44; Rena M., dau. age 23; Bacon, Theodore H, boarder, age 42, laborer sawmill; Eaton, Harry, boarder, age 30, laborer sawmill."

87. Bacon, Elizabeth, *Bacon (Henry & Elizabeth) Family Bible Births*, 10 May 1878.

88. Vital Records Inquiry, Emmet County, Michigan Deaths, Bacon, Lib/Fol: 60/11.

89. Greenwood Cemetery, Greenwood Cemetery Records, Lot Seq #3105-10. "Sec K, Blk 90, Lot 19, Grave 11b."

90. Marriage Records of Emmet County, Michigan 1900-1906, Vol. 1, Page 313, Rec. # 58, Family History Library, 35 North West Temple, Salt Lake City, Utah 84150, Micorfilm #0966507. "Walter: age 28, resides in Bay Springs, carpenter, parents: Andrew Wheaton & Eliza Jane B; Lillie: age 26, resides in Resort, teacher, parents: Henry Bacon & Elizabeth Couch; neither previously married; Witnesses: W Wheaton & Lucy Bacon." [WWD041, 1]

91. Wheaton Family Bible (Walter & Jennie), Copied by Veda Wheaton (dau.), Unpublished, Page 1, The Collection of Dean Wheaton, 5976 Kungle Road, Clinton, OH 44216-9317. Received in a letter from Veda (Wheaton) Anderson 29 Oct 1992. [WVE001, 2]

92. County Clerk, Death Records of Emmet County, Michigan 1931-1956, Surnames S-Z, Page 62, Rec. #74, Family History Library, 35 North West Temple, Salt Lake City, Utah 84150, Microfilm #09660505. "PoD: Lockwood Hospital, Petoskey; spouse Lillie; DoB 18 Apr 1875; DoD 28 Apr 1945; age 70y 0m 10d; carpenter & farmer; coronary thrombosis; burial 1 May 1945 at Greenwood; RL Peters, undertaker." [WWD107, 4]

93. Greenwood Cemetery, Greenwood Cemetery Records, Lot Seq #3105-12. "Sec K, Blk 90, Lot 19, Grave 12."

94. City Clerk, Burial Permit for Walter R. Wheaton, City of Petoskey, #71, The Collection of Dean Wheaton, 5976 Kungle Road, Clinton, OH 44216-9317. "Walter R Wheaton, DoD 28 Apr 1945, age 70, coronary thrombosis, Dr. Lashmet, Undertaker: Ralph L. Peters."

95. P.A. & J.W. Myers, Surveyors and Draughtsmen, *1902 Plat Book of Emmet County Michigan* (The Consolidated Publishing Company, 610 Boston Block, Minneapolis, Minnesota, E.P. Noll & Co., Map Publishers, No. 9 North 6th Street, Philadelphia, Pennsylvania, 1902), Page 8, The Collection of Dean Wheaton, 5976 Kungle Road, Clinton, OH 44216-9317. Republished as *Grandfather's Land*, PO Box 8, Hemlock, Michigan 48626, 1973 in 8.5" X 11" paperback format without attribution to the original.

96. *Directory, Petoskey City & Emmet County*, Vol. 1903, Page 350.

97. *Directory, Petoskey City & Emmet County*, Vol. 1909-1910, Page 358.

98. 1910 U.S. Census of Michigan, Charlevoix County, Boyne City Village, Page 266, Lines 4-6, 20 Apr1910, Family History Library, 35 North West Temple, Salt Lake City, Utah 84150, Microfilm #1364653. "Wheaton, Walter R., North Lake Street, head, age 34, married once for 5 yrs, laborer on lumber dock, ownes home has mortgage; Lillie M.H., wife, age 32, 1 child living; Mamie, dau., age 3." [WWD182, 8]

99. Wheaton, Dean, Interview of Bertie Foster (notes), Unpublished , Page 1, The Collection of Dean Wheaton, 5976 Kungle Road, Clinton, OH 44216-9317. "Postcards written by Walter & Jennie: 22 Aug 1912 and 23 Aug 1912 from Winnipeg." Travel was by train, Walter & Jennie Wheaton with children Mamie & Veda, Albert & Ella Bacon (Jennie's brother & sister-in-law) to Crandall, Manitoba to visit Jennie's and Albert's Uncle John Bacon; Walter's 3rd child was named Virden for Virden, Manitoba. [FRM002, 1]

100. *Directory, Petoskey City & Emmet County*, Vol 1919-1920, Page 380.

101. 1920 U.S. Census of Michigan, Emmet County, Friendship Township, Page 48, lines 38-42, 20 Jan 1920, Family History Library, 35 North West Temple, Salt Lake City, Utah 84150, Microfilm #1820763. "Wheaton, Walter R., head, age 45, farmer; Lillie M.H., wife, age 41, public school teacher; Mamie, dau., age 13; Veda L.D., dau., age 7; Virden, son, age 5." [WWD190, 47]

102. *Directory, Petoskey City & Emmet County*, Vol. 1925, Page 370-371.

103. *Directory, Petoskey City & Emmet County*, Vol. 1925, Page 311. Listed in the names of W.R. & Lillie Wheaton.

104. County Clerk, Death Records of Emmet County, Michigan 1931-1956, Surnames A-K, Page 12C, Rec. #127. "Dollie: unmarried, DoD 16 Jun 1945 at Traverse City; age 66; chronic myocarditis; informant: Traverse City State Hospital records."

105. Greenwood Cemetery, Greenwood Cemetery Records, Bacon Extract, Lot Seq #1374-6. "Dollie: DoD 16 Jun 1945; age 66y 1m 16d; buried 19 Jun 1945 in Sec F, Blk 84, Lot 10, Grave 6; Funeral: Stone Funeral Home, Petoskey, 19 Jun 1945."

106. Notes Book of Warner & Lucy Wheaton, Unpublished, Page 2, The Collection of Dean Wheaton, 5976 Kungle Road, Clinton, OH 44216-9317. "Nov. 26, 1918 Tuesday, Mable taken to Traverse City; Taken to Charley Miller's Nov 23, 1918." Mabel was mentally handicapped either from birth or an illness at age 3. She was committed to the State Hospital when she struck Sarah (Albert's wife?) with a stick of wood. Apparently there had been other "incidents". Henry Pagel(s) (husband of Emma Bacon) was her guardian. [WWA001]

107. Wheaton, Dean, Interview with Ruth Bacon Bates, 20 Jul 1994.

108. County Clerk, Birth Records of Emmet County, Michigan, Vol 1, Page 93, Rec. #1316, 28 May 1884, Family History Library, 35 North West Temple, Salt Lake City, Utah 84150,

Microfilm #0965394. "Emma: "Emerson" A.F. Bacon; DoB 7 Sep 1883; parents: Henry & Elizabeth Bacon." [WWD047, 13]

109. Bacon, Elizabeth, *Bacon (Henry & Elizabeth) Family Bible Births*, 07 Sep 1883.

110. Greenwood Cemetery, Greenwood Cemetery Records, Pagel Extract, Seq #174-7. "Emma; DoD 25 Nov 1974, age 91; funeral & burial 27 Nov 1974 by Stone Funeral Home, Petoskey in Greenwood Cemetery in Sec D, Blk 18, Lot 7, Grave 7."

111. Marriage Records of Emmet County, Michigan 1900-1906, Vol. 1, Page 222, Rec. #155. "Henry: age 24, resides in Resort, farmer, parents: Christian Pagels & Massie?; Emma: age 22, resides in Resort, housework, Parents: Henry Bacon & Elizabeth Couch; first mariage for both, Frank H Boyles, Clergyman, Witnesses: Huston Bacon & ? Pagels."

112. Cushing, Avis (Pagel), Family Records: Cushing, Avis to Wheaton, Dean, Page 2. "PoB Saginaw, DoB 6 Jul 1882." This date and place of birth conflict with Charlevoix County birth record.

113. County Clerk, Birth Records of Charlevoix County, Michigan 1868-1906, Unpublished, Vol 1, Page 89, Rec. #1251, 06 Jun 1883, Family History Library, 35 North West Temple, Salt Lake City, Utah 84150, Microfilm #0965394. "DoB 6 Jul 1882, PoB Petoskey, parents: Christ & Mary Pagel of Resort." [WWD047, 11]

114. Greenwood Cemetery, Greenwood Cemetery Records, Pagle Extract, Seq #174-8. "Died 15 Mar 1972 at age 90, Funeral 18 March 1972 by Stone Funeral Home, Petoskey, burial 18 Mar 1972 in Sec D, Blk 18, Lot 7, Grave 8 with marker." The burial date is given as 5/18/1972 which is probably a typo and should be 3/18/1972.

115. Emmet County Abstract & Title Company, 22 Oct 1934, Abstract of Title to T34N R5W, Sec 19, E 3/4 of N 1/2 of SW 1/4 (60 acres), No. 17081, Instr. # 14, Page 6, 15 Mar 1904, The Collection of Dean Wheaton, 5976 Kungle Road, Clinton, OH 44216-9317. Purchased by Henry C. Pagel(s) from Guy D. Carpenter. [DW0064]

116. 1910 U.S. Census of Michigan, Emmet County, Resort Township, Page 277, Lines14-19, 25 Apr 1910. "Pagels, Henry C., head, age 28, married once for 4 yrs, farmer; Emma A.F., wife, age 26, married once for 4 yrs, one child living; Edith M., dau., age 6/12; Christian, father, age 64, married 2nd for 5 yrs, farmer; Josephine, step-mother, age 59, married 2nd for 5 yrs, Ella, sister, age 20."

117. Emmet County Abstract & Title Company, 22 Oct 1934, Abstract of Title to T34N R5W, Sec 19, E 3/4 of N 1/2 of SW 1/4 (60 acres), No. 17081, Instr. # 15, Page 6, 10 Jun 1919. Sold by Henry C. & Emma A. Pagel(s) to Warner A. and Lucy V. Wheaton.

118. 1920 U.S. Census of Michigan, Emmet County, Resort Township, Page 159, 02 Jan 1920. "Pagels, Henry C., head, age 38, farmer; Emma A., wife, age 36; Edith M., dau., age 11; Leo G., son. age 7; Avis E., dau., age 1 7/12."

119. Morford, William H., *Henry & Emma (Bacon) Pagel* (Unpublished, 1965), Page 1, 1965, The Collection of Dean Wheaton, 5976 Kungle Road, Clinton, OH 44216-9317, WMH001, 6. Written for the Bacon-Morford-Wheaton Reunion. [MWH001, 6]

120. *Henry & Emma Pagel Celebrate 64th Wedding Anniversary* (Petoskey News-Review, 19 Nov 1969), Page 2, 19 Nov 1969, The Collection of Dean Wheaton, 5976 Kungle Road, Clinton, OH 44216-9317. Story has Henry's name as Leo in bold header. [DB0008]

121. County Clerk, Birth Records of Charlevoix County, Michigan 1868-1906, Vol. 1, Page 146, Rec. #101, 30 Apr 1887.

122. County Clerk, Death Records of Emmet County, Michigan 1931-1956, Surnames S-Z, Page 61, Rec. #209, 02 Sep 1939. "PoD: Little Traverse Hospital, Petoskey, married, spouse Warner Wheaton, DoB 30 Jan 1886, age 53y 7m 0d, housewife, father: Henry Bacon, mother: Elizabeth Couch, informant: Warner Wheaton, Burial: 3 Sep 1939, Greenwood Cemetery, Ralph L. Peters, undertaker, Cause of death: coronary thombosis." Lucy had a large goiter which she went into the hospital to have it removed. During or immediately after the surgery she died. Dr. Dean C. Burns was the surgeon (later well known for his Burns Clinic) he did not sign the death certificate (it is unsigned) although he is listed on her Burial Permit as the medical attendant. Son Alton was very angry and bitter about what happened and would never go or allow any of his family to go to either the Burns Clinic or the Little Traverse Hospital.

123. City Clerk, Burial Permit for Lucy V. Wheaton, No. 127, 02 Sep 1939, The Collection of Dean Wheaton, 5976 Kungle Road, Clinton, OH 44216-9317. "DoD: 30 Aug 1939, age 53, coronary thombosis, medical attendant: Dr. Dean C. Burns. Burial: Greenwood 2 Sep 1939, Undertaker: Ralph L. Peters, Petoskey." [GGC097, 3]

124. Greenwood Cemetery, Greenwood Cemetery Records, Wheaton Extract, Seq #26-3. "Lucy: DoD 0 Aug 1939, age 53, Funeral & Burial: 2 Sep 1939 by Peters Funeral Home, Petoskey; Greenwood Sec A, Blk 7, Lot 6, Grave 3."

125. Marriage Records of Emmet County, Michigan 1900-1906, Vol. 1, Page 313, Rec. #167. "Warner: age 21, resides in Petoskey, farmer, parents: Andrew Wheaton & Eliza J. Benway; Lucy, age 20, resides in Resort; first marriage for both, Samuel W. Large, Clergyman, witnesses: Maude Hall & Edgar Wheaton." An Original Marriage Certificate on heavy paper is in the Library of Dean Wheaton (DB0073).

126. County Clerk, Certificate of Birth of Warner Wheaton (Certified), Li. 1, P 124, Rec. #1779, 26 Aug 1886, The Collection of Dean Wheaton, 5976 Kungle Road, Clinton, OH 44216-9317. "Warner Abner Wheaton: 12 Aril 1885, Legit, Norwood, parents: Andrew Wheaton, Norwood, born in New York, farmer; Eliza Benway, Norwood, born in Denmark; Date of copy: 4 Jun 1962." Both parent's PoB is wrong, should be Canada for both. [GMI001]

127. County Clerk, Birth Records of Charlevoix County, Michigan 1868-1906, Vol., 1, Page 124, Rec. #1779, 26 Aug 1886. "Andrew Wheaton: 12 April 1885, Norwood, parents: Andrew Wheaton, Norwood, Born in New York, farmer; Lizzie Wheaton, Norwood, born in Denmark." Compare this record to the certified copy of it and wonder where the information on the certified copy came from.

128. Vital Records Inquiry, Emmet County, Michigan Deaths, Bacon, Lib/Fol: 67/C16.

129. Greenwood Cemetery, Greenwood Cemetery Records, Wheaton Extract, Seq #26-2. "DoD 28 Apr 1967, age 82y 0m 16d, Burial 1 May 1967, Sec A, Blk 7, Lot 6, Grave 2, Stone Funeral Home, Petoskey."

130. *Boyne Citizen* (Boyne City, Michigan), 18 Jun 1907, The Collection of Dean Wheaton, 5976 Kungle Road, Clinton, OH 44216-9317. "Mr. and Mrs. Warner Wheaton of Resort have arrived in the city and will spend the summer here, Mr. Wheaton having secured employment here." [FR_004]

131. 1910 U.S. Census of Michigan, Charlevoix County, Boyne City Village, Page 268, Lines 2-3, 22 Apr 1910. "Wheaton, Warner A., head, age 25, married once for 3 yrs, laborer at the chemical plant, renting a house at 508 North Park Street; Lucy V., wife, age 21, married once for 3 yrs, no children."

132. Emmet County Abstract & Title Company, 22 Oct 1934, Abstract of Title to T34N R5W, Sec 19, E 3/4 of N 1/2 of SW 1/4 (60 acres), No. 17081, Instr. 15, Page 6, 10 Jun 1919. "Recorded in Book 67 of Deeds on page 440." Purchased by Warner A. Wheaton from Henry C. and Emma Pagel(s).

133. Emmet County Abstract & Title Company, 22 Oct 1934, Abstract of Title to T34N R5W, Sec 19, E 3/4 of N 1/2 of SW 1/4 (60 acres), No. 17081, Instr. #38, Page 13, 10 Jun 1919. "Book 67 of Deeds, Page 439." Sold by Francis P. and Mary Ann Coveyou to Warner A. & Lucy V. Wheaton.

134. Emmet County Abstract & Title Company, 22 Oct 1934, Abstract of Title to T34N R5W, Sec 19, E 3/4 of N 1/2 of SW 1/4 (60 acres), No. 17081, Instr. #40, Page 13, 10 Jun 1919. "Book 30 of Mortgages, Page 304." by Warner A. and Lucy V. Wheaton to Albert Fochtman for five years at 7% per year.

135. 1920 U.S. Census of Michigan, Emmet County, Resort Township, Page 163, Lines 89-92, 02 Jan 1920. "Wheaton, Warner A., head, age 34, farmer; Lucy V., wife, age 33; Alton A., son, age 4; Lloyd B., son, age 0."

136. *Directory, Petoskey City & Emmet County*, Vol. 1925, Page 371. Name is given as "Warren" instead of "Warner".

137. Emmet County Abstract & Title Company, 22 Oct 1934, Abstract of Title to T34N R5W, Sec 19, E 3/4 of N 1/2 of SW 1/4 (60 acres), No. 17081, Instr. #44, Page 15, 24 May 1933. "Release of Right of Way in Book 91 of Deeds, Page 155."

138. Registrar of Deeds, Chattel Mortgages of Emmet County, Michigan, Page 77, No. 384, 01 Sep 1934, The Collection of Dean Wheaton, 5976 Kungle Road, Clinton, OH 44216-9317. "Conditional Sale Contract & Order, Massey Harris Cultivator; Mortgagors: Warner Wheaton; Mortgagees: Massey-Harris Company; When given: 25 Aug 1934; RFD 1, Petoskey; Discharged." There is no date given for the discharge. [GEM001]

139. Emmet County Abstract & Title Company, 22 Oct 1934, Abstract of Title to T34N R5W, Sec 19, E 3/4 of N 1/2 of SW 1/4 (60 acres), No. 31534, Instr. #1, Page 1, 26 Dec 1934. "Mortgage in Book 38 of Mortgages, Page 319; $1,000 at 5% per year interest ($50 + int.) payable semi-annually on May 1 and Nov 1 from 1 May 1935 to 1 Nov 1944." Warner A. & Lucy V. Wheaton to Land Bank Commissioner for the Emergency Farm Mortgage Act of 1933.

140. County Registrar, Deed of Sale: Couch, Josiah to Wheaton, Warner & Lucy, Liber 621, Page 160, 19 Nov 1934, The Collection of Dean Wheaton, 5976 Kungle Road, Clinton, OH 44216-9317. Why Josiah sold this lot to Warner & Lucy and what they did with it is unknown. [GGE001]

141. Emmet County Abstract & Title Company, 22 Oct 1934, Abstract of Title to T34N R5W, Sec 19, E 3/4 of N 1/2 of SW 1/4 (60 acres), No. 31584, Instr. #1, Page 1, 01 Feb 1935. "Discharge in Book 58 of Mortgages, Page 277 of a Mortgage recorded in Liber 30 of Mortgages, Page 304." Mortgage of $1,050, No. 17081, Instr. #40, Page 13. Albert Fochtman assigned mortgage to Johanna Steffel on 14 Jun 1919. Johanna Steffel died 19 Apr 1934 and Fred Stfefel made Administrator of her estate.

142. Emmet County Abstract & Title Company, 22 Oct 1934, Abstract of Title to T34N R5W, Sec 19, E 3/4 of N 1/2 of SW 1/4 (60 acres), No. 35918, Instr. # 4, Page 3, 30 Oct 1946. "Land Bank Commissioner to Warner A. & Lucy V. Wheaton, Discharge of Mortgage bearing date 1 Nov 1934 recorded in Liber 38 of Mortgages on Page 319 on 26 Dec 1934."

143. Emmet County Abstract & Title Company, 22 Oct 1934, Abstract of Title to T34N R5W, Sec 19, E 3/4 of N 1/2 of SW 1/4 (60 acres), No. 40668, Instr #3, Page 2, 25 Oct 1948. "Deed recorded in Liber 129, Page 577." Warranty Deed from Warner A. & Bertha A. Wheaton to Alton A. & Ruth C. Wheaton.

Modified Register for Joseph Bacon, Sr.

Second Generation - Mary Jane

12. **Mary Jane Bacon** was born[1,2,3] 22 Jan 1847 in Middletown Township, Middlesex County, Canada West. She died[4] about 1905.

Mary purchased land[5] Con 5 Lot 6 (100 acres) from William Bacon, her brother, for $600 on 21 Apr 1864 in Brant Township, Bruce County, Canada West. She was enumerated in a census[6] 1881 in Brant Township, Bruce County, Ontario. She purchased land[7] jointly with William James Guinn (her son), Con 1 NDR, Lot 16 (50 acres) from the heirs of William Guinn Jr. for $1 on 22 Mar 1895 in Brant Township, Bruce County, Ontario. She gave a mortgage[8] jointly with William James Guinn on Con 1 NDR, Lot 16 (50 acres) to Sarah Holmes for $800 on 10 Apr 1895 in Brant Township, Bruce County, Ontario. She gave a mortgage[9] jointly with William James Guinn on Con 1 NDR, Lot 16 (50 acres) to Sarah Holmes for $100 on 15 Aug 1895 in Brant Township, Bruce County, Ontario. She gave a mortgage[10] jointly with William James Guinn on Con 1 NDR, Lot 16 (50 acres) to Sarah Holmes for $108 on 23 Jan 1897 in Brant Township, Bruce County, Ontario.

Mary married[11,12] **William Guinn Jr.**, son of William Gwynne Sr. and Jane Willis, on 13 Feb 1866 in Brant Township, Bruce County, Canada West. William was born[13] about 1834 in Montreal, Ile de Montreal, Quebec. He died[13] 28 Sep 1876 in Walkerton, Bruce County, Ontario.

William received a Crown Patent[14] Con 1 NDR, Lot 16 (50 acres) on 18 May 1854 in Brant Township, Bruce County, Canada West. He purchased land[15] Con 1 NDR, Lot 17 (50 acres) from James Guinn on 19 May 1859 in Brant Township, Bruce County, Canada West. He was enumerated in a census[16,17] in 1871 in Brant Township, Bruce County, Ontario. He sold[18] Con 1 NDR, Lot 17 (50 acres) to James Guinn for $2000 on 10 Feb 1876 in Brant Township, Bruce County, Canada West. He signed a will[19] 29 Nov 1876 in Bruce County, Ontario.

They had the following children:

95 F i. **Mary Guinn** was born[20] about 1866 in Brant Township, Bruce County, Canada West. She died[20] 05 Jun 1934 in Toronto, Ontario and was buried[21] in Mount Pleasant Cemetery, Toronto, Ontario.
Mary resided[22] 22 Mar 1895 in City Of Toronto, York County, Ontario.

Mary married[23] (1) **Thomas Bruce Clarke**, son of Richard Clarke and Eleanor Reynolds, on 05 Jun 1934 in Toronto, Ontario. Thomas was born about 1856 in Bailieborough, County Cavan, Ireland. He died[23] 28 Jan 1908 in Toronto, Ontario.

Mary and Thomas had seven children, two died without being named and three boys and two girls, born 1890-1905, lived through adulthood.

Mary also married[23] (2) **? Walsh** about 1915 in Toronto, Ontario.

96 M ii. **William James Guinn** was born[24] 1868 in Brant Township, Bruce County, Canada West.

William purchased land[24] jointly with Mary Jane Guinn Con 1, Lot 16 NDR (50 acres) from the heirs of William Guinn, Jr. for $1 on 22 Mar 1895 in Brant Township, Bruce County, Ontario. He gave a mortgage[25] jointly with Mary Jane Guinn (his mother) on Con 1 NDR, Lot 16 (50 acres) to Sarah Holmes for $800 on 10 Apr 1895 in Brant Township, Bruce County, Ontario. He gave a mortgage[26] jointly with Mary Jane Guinn on Con 1 NDR, Lot 16 (50 Acres) to Sarah Holmes for $100 on 15 Aug 1895 in Brant Township, Bruce County, Ontario. He gave a mortgage[27] jointly with Mary Jane Guinn on Con 1 NDR, Lot 16 (50 Acres) to Sarah Holmes for $108 on 23 Jan 1897 in Brant Township, Bruce County, Ontario.

William and Susan had two boys, one born in 1893. Subsequent Land Instrument Index entries for Con 1 NDR, Lot 16 are on page 885 of the Bruce County records.

William married[27] **Susan Ritter**. Susan was born[27] in Walkerton, Bruce County, Canada West. She died[27] 21 Feb 1923 in Edmonton, Alberta.

97 F iii. **Susannah Jane Guinn** "Susan" was born[27] about 1870 in Brant Township, Bruce County, Canada West.
Susan resided[27] 22 Mar 1895 in Village Of Britton, Marshall County, South Dakota.

Susan married[27] **Robert McCarter**.

98 M iv. **Richard Guinn** was born[27] 04 Oct 1871 in Brant Township, Bruce County, Canada West.

Richard received a Crown Patent[28] Con 1 NDR, Lot 19 (50 acres) 18 May 1854 in Bruce Township, Bruce County, Canada West. He sold[29] Con 1 NDR, Lot 19 (50 acres) to Hugh H. Todd 28 Jul 1858 in Bruce Township, Bruce County, Canada West. He purchased land[30] Con 1 NDR, Lot 19 (50 acres) from Hugh H. Todd 19 Mar 1866 in Bruce Township, Bruce County, Canada West. He sold[31] Con 1 NDR, Lot 19 (50 acres) to Andrew Thompson 08 Jul 1874 in Brant Township, Bruce County, Ontario.

99 F v. **Elizabeth Guinn** was born[31] in 1875 in Brant Twp, Bruce County, Canada West.

Elizabeth resided[31] 22 Mar 1895 in Toronto, Ontario.

Elizabeth married[32] **Frederick William Marshall** on 18 Sep 1895 in Toronto, Ontario. Frederick was born[32] 1874 in Weston, Ontario.

100 M   vi. **George Henry Guinn** was born[32] about 1876. He died[33] before 22 Mar 1895.

Source References - Mary Jane

1. Taylor, Elaine, Guinn Family Records: Taylor, Elaine to Clarke, Roger; CC: Wheaton, Dean, Descendants of William Guinn, Unpublished, Page 2, The Collection of Dean Wheaton, 5976 Kungle Road, Clinton, OH 44216-9317, CR_002. Mary Jane DoB: Taylor has 1849, Clarke has 1847, computed from 1871 Census: 1946, computed from marriage registration: 1845.

2. Wheaton, Dean, Interview with Ruth Bacon Bates, Conducted 20 Jul 1994 in Kentwood, Michigan, Unpublished , Page 1, The Collection of Dean Wheaton, 5976 Kungle Road, Clinton, OH 44216-9317, WWD079. "Mary Jane is the daughter of William Bacon [2], son of Joseph Bacon [1], who's wife died at Mary Jane's birth. Mary Jane was adopted by her grandparents, Joseph & Susannah Bacon."

3. Clarke, Roger, Descendants of William Gwynne (Clarke), Modified Register Report, 51 Pages, Unpublished, Page 2, CRB001, 2, The Collection of Dean Wheaton, 5976 Kungle Road, Clinton, OH 44216-9317. Via email 2 Mar 2003. Mary Jane DoB: 22 Jan 1847.

4. Clarke, Roger, Descendants of William Gwynne (Clarke), Page 2.

5. Bruce County Registrar, Land Records of Bruce County, Ontario, Microfilm Series A, Microfilm Records, Instrument #498, Page 539, 28 Apr 1864, Bruce County Registry Office, 203 Cayley Street, Walkerton, Ontario N0G 2V0. Witnessed by Elijah Bacon and Isaac Bacon. [OBC001]

6. 1881 Canadian Census of Ontario, Bruce County, Brant Township. "Guinn, Mary Jane, Wesleyan Methodist; Children: Mary, William, Richard, Elizabeth." [CR_002, 2]

7. Bruce County Registrar, Land Records of Bruce County, Ontario, Reel A-87, Instr. #10056, 11 Apr 1895. Land willed by Wm Guinn, Jr. to wife & children to be sold when youngest child reaches age 21 yrs. Purchased jointly by wife Mary Jane and son Wm James Quinn.

8. Bruce County Registrar, Index of Land Instruments for Bruce County, Ontario, Microfilm A-3-9, Page 250, Instr. #10057, 11 Apr 1895, Walkerton Branch Library, 253 Durham Street East, Walkerton, Ontario N0G 2V0. William James Guinn was co-grantor. [OBC002]

9. Bruce County Registrar, Index of Land Instruments for Bruce County, Ontario, Microfilm A-3-9, Page 250, Instr. #10144, 10 Aug 1895. William James Guinn was co-grantor.

10. Bruce County Registrar, Index of Land Instruments for Bruce County, Ontario, Microfilm A-3-9, Page 250, Instr. #10697, 29 Jul 1897. William James Guinn was co-grantor.

11. County Clerk, Marriage Registers, Bruce County, Ontario. "Wm Guinn age 29 of Brant Township, born Canada West, son of Wm. and Jane Quinn. Mary Jane Bacon age 19 of Brant Township, born Canada West, daughter of Joseph and Susannah Bacon. Married 13th February 1866 by Rev. John David Gilbert, Primitive Methodist. Witesses: John Gauger Sarah

Ann Wilson." From Taylor, Elaine, "Descendants of William Guinn", Page 1. Compute DoB for Mary Jane: 1866 - 19 = 1845. [CR_002, 4]

12. Ontario District Marriages, Bruce County, Ontario, No Page or Reg. #'s (Guinn), Archives of Ontario, 77 Grenville Street, Unit 300, Toronto, Ontario, Canada, M5S 1B3, RG 8, Series 1-6-B, MS 248 Reel 5. "Groom: William Guinn, age 29, resident of Brant, born Canada East, parents: Williams & Jane Guinn; Bride: Mary Jane Bacon, age 19,resident of Brant, born Canada West, parents: Joseph & Susannah Bacon; Witnesses: John Grainger, Sarah Anne Wilson, Date of marriage: 13 Feb 1866." Copy of registration from Betty Allen, 2001. [LLE002, 6]

13. Taylor, Elaine V., Descendants of Willian Guinn (Taylor), Modified Register Report, 4 pages, Unpublished, Page 1, The Collection of Dean Wheaton, 5976 Kungle Road, Clinton, OH 44216-9317, CR_002.

14. Bruce County Registrar, Index of Land Instruments for Bruce County, Ontario, Microfilm A-3-9, Page 250. No activity takes place on the Lot until 1 Sep 1894 when William James Guinn (probable heir to William Guinn, Jr.) Assigns it to Mary Jane Quinn, Instr. #9873. On 22 Mar 1895 a DEED was granted (Instr. #10056) by William Guinn's children as heirs to William James Guinn and Mar Jane Guinn for $1.

15. Bruce County Registrar, Index of Land Instruments for Bruce County, Ontario, Microfilm A-3-9, Page 251, Instr. #202, 23 May 1859.

16. 1871 Canadian Census of Ontario, Bruce County, Brant Township. "Quinn, William, Wesleyan Methodist; Mary Jane, wife, age 25; Children: Mary, William James, Susannah." Computed DoB for Mary Jane: 1871 - 25 = 1846. [CR_002, 2]

17. 1871 Canadian Census of Ontario, Bruce County, Brant Township. "Guinn, William, age 36; Mary Jane, wife, age 24; Mary, dau., age 5; Wm James, son, age 3; Susannah Jane, dau., age 1." Researched by Betty Allen, Langley, British Columbia.

18. Bruce County Registrar, Land Records of Bruce County, Ontario, Reel A-69, Instr. #3832.

19. Bruce County Registrar, Land Records of Bruce County, Ontario, Reel A-87, Instr. #10056, 11 Apr 1895. "... will was registered in the Registry Office of the County of Bruce on the twenty-ninth day of November A.D. 1876 as number 191 for the general register." William Smith (husband of Mary Ann Guinn, granddaughter and daughter of son Richard) and Richard Guinn (son) were executors.

20. Clarke, Roger, Descendants of William Gwynne (Clarke), Page 5.

21. Clarke, Roger, Descendants of William Gwynne (Clarke), Message, Page 1, 01 Mar 2003.

22. Bruce County Registrar, Land Records of Bruce County, Ontario, Reel A-87, Instr. #10056, 11 Apr 1895.

23. Clarke, Roger, Descendants of William Gwynne (Clarke), Page 5. Clarke cites Marriage Registration, Archives of Ontario, #104095.

24. Clarke, Roger, Descendants of William Gwynne (Clarke), Page 6.

25. Bruce County Registrar, Index of Land Instruments for Bruce County, Ontario, Microfilm A-3-9, Page 250, Instr. #10057, 11 Apr 1895. Mary Jane Guinn was co-grantor.

26. Bruce County Registrar, Index of Land Instruments for Bruce County, Ontario, Microfilm A-3-9, Page 250, Instr. #10144, 15 Aug 1895. Mary Jane Guinn was co-grantor.

27. Bruce County Registrar, Index of Land Instruments for Bruce County, Ontario, Microfilm A-3-9, Page 250, Instr. #10697, 29 Jul 1897. Mary Jane Guinn was co-grantor.

28. Bruce County Registrar, Index of Land Instruments for Bruce County, Ontario, Microfilm A-3-9, Page 253.

29. Bruce County Registrar, Index of Land Instruments for Bruce County, Ontario, Microfilm A-3-9, Page 259, Instr. #150, 02 Aug 1858.

30. Bruce County Registrar, Index of Land Instruments for Bruce County, Ontario, Microfilm A-3-9, Page 259, Instr. #671, 23 Mar 1866.

31. Bruce County Registrar, Index of Land Instruments for Bruce County, Ontario, Microfilm A-3-9, Page 259, Instr. # 3101, 11 Jul 1878.

32. Clarke, Roger, Descendants of William Gwynne (Clarke), Page 2. Clarke cites Marriages in Ontario 1895, Archives of Ontario, Reg. #014944.

33. Bruce County Registrar, Land Records of Bruce County, Ontario, Reel A-87, Instr. #10056, 11 Apr 1895. Not mentioned a being among the only surviving children of William Guinn, Jr.

Genealogy Index of Names

A

Allen
Thomas 107
Thomas (3S - b.1819) 107
Armstrong
Mary 189, 201
Atkins
Thomas (9S) 168

B

Bacon
Agnes (67 - b.1866) 168
Agnes Jane (51 - b.1858) 142
Albert Edward (87 - b.1867) 189, 202
Alice Alivena (52 - b.1860) 143
Benjamin (32 - b.1858) 130
Bethia (33 - b.1859) 130, 133
Charlotte (5 - b.1827) 95, 135, 139, 140
David (35, 9S - b.1869) 132, 170, 171
Dollie Mabel (92 - b.1881) 194
Elijah (9 - b.1833) 96, 132, 149, 167, 217
Elizabeth (58 - b.1856) x, 5, 10, 47, 51, 100, 144, 153, 158, 166, 200, 202, 203, 208
Eliza Jane (71 - b.1872) 169
Emily Louise (36 - b.1870) 132
Emma Alice Franklin (93 - b.1883) 194
Emma Jane (10 - b.1836) 96, 175
George (34 - b.1836) 131
Henry (11 - b.1839) xi, xiii, 27, 35, 39, 45, 51, 54, 61, 67, 130, 200, 201, 202, 204, 206, 208, 209
Hiram William John (13 - b.1855) 101
Husley Hannah (62 - b.1863) 160
Isaac (86 - b.1864) 12, 24, 88, 156, 157, 158, 159, 160, 161, 162, 163, 164, 165, 166, 188, 217
Isaac Elisha (60 - b.1860) 95, 155, 160, 162, 166
Isaac Elisha (64 - b.1874) 95, 155, 160, 162, 166
Isaac Elisha (8 - b.1833) 95, 155, 160, 162, 166
James (69 - b.1870) 11, 29, 33, 40, 45, 46, 55, 93, 95, 129, 132, 169, 170
James A (70 - b.1871) 169
James Jr. (29-b.1850) 129
James Sr (4 - b.1825) 95, 129, 170
Jane Algerina (89 - b.1872) 192
John (7 - b.1831) 95, 101, 141, 152, 168, 207
John William (57 - b.1855) 157
Joseph (73 - b.1880) iii, v, x, xiii, 1, 2, 5, 6, 10, 11, 12, 17, 28, 40, 46, 54, 56, 61, 77, 89, 90, 93, 95, 97, 98, 100, 101, 129, 135, 141, 155, 167, 170, 175, 181, 185, 187, 198, 203, 213, 217
Joseph Elias (88 - b.1870) 54, 191, 203
Joseph Henry (30 - b.1853) 130
Joseph Jr. (6 - b.1829) 95
Joseph Sr. (1 - b.1795) 93
Lillie Mary Hope (91 - b.1878) 193

Lucy (68 - b.1867) 169, 206
Lucy Violet (94 - b.1886) xiii, 195
Margaret (63 - b.1866) 160, 162, 166
Maria (4S, 74 - b.1882) 132, 170
Mary Ann (85 - b.1863) 88, 166, 188
Mary Ellen (56, 9S - b.1862) 149, 168
Mary Jane (12 - b.1847) 61, 79, 96, 213, 217, 218
Mary Maud (28 - b.1848) 129
Minnie Elizabeth (55 - b.1867) 144
Richard (31 - b.1856) 130
Robert (7S, 66 - b.1863) 149, 168
Robert Hunter (53 - b.1862) 143
Ruth Rebecca (59 - b.1858) 12, 159, 166
Susanna (61 - b.1863) x, xi, 35, 58, 60, 63, 160
Susan (3 - b.1823) 10, 11, 44, 91, 95, 105, 106, 108, 109, 110, 111, 112, 113, 114, 115, 116, 117, 118, 119, 120, 121, 122, 123, 124, 125, 126, 127, 128, 170, 173
Susan (72 - b.1875) 10, 11, 44, 91, 95, 105, 106, 108, 109, 110, 111, 112, 113, 114, 115, 116, 117, 118, 119, 120, 121, 122, 123, 124, 125, 126, 127, 128, 170, 173
Sussanna Franklin (54 - b.1864) 144
Theodore Huston (90 - b.1875) 193
William (2 - b.1821) 54, 94, 101, 103, 157, 213, 217

Benway
Eliza Jane (- b.1853) 193, 195
Boden
E. 135
Bown
Andrew 142
David (7S - b.1858) 142
Boyle
James 130
William (4S - b.1840) 130, 133
Brayman
Nancy A. (2S - b.1861) 102
Brown
John 192, 204
Sarah A. (11S - b.1877) 192
Bryant
Nancy Jane 121
Bull
Marie 195
Bunsell
Elizabeth 175, 179, 185

C

Carber
Fanny 179
Carlton
George Louis (10S - b.1853) 176
Chesney
Henry 135
Martha Jane (5S - b.1855) 135
Robert (5S - b.1846) 136
Clarke
Richard 214
Thomas Bruce (12S - b.1856) 61, 214
Clohessy
David (9S) 132, 171
Couch
Christopher (-b.1809) 5, 10, 51, 178, 188
Elizabeth Franklin (11S - b.1843) 188

Mary Anne 178
Cox
George (7S - m.1879) 152, 153
Crandall
Lucy Lucinda (10S - b.1871) 179
Merrill C. 179
Cromar
George (5O - b.1880) 45, 138
James (5S - b.1836) 11, 35, 39,
47, 46, 138, 140

D

Demming
Anna Patience 190
Denny
(8S) 160, 161
Dickerson
Francis Louise 192

E

Elmslie
Jane 144
Emma v, x, 5, 6, 11, 17, 35, 39, 49,
50, 90, 96, 113, 114, 136, 158,
166, 175, 180, 181, 183, 185,
190, 194, 195, 207, 208, 209,
210

F

Fanan
Ella (11S - b.1873) 190
James 190
Fleet
George 159
William (8S - b.1855) 12, 159,
166
Flewelling
James Morrice 144
Robert David 144
Fortune
Robert (3S - m.1871) 110
Franklin

Henry (-b.1755) 13, 94
Susannah (1S - a.1798) xiii, 2, 13,
94, 100
French
Philena 137

G

Galloway
David 178
Jane Ellen (10S - b.1859) 178
Garrett
Mildred Lillian (3S - b.1875) 121
Wallace Edgar 121
Gooding
James 158
Stephen (8S - 1850) 158, 166
Gordon
Arthur William (5S - b.1845) 136
Guinn
Elizabeth (99 - b.1875) 215
George Henry (100 - b.1876) 216
Mary (95 - b.1866) 214
Richard (98 - b.1871) 215, 218
Susannah Jane (97 - b.1870) 215
William James (96 - b.1868) 213,
214, 217, 218
William Jr. (12S - b.1834) 213
Gwynne
William Sr. (-b.1791) 213

H

Haddow
Jane 142
Harkness
Sarah 179, 184
Hart
Agnes 142
Hattie 192, 204
Hill
Thomas (3S - b.1848) 11
Hilts
Susanna 135

Hoar
  Carrie (76) 175
  David B. (10S - b.1844) 50, 179
  Elizabeth Jane (81 - b.1862) 178
  Esell H. (84 - b.1869) 179
  Jennie (75) 175
  John (80 - b.1858) 49, 175, 177,
    178
  Joseph (83 - b.1868) 179
  Lucy (77) 175
  Mary (78 - b.1855) 175
  Samuel 6, 11, 35, 39, 109, 175,
    179, 183, 185
  Samuel John Jr. (82 - b.1864) 178
  Samuel John Sr. (10S - b.1864)
    175
  Susanna (79 - b.1856) 176
Holderness
  Austin (3S - b.1835) 114
Hunter
  Elizabeth (7S - b.1837) 35, 47,
    142, 168
  Elizabeth (- b.1837) 35, 47, 142,
    168
  Jeanette 144
  William 142

J

Johanna
  Jacoba Dorothea (8S - m.1921)
    163

K

Kennedy
  Mary Ellen (4S) 130
Kiley
  Margaret Rachel (2S - b.1860)
    102

L

Leas (5S - m.1879) 137

Levar
  Benjamin 161
Lewis
  Thankful 192, 204

M

Marshall
  Frederick William (12S - b.1874)
    216
Mary v, 5, 10, 11, 12, 13, 14, 33, 35,
    36, 39, 43, 44, 45, 48, 53, 54,
    55, 60, 61, 79, 88, 93, 96, 101,
    112, 113, 124, 129, 130, 132,
    133, 135, 142, 143, 144, 146,
    147, 148, 149, 152, 153, 156,
    157, 158, 159, 166, 167, 168,
    170, 173, 175, 176, 178, 180,
    182, 188, 189, 193, 200, 201,
    206, 208, 210, 213, 214, 217,
    218, 219
Mary (8S - b.1855) 158, 175, 182
Matilda (4S - b.1858) 130
McCallum
  Jane 107
McCarter
  Robert 215
McIntyre
  James (- b.1830) 144
  Mary Elizabeth (7S - b.1862) 144
McLeod
  Archibald (3S - b.1840) 111
McNeil
  Jno. 167
  Maria (9S - b.1844) 35, 48, 132,
    149, 167
  Maria (- b.1844) 35, 48, 132,
    149, 167
McPherson
  Thomas (5S - b.1869) 138
Mead
  Annie Edenore (4S - b.1868) 131
Miller
  Clara 190

Minorgan
  John 116
Morford
  Edwin Alfred (11S - b.1866) 192,
    205
  William Lane 192
Morrison
  Alexander (9S - b.1857) 169
  Donald (9S - b.1871) 169
  John McPhee (9S - b.1882) 170

N

Nelson
  Sara (11S - m.1952) 192
Newville
  Bernice Grace (11S - b.1873) 190
  Frank 190, 202
  John A. 190
  Sarah Louise (11S - b.1878) 190
Norris
  Mary (4S - b.1827) 33, 35, 45,
    129, 170
  Mary (- b.1827) 33, 35, 45, 129,
    170

P

Pagel
  Henry C. (11S - b.1882) 195,
    208
Pagels
  Christian 195, 208
Pavers
  Ellemena (2S - b.1813) 35, 101
Porter
  James (9S - m.1894) 170
  Mary 130
Pretorius
  Wilhelmina Francina (8S -
    m.1904) 163
Prior
  Charlotte S. (23 - b.1859) 118
  Elijah (21 - b.1855) 115, 116,

  117, 127
  Elizabeth Anne (14 - b.1859) 11,
    105
  George A. (26 - b.1866) 122
  James (3S - b.1815) 10, 11, 35,
    42, 105, 114
  James Arthur #1 (20 - b.1854)
    115
  Jane Emma (19 - b.1852) 113
  Jemima Louise (27 - b.1871) 123
  Lucy Mimie (15 - b.1844) 108
  Mary Margaret (18 - b.1850) 11,
    112
  Phoebe (24 - b.1861) 120
  Sarah Ann (17 - b.1847) 110
  Thomas Henry (22 - b.1856) 113,
    114, 119, 123
Prout
  John 178
  Levi A. (10S - b.1862) 178

R

Rathburn
  Jane 178
Reed
  William John (10S - b.1855) 177
Reid
  Margaret 161
Reynolds
  Eleanor 214
Ridgley
  David Henry (5S - b.1839) 137
  Jonathon 137
Ritter
  Susan (12S - d.1923) 215
Routledge
  George Walton 145
  William (7S - b.1865) 145, 148,
    149

S

Sarah (4S - b.1959) 130
Shannon
  Henry 189, 201
  Mary (11S - b.1873) 189
Shrock
  Lillie Mae (10S - b.1875) 179
  Peter 179
Smith
  Bleakney 135
  Charlotte (48 - b.1869) 137, 139
  Elizabeth (44 - b.1861) 136
  Emma (42 - b.1857) 136
  George (5S - b.1814) 39, 45, 135,
    139
  Gideon (43 - b.1859) 136
  Joseph (47 - b.1867) 137
  Margaret (45 - b.1863) 137
  Maria (46 - b.1865) 137
  Martha Mary (5S - b.1851) 135
  Mary Ellen (4S - b.1861) 129,
    132
  Mary Jane (37 - b.1846) 135
  Samuel (39 - b.1859) 135
  Sarah (41 - b.1855) 136
  Susan (40 - b.1853) 136
  Un-named Infant (49) 138
  William (38 - b.1848) 135, 218
Steel
  Joseph 192

T

Tighe
  Mary Ann (- b.1816) 188

V

Vaux
  Ann Elizabeth 145

W

Walsh
  ? (12S - m.1915) 214
Watson
  Mary Margaret (8S - b.1836) 156
Welch
  Rose Viola (9S - b.1883) 170
Wheaton
  Andrew (- b.1849) 193, 195,
    206, 209
  Walter Rhynear (11S - b.1875)
    193
  Warner Abner (11S - b.1885) xiii,
    195, 209
Willis
  Jane (- b.1800) 213